# Be Financially Free

# BE
# FINANCIALLY
# FREE

## how to become salary independent
## in today's economy

**Morten Strange**

Marshall Cavendish
Business

Published in 2016 by Marshall Cavendish Business
An imprint of Marshall Cavendish International
1 New Industrial Road, Singapore 536196

Other Marshall Cavendish Offices:
Marshall Cavendish Corporation. 99 White Plains Road, Tarrytown NY 10591–9001, USA • Marshall Cavendish International (Thailand) Co Ltd. 253 Asoke, 12th Flr, Sukhumvit 21 Road, Klongtoey Nua, Wattana, Bangkok 10110, Thailand • Marshall Cavendish (Malaysia) Sdn Bhd, Times Subang, Lot 46, Subang Hi-Tech Industrial Park, Batu Tiga, 40000 Shah Alam, Selangor Darul Ehsan, Malaysia.

Marshall Cavendish is a trademark of Times Publishing Limited

National Library Board, Singapore Cataloguing-in-Publication Data:
Name(s): Strange, Morten.
Title: Be financially free : how to become salary independent in today's economy / Morten Strange.
Description: Singapore : Marshall Cavendish Business, 2016.
Identifier(s): OCN 946967988 | ISBN 978-981-47-5137-7 (paperback)
Subject(s): LCSH: Finance, Personal. | Investments.
Classification: DDC 332.024–dc23

Printed in Singapore by NPE Print Communications Pte Ltd

# Contents

# Preface

*"If there's a book you really want to read,*
*but it hasn't been written yet,*
*then you must write it."*

— TONI MORRISON

A few years ago I attended a lecture at the Singapore Botanic Gardens by Ashleigh Seow about tiger conservation in Malaysia. Ashleigh has a university degree from Australia in politics and economics, but he has reinvented himself as a naturalist. At the event he called himself a "citizen scientist". He said that science was too important to be left to the scientists; we citizens had to participate.

I thought of that. I was a naturalist at the time; I published nature books. But I was getting more and more interested in finance and economics. So now, like Ashleigh, except the other way around, I have reinvented myself. Now I consider myself a "citizen economist". Economics and finance is too important a subject to be left to the professionals.

I wrote this book for two reasons: To share with my friends and with the public in general my experience in finance, and to say to you, You can do it too! You can set yourself free – free from consumerism and financial worries, free to do what you really want. But it won't happen automatically. You have to understand how to do it and use the tools at your disposal correctly. In this book I show you how to do that. The final choice, how you want to prioritise, is up to you.

The other reason for the book is: I want to share the insights I have gained about our current economic situation. My experience with economics and social affairs goes back some 50 years – I actually vividly remember the oil crisis in 1973 and the stock market crash in 1987. Living through these events is different from studying them in a business course textbook (I have crammed a few of those too). Together with my interest in natural resources and the environment, I have come to the conclusion that all is not as it appears in the economy of today.

We are reaching some limits, and that is why I devote the longest chapter in the book, chapter 10, to dealing with these limits. These limits have a direct bearing on your ability to become – and stay – financially free. I feel I have to share this material with others. It is amazing how these factors are consistently left out by mainstream financial analysts and political decision-makers. The facts are staring us in the face, but they are ignored by most. I urge you to take the time and study chapters 10 and 11 carefully. Armed with this new insight, you will be better equipped to protect yourself against the limits we are facing, to position yourself financially, and to gain your freedom from consumerism and economic worries.

Some practical matters: The monetary references here are mainly in $, meaning US$ or USD. Where I refer to Singapore dollars, I will make that clear with S$ or SGD. Currently US$1 is about S$1.40. I don't cite every single statement I make; this is not an academic work and much of what I write is easily checked on the internet. For specific – possibly contested – assertions, I use a basic reference to the source. I also don't list every single person or book I refer to, so as not to clutter the material, but I do explain who and what most of them are, so that you can go on and explore in more detail if you like.

Before printing I showed the manuscript to a few people to get their input and their reaction – I thank them all, especially Dr Marc Faber, who allowed me to use his comments in the book.

On the television show MythBusters, two dudes in northern California test the validity of various myths suggested by the public. The myths are either busted, plausible or confirmed.

Here are some economic myths that we often hear:

- You can make money by trading financial futures.

- Higher GDP is good for everyone.

- Population growth is positive for society.

- Electric cars are good for the environment.

- We will get back to economic growth soon.

All these statements are repeated incessantly by mainstream economists and financial commentators. But I will bust these myths. Sometimes it takes an outsider to see things clearly, a citizen economist. I will show you that financial futures and options trading is zero-sum, and only the trading platform is sure to make money; higher GDP is sometimes bad; population increase stifles development; electric cars are bad for the environment; and most importantly, economic growth as we know it cannot go on forever.

But there is one myth that I will confirm: You can make your money grow – if you invest in a good company of honest and hardworking people who provide a competitive product or service that others are willing to pay for. And by controlling your spending at the same time, you can soon be free forever. I will show you how to get there.

Good luck!

Morten Strange
Singapore
April 2016

**1**

# Retire at 30?

*"There must be more to life than
having everything!"*
— MAURICE SENDAK

### A lucky break

When I was 25 years old I lived in Aberdeen, Scotland. The Granite
City, they called it – many of the old buildings downtown were
built out of large solid stone blocks. People spoke with a funny
accent, but they were always nice and I liked it there. I bought a
small apartment on Jamaica Street. It was on the top floor and
had slanting ceilings near the outer walls.

That was in 1978. I didn't spend that much time in the apartment, though. I worked offshore on the oil rigs and platforms in
the North Sea. In between jobs I was at the office and workshop to
prepare for the next offshore assignment, and to train on all the
new equipment we had. We collected and analysed down-hole data
from both exploration and production wells. Each job was usually
on a new location, so I travelled a lot and met a lot of different
people during that period.

On one of the rigs I chatted with an American guy, who was
a few years older than me. He told me he had just been through
a divorce and was planning to marry again. So I tried to be a bit
supportive and said: "They say the second marriage is usually
better". He replied: "Don't believe it – that was my second wife

I just divorced." Anyway, he planned to retire before he was 30. I thought that sounded pretty cool. I loved my job, and I really had nothing better to do. But just the thought of it – the power of being financial independent at 30 – it stayed on my mind.

I quit my job in the UK two years after that. I wanted to work overseas. I had saved some money and put myself through a training course in oil well drilling and completion. Since we worked so closely with the drilling crews in the service business, I felt I had to know more about that part of the business. But that was in Stavanger, Norway, and I didn't want to live there. I wanted to see the world.

There was lots of work in the Middle East at the time, but the region just didn't appeal to me. Nothing but sand all around. Expats living in gated camps with nowhere to go after work.

My wife at the time had heard of Singapore, and she urged me to find a job there. Other oilfield wives had told her it was Heaven on Earth. I wasn't sure where Singapore was – I confused it with Hong Kong and Shanghai. We didn't have smartphones with Google Earth installed at the time.

Sometimes you just get a lucky break. If you keep trying and keep looking for opportunities, the breaks will come to you. Singapore was one of mine. Warren Farley hired me from the Core Laboratories Ltd office in England, and I will always be indebted to him. Landing in Paya Lebar one night in October 1980, I found a country full of prospects and possibilities, and with the most beautiful and diverse natural world you can find anywhere.

No, I didn't retire at 30. But I did take the option to retire from the oil industry some years later in 1986. I was 33 years old then. Life on the rigs had lost its allure. I tried to move into middle management for a while, but I just didn't really believe in our mission anymore; I had lost the passion for the oil industry. If you don't have the passion, don't do it, it's not worth it. I have done many things since then, but I never worked in industry again.

How is that possible? How can you retire at 30, or 33? You can, and I am not talking about some young kid who establishes an internet company, sells it off to Google for millions of dollars and then buys a ticket to the International Space Station. Those cases make the headlines, but they are not many. The rest of us have to do it the hard way: By working for other people, living within our means and investing wisely.

But I am not the only one in the world to have done this, to quit the corporate life early. Lots of people I know retired from their careers early in life. Or they changed direction and found a new and more fulfilling path. As we shall see later, for some macro-economic reasons it might have been easier to do this 30 years ago. Interest rates were higher then and taxation was lower. But you still can – if you put your mind to it, and if you want it bad enough – do as Johnny Paycheck did, and say: "Take this job and shove it."

## The key to financial freedom

There are three things you need to do to gain financial freedom and retire early. You need to:

1. Make some money
2. Spend less than you make
3. Save the rest and make it grow

## Make more

I will not dwell on the first point here too much. Most people realise when they set out in life that they have to have a good income. In fact, most young people study really hard, try to get into the best schools and look for jobs where they can make lots of money. It comes fairly naturally to most people and yes, it is important.

But I would argue that it is even more important how you manage the money that you do make. It seems obvious enough when you think about it, but it is surprising how many people get it wrong at that stage.

That's because, even if you make millions, it won't be enough if you spend even more. Think of all the people who made a boatload of money, lived in style ... and then went bankrupt.

In fact, many of the people I know who retired early did not even make that much cash during their working careers. I was never that highly paid. When I started that job in Aberdeen, I was just a wireline assistant and a trainee engineer, even though I actually had two years of offshore oilfield experience working in the Norwegian sector of the North Sea, where I made much more money. I liked the job in Scotland because I got to work with the latest technology, and the great crew of American colleagues taught me everything they knew. I was paid by the week, and one Friday afternoon my boss, Eddie Rankin, asked me if I had been paid that week. I hadn't, and our accountant in the small front office had gone home. So Eddie asked me how much I made, and I said, "80 pounds per week, around 60 pounds after tax." He took a big bundle of banknotes out of his pocket and peeled off 60 pounds for me. I was paid with my boss' pocket money!

Sure, your income is important. Of course you should try to maximise it; and if you do well, it will help you reach your financial freedom faster. I sold photographs of birds when I was young, and it gave me an extra income. I authored a few small bird books, and the revenue from public lending rights turned out to be substantial. Wherever I went, I would take pictures and write an article about the place for travel and nature magazines. When I started working in the oilfields, I photographed the rigs and the work we did on them, and sold the photographs to newspapers and book publishers. I don't recall ever seeing another person with a camera among the oilfield crews in those days.

This is just an example – obviously that business model has gone the way of the Polaroid camera, i.e. it has disappeared. You can't make money from selling photographs today. Everyone has his or her own camera, and photographs in general don't really have a commercial value anymore. But there are now other opportunities. The same technological developments that destroyed one business model have generated many new ones. Via the internet it is now possible to make extra money from home, working freelance as and when it suits you, whether it's in writing, design, web development, online tutoring, data entry or social media marketing. Writing a blog and endorsing products, playing video games competitively – such ways of making money would have been inconceivable in the past.

So there are lots of ways you can enhance your income. If you work for someone else, do overtime or volunteer to work over Christmas and New Year for a little bit extra. Do double shift. Pick up extra projects and freelance assignments that come along. Go through your stuff and sell off what you don't need online.

## Don't listen to them

All this is good, making some money. But like I have emphasised, this is not the key to financial freedom. The key is to spend less than you make.

It is not as easy as it sounds. Every day you are being bombarded with exactly the opposite message: Buy stuff! Sales agents contact you and urge you to buy cars, insurance, property. These agents go to school to learn a whole range of techniques to persuade so-called "prospects" (that is you) to buy stuff they don't really want and don't really need. There is a whole industry out there teaching sales people how to sweet-talk customers, in order to "close the sale" fast.

You probably don't even notice it, but each time you open up the morning paper, check your smartphone, browse the internet on your computer, listen to the radio or click through the cable TV stations at night, advertisements are trying to get you to buy more stuff. Most of which you can easily live without. Does it work, advertising? Of course, otherwise the companies wouldn't do it. And governments wouldn't find it necessary to restrict advertisement for products they find objectionable, like cigarettes and booze. You could argue that advertisements for cars should be banned as well, as more cars add to road congestion, pollution and the 1.24 million people killed in traffic every year.[1] But we are not quite there yet.

In 2015 the Monetary Authority of Singapore (MAS) proposed tightening the requirements for financial institutions and insurance companies when they sell their products in public places such as shopping centres and MRT stations.[2] MAS was afraid that the sales people would aggressively push credit cards and life insurance schemes on the unsuspecting public, poorly prepared to resist the sales pressure. It is nice that we have the government to protect us from unscrupulous sales people. But wouldn't it be even nicer if we all developed enough financial savvy and common sense to say no?

I don't want to pick on advertisers. I have worked with many of them; in fact, I spent many years working in marketing and sales myself. Like the rest of us, marketing people are just out there trying to make a living. They are very much part of the modern economy. All I am saying is: Don't listen to them. Don't be swayed by their slick commercials. Let all the others buy this stuff if they want to. You should ignore them all and stand firm. Don't buy that watch or car or handbag or diamond ring or soft drink just because some company with a clever presentation wants to convince you that you cannot live without it. You don't need it. Free yourself from manipulation and peer pressure. Buy a dividend-paying stock with your extra funds instead, and watch your money grow to secure your freedom.

## A case study

As I mentioned, I know lots of people who did more or less what I did – retired early or simply just quit their jobs and found something more meaningful and rewarding to do. My wife and I were at a lunch at the Shangri-La Hotel recently and virtually everyone around the table fell into that category. There was a nature photographer and his wife there, who both quit the corporate life early to do what they loved and still have a reasonable standard of living; he travelled the region taking pictures of wildlife, she spent more time with their kids. The wife, a former banker, said to me: "The secret is to control your spending." It was music to my ears!

And if you need any more convincing than this, consider Iain Ewing's story. Iain was born in Scotland and grew up in Canada, where he graduated from the University of Toronto with a degree in philosophy and English literature. In 1985 he got a job at the Singapore Polytechnic teaching media skills, and as a pastime he became active in the Nature Society of Singapore. He had a passion for nature, environmental issues and especially for bird-watching. I met Iain on birding excursions that I conducted in those years for the Nature Society; he was in his prime, active, handsome, well-spoken. He came to Singapore with just a shirt on his back and his four-year-old son Tejas to take care of, his marriage in India having broken down.

So far nothing extraordinary about that, right? But Iain was unusually knowledgeable and articulate. You could immediately sense that he was a driven and ambitious individual. He felt his supervisor at work was holding him back. He wanted more out of life than "just" being an ordinary teacher.

True enough, in 1991 Iain started his own company, Ewing Communications Pte Ltd, which he grew over the years to become a major player in training corporations and government organisations in media skills, presentation techniques and sales. During that time, Iain worked incredibly hard, and by the end of that decade he had become somewhat of a big shot. He had built his company from out of nothing into a sizeable organisation with some 12 employees; he bought his own office building, and he and his staff did lectures and seminars here as well as in many other countries. Iain said later in 2008, during an interview with the *Sunday Times*, that he came to Singapore with S$33,000 in the bank and grew that to S$20 million by carefully spending less than he made and investing wisely. At that point he was free, financially independent.

2008 was also the year Iain was diagnosed with cancer. But he could now use his freedom to do what he liked. He scaled down his workload gradually and started travelling the world, this time looking for beautiful wild locations, birds and animals, from Svalbard in the Arctic to the Antarctic and many wild places in between. Usually in the company of his son. His last trip was to the Galapagos Islands in August 2014. He lost his battle with the disease in October that year. Throughout his ordeal, Iain kept up a remarkable spirit and he often told me how happy he was about the way he had turned his life around, and about the freedom he enjoyed by not having to worry about money.

So, if the key to financial freedom is spending less, let us see how you can go about that in more detail.

# Spend Less

*"It's not how much money you make,*
*but how much money you keep."*

— ROBERT KIYOSAKI

**Why would you ... spend less?**

I am not the only penny-pinching adviser out there urging people to spend within their means. We are many of us. In fact, some members of the public are a bit tired of us. I have seen comedy programmes on television occasionally poking fun of the goofy-looking financial adviser running around with his oversized pocket calculator shouting, "Time is money!"

I will accept that. I know it is hard to control your spending. Like everyone else, the first thing I bought when I started making a bit of money on the North Sea was a car, of course! An Opel stationwagon that I could sleep in when I drove out to photograph birds during my days off. When I transferred to Scotland, I moved up and bought a Ford Mustang V8 to go with my oilfield image; it was the only one of the American muscle cars at the time that was delivered with a right-hand steering column for the UK market. Today I don't own a car, though I occasionally drive my wife's Toyota Prius hybrid; that goes to show how times change!

Sure, if you are young and finally make a buck, you want to spend it, I can understand that. But what if you don't have the money, but still want to buy that really cool thing? Should you borrow money to buy it, i.e. spend more than you make? I strongly urge every young person never to do that. It is the surest way, not to financial freedom, but to financial prison.

By limiting your spending to what you make, it may seem like you're denying yourself many of life's pleasures. But that's not the case. What you're doing is *delayed gratification*. Yes, for the moment you are deprived of that pleasure, but it is for the sake of a greater future reward.

This is a process that has to be learned. A baby doesn't know how to delay gratification. It must have food immediately if it feels hungry. You cannot tell a two-year-old that you will now take his toy tractor away, put it over here and then Baby can play with it when Baby is four – even if you promise *two* tractors instead of just one when the time comes. Try it and see what happens, then you will know what I mean.

But as we get older, we learn to manage our needs and to delay rewards and enjoyment. It is something you have to make a conscientious effort to do. When you get your bonus, try not to spend it at all. Put it in the bank and do nothing. When you have some capital, invest it and watch it grow. I have met people who could do that, and I have met people who couldn't. In my experience, the people who waited and saved their money ended up in a position where they could buy many more nice things than the people who couldn't wait.

Like I said, I am not the only one with this bright idea, that you should save instead of spend. An excellent source of inspiration is *Your Money Or Your Life* (by Vicki Robin and Joe Dominguez), which offers a detailed guide to "transforming your relationship with money" in 9 steps. In *Life Or Debt*, Stacy Johnson provides a complete hands-on, step-by-step programme to get out of debt and secure financial freedom.

I can confirm much of what Johnson preaches from my own experience. However, I find his 205 ways to save money a bit over-the-top and most of his ideas are things we do anyway, like bargaining for discounts and keeping the family car tuned. So I have come up with a simpler 13-step guide[1]:

## 13 ways to spend less

**(1) Shop wisely.** In the supermarket, use a shopping list and only buy what's on the list. Take advantage of special offers, but only for items that can be stored and which you would need to buy in the future anyway. Don't buy that box of candy just because it is on sale; but if your favourite washing powder is on offer today at three-for-the-price-of-two, buy a few boxes and store them away.

**(2) Sometimes pay more now to save later.** Cheap is not always better; quality items tend to last longer and save you money in the long run. That cheap, nice-looking frying pan may appear OK, but if you have to throw it away next month because the Teflon coating is gone, it wasn't such a good deal after all. Sometimes quality food or an organic alternative is better for you, so by spending more now you save on hospital bills later!

**(3) Buy used.** The old mantra: Reuse. Why not support the Salvation Army by buying used stuff from them? Refurbished old furniture has a lot of character. Reusing is also good for the environment. Baby stuff and children's clothes you can usually get for free; pass them on when your child grows out of them. Get over the hang-up that you shouldn't use stuff from dead people; that is exactly what you should do. Use your parents' or grandparents' old plates and cutlery and wristwatches and jewellery. These antiques have a lot of history, and you respect and commemorate your family by using their things. I have never spent money on a handphone in my life, although I have had a few given to me. The phone I use now is a Doro PhoneEasy 605 from Denmark that I selected out of my mother's estate when she died in 2012. We had a local SIM card installed that I top-up now and then, and I enjoy using it.

**(4) Buy yesteryear's technology.** In 1999 I bought the latest digital camera model, a Nikon Coolpix 990 with 3.34 megapixels. If memory serves me right it cost around S$1,700. Three months later Nikon came out with a newer model, with more features and more storage capacity, and the price was S$1,400! Today you can buy a digital camera with much better features for a few hundred bucks. My wife and son both have a collection of these. Me, I still use the old Coolpix. If you are a gadget-lover, good for you. The rest of us can save a lot of money by not buying the latest smart-phone or smart TV or smart car. Wait till the older and simpler version is put out for stock clearance sale. I am sure it will do the job for you, and it will help you be free so much sooner.

**(5) Attend free events.** In Singapore you can catch free concerts at the Esplanade outdoor theatre, the Botanic Gardens, and the Conservatory of Music, to name a few venues. Museums regularly open their doors to certain groups or for special events. Why pay for something you can get for free? In fact, the free events can be nicer to attend than the paid ones, with their informal atmosphere and hassle-free access.

**(6) Get knowledge and skills and entertainment for free.** When I was a kid, we had door-to-door sales people visiting us, proposing that we subscribe to various encyclopedias. My mother wasn't stingy with books, so she bought a five-volume set about animals of the world, one on art, one on music, another one on the history of the world, etc. Soon our living room was half-filled with bookcases and nicely bound works. I learned a lot from those books, but my, they took up a lot of space. Long after I left home, my mother invested some DKK40,000 (about $5,700) in *Den Store Danske Encyklopædi*, an enormous work in 24 large volumes with its own storage cabinet.[2] When she died in 2012 her extensive book collection had no commercial value whatsoever; we gave it all away. Today all this knowledge and so much more is available online for free, continuously updated. Imagine the money (and the space!) young people save by not having to pay for reference books, dictionaries and encyclopedias.

And you can take this one step further and find free classes and training courses online in virtually anything you might want to learn or do. Need a guitar tuner? Don't buy one, find one on YouTube. My son uses his mother's iPad mini as a keyboard, we don't have to buy a piano for him! Young people find movies and music for free online; I am not sure if it is all legal, but that is what they do. I still have some of the LP records I bought in the 1960s and 70s, and the turntable I used then still works. We still occasionally watch DVDs on a DVD player. But my kids will never have to spend all that money on music and movies or haul all that stuff around with them ever again. Their world can fit into a thumbdrive.

**(7) Don't pay to exercise.** It is silly to pay for a gym membership when you can get the same result for absolutely free. Your condo or your housing estate surely has an exercise ground; otherwise find one in a nearby park. To stay fit, you really only need two exercises, which together will work all your muscle groups as well as your cardiovascular system. (1) Pull yourself up by your arms (chin-ups); if you can't do that, just hang by your arms like a gibbon and lift your knees up as high as you can. (2) Walk up steps. That's all! Forget all those torture machines and intricate weightlifting and running devices they have in overpriced health clubs. If you want to be featured in the "Hot Bods" section of your local newspaper, you might consider those. For all the rest of us, the best way to stay in shape is to walk up any staircase you come across – and Singapore has a lot of them!

**(8) Stay healthy in general.** This is the best way to save money. I know, we are not all blessed with perfect health. I have known fit and slim non-smokers who developed cancer or fell over one morning and died of a cardiac arrest. Your health is very much a game of chance, but you can do a bit to improve the odds. Don't shoot yourself in the foot by smoking or over-eating or over-drinking. You don't need that, and you just harm yourself and the environment with your indulgence. Life is too precious. If you are healthy, you not only save money by not gorging on things you don't need, you are also more productive and end up making more money.

**(9) Don't buy insurance.** I am serious, it will work against you. Don't buy life insurance or house insurance or travel or comprehensive car or health or any other insurance. I will come back to this in more detail in chapter 9 when we consider how you should balance your investment portfolio and organise your finances.

**(10) Don't gamble.** I know this is not for everyone. Even fairly sensible people I know like to buy a few 4D tickets from time to time or bet on a football game. That is your choice. But you should know that overall as a group gamblers always lose, and I will prove that mathematically later on in chapter 4.

During my army days in Denmark I loved soccer. Denmark was playing the mighty Soviet Union in a big game in Copenhagen, and I considered betting on the game, because I was sure Denmark would surprise everyone and win, and the odds that the bookies offered were good. But I didn't. In the end Denmark did win 2–0, but I didn't feel frustrated that I'd missed out. In fact, I was glad I didn't bet – the winnings wouldn't have made any difference to me. I got so much more enjoyment from money I had *earned*, from serving in the army or from selling photographs and magazine articles as I did back then in my spare time. So I felt very relieved that I didn't bet after all, and have never considered it again since.

I went to a casino once, with a colleague who liked to gamble a bit. He was a computer programmer and liked number games, although he should have known that you cannot beat the house consistently. I didn't try, although I did have a free drink; in general I didn't feel comfortable there at all. That was a great decision I made back then in the 1970s, never to gamble, not even for fun or for "free". I urge you to do the same; it will be a relief for you. The great danger is becoming addicted to gambling. When you're addicted to something, you become its slave. Addiction is the opposite of freedom.

**(11) Do it yourself**. Do you really need that maid or gardener or repair man? It can be fun to do things for yourself, to mow the lawn or repair a broken cabinet. Yes, you will need a few tools, but they will last you a lifetime.

As for maids ... I know, some families cannot function without one. But 8,000 households here have two or more. In total there were some 214,500 maids in Singapore in 2013 according to the Ministry of Manpower.[3] It seems excessive. In my estate I see maids down in the car park washing the family car every day at 7am, Sundays included – is that really necessary? You can run your car through a car-wash once a month for $5; or better still, wash it yourself. We had a part-time cleaner in our household for a while; but when she quit a few years back, we found that it was actually easier and more convenient if we did our own cleaning, and cheaper too of course.

**(12) Turn off your water heater.** Even when you are in a cold climate, cold showers are better for you as they build up your body's resistance and immunity system. My older sister back in

Denmark had problems with flu and sinus issues for many years until she discovered the wonders of winter swimming. You know, in extreme cases participants go out on the sea ice and break a hole to swim. Now she swims all through the year in the freezing cold Nordic waters and feels much better. In the tropics, a water heater makes no sense at all. Why have a warm bath and sleep in air-conditioning when a cool shower and sleeping with a fan is much better for you, as well as for your finances and the environment?

**(13) Drive slowly.** Sometimes when I am early for an appointment I drive as slowly as I can. Someone wants to get into my lane? I let them. I keep a long distance from the car in front of me so that I can decelerate gradually at the red lights. I try to never come to a complete stop. The rule is that I am not allowed to impede traffic, just to follow it as slowly as I can in the middle lane. I listen to the news and relax; it is almost pleasant to drive this way. Sure, I will miss a light occasionally, maybe two or three over the course of the journey. That is still less than 5 minutes wasted and it doesn't really matter; our hybrid car shuts down and doesn't consume energy when stationary. I save a lot of fuel and wear on the pads by hardly having to brake at all. I get no speeding tickets. I am also less likely to get into an accident and have my car and myself dented, so I save on insurance and medical bills as well. And best of all, not only do I save money, but I feel a lot less stressed and frustrated. Try it for yourself one day.

On top of these 13 ways, Stacy Johnson in *Life Or Debt* goes one step further and urges us to never use credit cards! This is a tall order in a place like Singapore where most people carry a wallet full of cards and use them extensively to get discounts and freebies. Let's face it, leaving your credit cards at home wouldn't work here. However, Johnson does have a point that using cards makes it too easy to make impulse purchases. Most would agree that paying with cash is psychologically a bit more painful. So try to use cash more, especially in smaller family-owned restaurants or shops where the 2–3% that the bank charges the vendor for the credit card service might make a real difference to their bottom line.

Some of the money you save this way might appear like irrelevant amounts. I don't think any saving is insignificant. What is important is that you develop an attitude of respect for the numbers and make them work in your favour. Benjamin Franklin said: "Beware of little expenses; a small leak will sink a great ship." His portrait adorns the US$100 bill today.

There is one additional advantage to not spending too much on stuff. Stuff is a time-waster, it slows you down. I have moved a lot in my life, and the more stuff you have, the harder it is! Everything gets more complicated – the storing, the packing, the hauling around. Eventually you end up throwing most of it away anyway, and then it just ends up taking up space in the Semakau Landfill or whatever your local dump is called. Every time you get a new item or gadget, you find yourself fiddling with it and reading the instructions for hours. Well, some might enjoy that, but personally I would rather spend my time playing with my son, studying economics or going for a swim.

My best advice is: Simply ask yourself a question every time you are about to buy something. Not "Would I like to have this?" but instead: "Is there any way I can live reasonably comfortably and do my work without this?" If the answer is yes, don't buy it.

## The paradox of thrift

Yes, I am aware of this: If we all suddenly started to spend less, what would happen to the overall economy? Wouldn't it shrink? Wouldn't everything come to a grinding halt if we all only bought what we needed? After all, we all depend to some extent on the overall health of our national economy.

This occurrence is called "the paradox of thrift" and has been considered by economists since John Maynard Keynes popularised it in the 1930s, though it had been identified in various forms by thinkers long before him. In his book *Economics*, Paul Samuelson devotes three pages to the phenomenon. The paradox is that in times of deflationary pressure and less than full employment in the economy, thriftiness by individuals could "reduce the amount of actual net capital formation in the community", to use Samuelson's words. The result is that the population's total saving might paradoxically *fall* – because of lower incomes and a weaker economy – even though people were individually being virtuous and thrifty.

This fall in aggregate demand and savings can be mitigated, however, for example by increased government stimulus of the economy (see the next chapter for details). A country with excess savings could also increase exports to other countries that might consume more, and in this way export itself out of the slowdown. Recently, Germany has done something to that effect.

In his 2014 book *The Age of Oversupply*, Daniel Alpert makes a case for higher savings. He writes: "The developed world must generate a higher rate of savings to cover internal investments rather than to continuously rely on capital inflows initiated at the whim of offshore investors. Furthermore, economies that invest more of their incomes tend to grow at faster rates. Consumption-driven economies therefore tend to crowd out investment spending, and that is not something that should be perpetuated in the age of oversupply."

Nevertheless, politicians sometimes give us the impression that it is somehow unpatriotic to save. This was famously put forward by George W. Bush, who after the 9/11 attacks in the US in 2001 urged all Americans to go out and shop and spend and eat, to help the American economy recover.

What can you say to this?

1.  Do right by yourself. Set yourself free, not just from finan-
    cial worries but also from the social pressure to consume. Let
    all the others go out and spend. They can contribute to the
    aggregate demand and keep the wheels of the economy turn-
    ing. Of course that won't work if everybody thought this way,
    but from experience I can say that this is highly unlikely. As
    we shall see later, there simply aren't enough resources in this
    world for everyone to be rich. So make sure you protect your
    wealth. If other people do not understand this point, then let
    them go ahead and spend heedlessly – they'll be contributing
    to the benefit of the economy and humanity.

2.  And then again, that is the other thing: Is all that spending
    really so great? Overconsumption is destroying the Earth. It
    might be a good thing if we all slowed down a bit. Rainforest
    depletion, habitat reduction, biodiversity loss, water shortage,
    global warming... all this can be traced back to overpopulation
    and too much consumption and wastage of food and energy
    and resources. So if you look at it this way, the patriotic thing
    is now to spend less.

3.  And finally, we are all so scared of a recession. What if a
    recession (or "degrowth", to use a better term) is not so bad?
    What if we just say: Bring it on! As we shall see later, there
    are researchers like Herman Daly, Saskia Sassen, Tim Jackson
    and Richard Heinberg who think that a slowdown of global
    economic activity is unavoidable and in fact in some ways
    desirable. Regardless of the outcome, things are likely to get
    tough in the future, so do yourself a favour and build up the
    financial muscle to fight it out.

## Five ways to grow your money

So whatever happens, you will need to protect and grow all those new savings of yours. It is the established view in finance that there are roughly five asset classes that you should understand before you make a decision about how to invest your capital:

1. Commodities

2. Bonds

3. Property

4. Shares

5. Derivatives

We will look at each of these investment opportunities in more detail later, although not in that order, as I will explain. But before that, let us consider briefly how the wider aspects of the economy work. The macroeconomic situation affects all of us, and we should consider it when we plan for the future. Having a basic understanding of the concepts involved will stand you in good stead.

## 3

# Interest in Economics

*"Economics is extremely useful*
*as a form of employment*
*for economists."*
— JOHN GALBRAITH

### Is economics boring?

When I graduated from high school in 1971, I didn't know whether
to study biology or political science, so instead I settled for economics. I figured that economics was pretty much the basis for
everything else, and the world would always need people who
could manage the subject.

The economics programme was five years, but after two years
I had had enough. This was boooring; I couldn't see myself sitting
behind a desk looking at mathematical equations and endless rows
of numbers for the next 40 years.

In my class was a guy who had worked as a roughneck on a
drilling rig in Arctic Canada – now that sounded a bit more exit-
ing! I was interested in nature, birds, resources and wild places.
I also assumed that we would always need plenty of oil, so this
was a business with prospects. I took the famous "gap year" and
travelled around Canada and Alaska, and when I came back from
that, I went up to Norway and started working on the rigs there,
offshore in the North Sea. That was in 1974. Oil had just been discovered a few years prior, in 1969. The fields were in the middle of

the ocean, near the British and the Danish sectors, and a challenge to locate and develop. But I felt this could be really big. And I was right. The oil in Norway did become a big deal and transformed the small northern nation.

So, I never went back to college, and I never became a hot-shot economist. But I did learn a bit before I quit. And I never threw away the textbook I was issued during my first semester in a subject called "National Economics": Paul Samuelson's *Economics*. I took it with me as I moved around all those years and finally dusted it off and read it again recently in 2014. What a difference 40+ years make and what a revelation! This wasn't boring at all; this was the essence of human civilisation. I bought the 2010 edition as well and read that too, to get all the latest data and case studies. Samuelson is to economics what David Attenborough is to natural history: an incredible communicator.

## How wealth is created

During my first year in college, a teacher told us something that stuck with me. He said: "To generate wealth, you really only need three things: labour, capital and productivity." I have thought about that often since, in the various projects I became involved in. You need to work, like digging in the ground. For that you need capital to buy a shovel, or a drilling rig if you want to go deeper. But that is not enough; you must also produce results. It is not enough to dig a hole and fill it in again, or drill one and the well comes out dry. Something must be produced. That is what gives you productivity and wealth.

Our teacher did simplify the matter a bit. It is generally accepted among economists that you need one more component: land, or rent, in other words a place to work. In fact, in earlier human history, land was more important than anything else. Up until the first Industrial Revolution started in Europe around 1760, societies around the world were mainly agricultural in nature, of course with some fishing, mining and small-scale production as well. Whoever controlled the land controlled the wealth. In feudal society, the landed class, the gentry, often related to or associated with the royal family, had absolute control and power; the landless peasants worked the farms but lived from hand to mouth.

Trade was also considered important during that period of early civilisation – globalisation as we talk about it today is far from a new phenomenon. The period of mercantilism developed in Europe in the 1500s and lasted up until the Industrial Revolution. This was a period of economic thought where wealth was no longer just land; it was now also money, and especially precious metals, in particular gold. Trade was regarded as a way to increase your wealth, much as it is today. However, the mercantilists then didn't see trade as a win-win situation but as win-lose; they favoured high tariffs to protect the domestic economy against imports, and an aggressive trade policy to bring wealth in from abroad and then hoard it at home in the form of gold and silver.

As a case in point, the Spanish trade with the newly found lands in the New World developed into a perverted kind of mercantilism that bordered on robbery and genocide. The peoples in the new lands were called Indians because Christopher Columbus in his wisdom thought he had reached the Asian continent when he landed in the Bahamas in 1492. He explored the coast all the way down to Venezuela but died not realising that he had in fact found two whole new continents. Anyway, the Indians in the new lands had gold, and they used the gold to make elaborate religious ornaments; but otherwise they had no use for it, as it was too soft to be used for tools, and they did not value it as money. They were interested in trading with the Europeans to get their much more useful tools made of iron.

In his book *Seven Elements That Have Changed the World*, John Browne describes vividly how the Spanish conquistadors, who followed Columbus a few decades later, raided South America in search of the elusive El Dorado, the land of untold riches in an area of what is now Colombia. They never found it, but they did find communities of Muisca and Inca Indians who mined gold, and they plundered them with unheard of brutality. During the 1530s and 1540s, the Spaniards stole gold ornaments from the Indians, melted down their prized works of art and shipped the bullion back to Spain, where it was minted into coins. The volume was enormous; the Spaniards travelled in convoys of 60 ships, each carrying 200 tonnes of gold.

It is part of the story that this period of mercantilism didn't end well for the colonisers. At home in Europe the wealth was wasted on extravagant luxuries and wars, and local industries stagnated. In an interesting reference to today's European economic situation, Browne writes: "Spain was quickly led into a spiral of debt and ultimately bankruptcy. As in the late 2000s, easy access to 'free money', today in the form of cheap credit, weakened their economy."

## From Adam Smith to Paul Krugman

It is no coincidence that with the onset of industrialisation, our view of the economy and how to generate and measure wealth also changed. Philosophy and reason tends to build on the physical situation we are in.

Adam Smith is generally regarded as the main spokesperson for that group of economists who have become known as the classical economists. For the first time, the role of labour was now emphasised in the generation of wealth. Which is somewhat ironic, as this was exactly the onset of the industrial era, where machinery and capital became equally important. Smith broke with the mercantilists by concluding that if gold and silver were just dead objects that could be bought and sold for merchandise, then the real source of wealth was that production of stuff and its components of labour, capital and land.

Adam Smith published his main work, *The Wealth of Nations*, in 1776. In this book, he described how market forces help allocate resources such as land, labour and capital in the most productive way to generate wealth for society as a whole. Smith believed that each industrialist and trader would act in the market motivated by self-interest rather than by benevolence. But – and this is the catch – *desirable* outcomes would emerge from these self-interested exchanges, as if each participant was "led by an invisible hand" to "promote an end which was no part of his intention".[1]

Voila, here is the famous invisible hand of the market place that benefits everyone. No wonder *The Wealth of Nations* became the bible for free-market devotees. Margaret Thatcher was said to carry a copy of it with her in her handbag.

Many interpretations of Smith's theories have appeared since its publication, but I find *Capitalism and Its Alternatives* (2014) by Chris Rogers particularly insightful. Rogers makes the point that Smith never believed that markets would solve all economic and social problems in society – a fact that has been somewhat overlooked by his supporters. Smith was a moral man, and his actors while acting in self-interest were not really selfish; they had strong moral principles and sympathised with each other. Smith also insisted that the state was absolutely essential for the operation of the economy. It was the state's role to create and preserve stable and peaceful conditions that would enable the division of labour and fair exchange of trade. Property rights and national borders had to be defended for the invisible hand to do its work.

Adam Smith never used the word "capitalism" but Karl Marx did; in fact, did he ever! His main work was called *Das Kapital*, the first and most important volume of which came out in 1867. Like Smith, Marx believed that labour was the key to producing wealth, and he went as far as to state that it was the only way to generate it. What owners of capital did was scoop up the difference between the value of the production and the wages paid to the workers who produced it, the so-called "surplus value". Workers were free to sell their labour at a price, but this freedom in Marx's view was somewhat of an illusion, as the alternative was charity, luck or to starve, none of which could be considered reasonable or acceptable choices (as explained by Rogers). Marx believed that competition between capitalists for market share and profits would tend to force wages lower in a downward spiral. Capitalists would also be inclined to replace labour with machinery to improve productivity, and this would in turn force labour into unemployment. All this would eventually lead to overproduction, lack of demand from impoverished workers/consumers and thus a crisis in the capitalist economy.

Much of all this is actually quite reasonable and holds true today. Where Marx went wrong was in his view of the role of the state. As we saw, Smith believed that the role of the state was to facilitate business and protect the owners of capital. Marx saw this as an oppressive mechanism. He believed that those who did the actual work – the working class – should seize control of the state from the bourgeoisie, who owned the means of production but who didn't really contribute anything of value. This should if necessary be done through a revolution where the working class, the proletariat, took over the means of production and set up a socialist state which would eventual lead to a communist one, a utopia where everyone worked according to his ability and was paid according to his needs.

Who said economics was boring? This is the most exciting stuff out there, at the core of everything else humans do. It is at the root of imperialism and industrialisation, the fight between capitalism and communism. Great wealth has been generated and lost, empires have emerged and crumbled, wars have been fought, over exactly these old ideas.

We all know what happened to Marxism and Communism. In the countries that adopted it, the system morphed into an oppressive dictatorship; and on top of that the planned economy was not able to provide the consumer goods that people expected.

The situation in Germany after the Second World War could not have made things any clearer. You take a country and cut it in half. On one side, the Soviet-occupied section, you have a planned economy, a workers' paradise where everyone works for the common good and there is no private ownership of the means of production. On the other side, the one the Allied forces liberated, you have a market economy. The planned economy produces a Trabant automobile, the market economy a Mercedes. People want the Mercedes and vote with their feet. The pure Marxist planned economy was dealt the final blow with the fall of the Berlin Wall in 1989 and the breakup of the Soviet Union a couple of years later.

Today only a few states such as Cuba and North Korea swear by the philosophy; it is generally accepted that others like China and Vietnam are communist in name only. I have on my shelf a beautiful vase that I got out of my mother's estate; at the bottom it says "Made in the DDR". The DDR, Deutsche Demokratische Republik, was East Germany. The country no longer exists. I keep it as a memento of a time gone by and an experiment that didn't work.

Capitalism has had to evolve as well. Since the 1929 stock market crash in the United States and the subsequent worldwide depression, it hasn't really existed in its pure form. With Franklin Roosevelt's New Deal in 1933 and the emergence of John Maynard Keynes in the same period, capitalism was modified with a good dose of state intervention – a prescription amount of socialism thrown in, if you wish.

Keynes formulated this concept of a "mixed economy" in his book *The General Theory of Employment, Interest and Money*, which came out in 1936, and it has really been the economic recipe for all successful countries ever since. Keynes lived till 1946 and had a profound influence on the way all countries conduct macroeconomic policies today. He was also instrumental in formulating the Bretton Woods agreements in 1944 which lead to a fixed currency exchange rate system and the establishment of the World Bank and International Monetary Fund. It is the otherwise somewhat conservative (i.e. free market proponent) economist Milton Friedman who is credited with the phrase, "We are all Keynesians now". Politicians and commentators have repeated this cliché ad nauseam since then.

There is of course still debate going on today amongst analysts, academics and politicians about how to move economic policy forward, but it tends to be about details rather than principles. In the conservative corner you find financial journalists like Rick Santelli with CNBC and his Tea Party friends in the libertarian movement within the American Republican Party who favour so-called laissez-faire free market capitalism. In the liberal corner are economists like the anti-austerity advocate Joseph Stiglitz and most prominently Paul Krugman.

Krugman, who writes for the *New York Times*, strongly favours state intervention in the economy, such as in the form of a high minimum wage and a welfare system, to mitigate inequality. He is on record as saying that as much as 50% state share of the economy would be acceptable to him, as the case is in France and the Scandinavian countries. His solution to a national debt crisis, like the one in Greece, is usually to simply just forgive the debt, so as to restore growth. Like other liberals, Krugman tends to find his supporters within the American Democratic Party and equivalent social democratic parties in Europe.

I think we have settled on the mixed economy simply because it has shown itself to produce the results people want: plenty of innovation, growth and jobs in the private economy, but with some state intervention in the form of tight regulation of businesses, control of monopolies, consumer protection and social policies to reduce inequality. Time and again we see the state providing the foundation for development, and the private sector grabbing the opportunities. The internet was developed by a state-funded US government initiative back in the 1960s and used mainly in academia until the 1990s. But look what happened when the private sector spotted the prospects for making money from it – think Microsoft, Apple, Google, Amazon, Facebook, the list is endless.

The debate between conservative and liberal economists hasn't ended, and it never will. As long as there are different interests and ideals and values out there, there will be different ideas and theories to formulate and promote them. That is what makes economics and politics exciting.

## Capitalism can set you free

Remember that Marx didn't think that the workers were really free? Well, first of all, you can still be fairly free to do what you want in a capitalist economy, even if you help some rich guy make even more money during working hours. The secret to that is simply to find an engaging job that you love and have a passion for. As the saying goes: "If you do what you love, you will never work a day in your life."

Secondly, and this is pretty much the theme of this book: If you can't beat them, join them! Be a capitalist, a "rentier" (we will define this term later). You know the cliché: "Don't work for money, let money work for you." We cannot all be Warren Buffett or Bill Gates; there simply aren't enough resources, as we shall see in chapter 10, for us all to be billionaires or even millionaires. That is impossible. But as I am trying to show here, we can all accumulate some capital. And with an interesting job and some return on our savings, we can work our way towards freedom.

I grew up in a liberal home. My mother, Ebba Strange, was a passionate socialist who entered politics and served over 20 years in the Danish parliament. She was the first woman in the country to chair a political party's group in parliament, and she served on many committees and councils, including the Nordic Council and as chair of the parliamentary legal committee. However, she never became a minister in government, somewhat to her disappointment; she was a bit too far to the left!

In high school and at university I mixed with left-leaning groups, and we explored alternatives to the capitalist system. I started high school in 1968, the height of the Vietnam War, the year Martin Luther King and Robert F. Kennedy were both assassinated. In Europe we had Portugal, Spain and Greece ruled by military dictatorships; there was an uprising by students in France and it spilled over into Germany and Denmark. Overseas, new countries were struggling for their independence. Surely there had to be a better system; capitalism and imperialism were the cause of so much evil and destruction in the world. Wars, famine, oppression, crisis, waste – couldn't you plan better? Couldn't we all live in peace? What if people took charge and owned all the factories and the banks, wouldn't everyone be happier?

After a year in North America and a few years working with Americans in the oil patch I became a different person. Americans weren't the arrogant racists and warmongers I thought they were, they were the best people on Earth. And maybe capitalism itself and the free market weren't so bad after all. I came to love the freedom it gave us young people. The freedom of movement and choice as students, workers and consumers. And sure, you could make money too, so with a bit of money you could travel where you wanted and work. In 1976, as my mother came back from the General Assembly meeting at the United Nations Headquarters in New York, I gave her a copy of Donna Fargo's patriotic record, "US of A" (*I believe in the red, white and blue...* – to this day I can still sing it to my son). My mother said: "Why thank you so much, that is very kind of you, Morten!" But I think she threw the record away after I left, I never saw it in her vinyl collection.

Young people like to go to the extremes, but maybe the truth is somewhere in between. Capitalism has been great for us; it has lifted me and millions, hundreds of millions, of others out of poverty or near-poverty. But there are big problems with the system that haven't been resolved, not even with the moderated mixed market economy of today. According to many observers, the biggest market failure of all has been the free market's inability to consider and value the natural world and price in the environmental externalities. We shall look at that in more detail later.

Winston Churchill has been quoted as saying: "Democracy is the worst form of government except all the others that have been tried."[2] Maybe the same is true for capitalism – it is the worst economic system except for all the others!

## A few macroeconomic concepts

As you make capitalism work for you, there are a few terms within the national economy that you should be familiar with. They will help you make the right decisions when you come to allocating your assets. You will be bombarded with this jargon if you just turn on CNBC or Bloomberg Television or read the business pages in your favourite newspaper or online. Some concepts are fairly obvious; others are more complex.

**Capital:** Capital must be the core of capitalism, right? It is indeed, but capital is many things. I like Samuelson's old-fashioned explanation: "To the extent that people are willing to save – to abstain from present consumption and wait for future consumption – to that extent society can devote resources to new capital formation." Samuelson concludes from this: "Economic activity is future-oriented. By the same token, current economic consumption is largely the consequence of past efforts." I wish that was so – Samuelson wrote this just before a new era set in, an era of unlimited capital creation via debt!

Both governments and private finance companies can create additional capital out of thin air, and they do. Banks by lending out funds beyond their reserve requirement, that way gearing the value of their deposits many times over. "Reserve requirements" refer to the liquidity ratio that most central banks impose on the local banks, i.e. the minimum ratio of deposits they must hold in relation to their lending. This should not be confused with "capital requirements", which refer to the equity within the bank required by regulators, i.e. the excess shareholder capital that the bank must have on its balance sheet to make sure it is solvent.

Capital is also used as an expression to describe physical capital goods, i.e. the wider assets within the economy, not just money, such as the means of production in terms of factories and office buildings. Even the people there are sometimes referred to as "human capital"! This becomes important in ecological economics, where writers like Herman Daly make a significant distinction between man-made and natural capital.

**Money supply:** Back to the money capital. The amount of money in a national economy is called the money supply, and there are typically four ways of measuring it. M0 is the actual currency in circulation, i.e. notes and coins. M1 is M0 plus bank reserves and check deposits not in circulation. M2 includes saving deposits and fixed deposits for individuals and is the key indicator for determining inflation. M3 is the broadest measure, taking into account institutional money market funds. Over the last few decades, the money supply, especially M2, has been allowed to expand steadily in all advanced economies, and this has vital ramifications for your investment decisions (see Fig. 1).

**Monetary policy:** This is the set of policies used by central banks to control the money supply and achieve growth and stability in the economy as well as price stability, moderate inflation and full employment. Central banks are independent institutions, but of course they operate in synchronisation with elected governments to steer the economy; the main economic tool of the government itself is *fiscal policy* (i.e. revenue collection and expenditure).

In the United States, the Federal Reserve System ("the Fed") conducts monetary policy; in the Euro zone, it is the European Central Bank; and in Singapore it is MAS.

The main tools in a central bank's toolbox are interest rates, banks reserve requirements and open market operations (buying/selling bonds to stimulate/slow down the economy). When central banks raise interest rates, sell bonds or raise capital reserve requirements for retail banks, they slow down the economy. They do this when the economy is overheating and inflation is building up. In a deflationary economic environment (low demand, low growth, high unemployment), central banks will do the opposite, i.e. keep interest rates low and purchase assets on financial

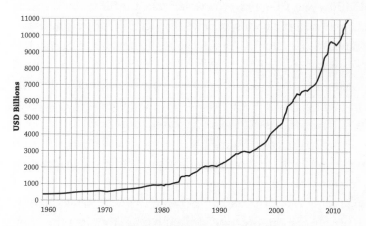

**Fig. 1: US MZM money supply**

Common to all developed countries is a financialisation of the economy, indicated by the enormous expansion of money supply that has taken place, especially so since the late 1970s. The graph above shows the ever-increasing MZM (money zero-maturity) money supply in the US. MZM is a measure of liquid funds – essentially M2 minus fixed deposits but plus money market funds.

markets to stimulate money supply and growth in what you might have heard of as "QE" (quantitative easing).

In Singapore, MAS is a bit different from other central banks in that due to the open nature of Singapore's economy, MAS does not set interest rates directly. This is done by the banks themselves, with rates here following international rates closely. MAS conducts monetary policy mainly by controlling the exchange rate of the Singapore dollar (SGD/S$) versus an undisclosed basket of currencies. MAS announces its stance on the currency twice a year, but also sometimes in between meetings. A higher S$ will tend to keep bond yields and prices down, while an easing is regarded as a somewhat inflationary stimulus of the local economy.

**Interest rates:** Interest is something we all hate to pay but love to receive. Why is there such a thing? Well, because money has a time value. If you had a choice between receiving $100 today and $100 a year from now, you would take the $100 now. To wait, you would expect a bonus, of say $3. So that would be your interest rate: 3% per annum. (In a recent development of completely perverse macroeconomics, some European banks have started to charge negative interest, i.e. penalising depositors for lending them money! And some societies do not appreciate interest for cultural reasons. We will leave such cases aside here.)

In most countries, central banks set an interest rate that they charge retail banks for borrowing; banks pay this and charge their customers a bit on top to make a buck. Deposit rates are lower than lending rates, the difference being the net interest margin. By lowering the interest rate, central banks stimulate the economy and promote growth and employment. Raising the rate cools an overheated economy that is experiencing excess demand, not enough production capacity and inflation.

In the United States, the central bank rate is called the federal funds rate and is an important tool for conducting monetary policy. Between December 2008 and the end of 2015 it was at a historic low of 0–0.25% per annum (or, 0–25 "basis points").

**Inflation:** Inflation, as most people realise, is when prices go up. But there is a bit more to it than that. Prices are usually measured using an index, most often the Consumer Price Index (CPI), which tracks a basket of consumer goods and the price increases over time. I say "increases" because prices always go up, don't they? Think back 10 or 20 years, was anything more expensive then than now? Probably not. Well, maybe airline tickets. Over a shorter period of time, however, say a few months or even a few years, it is possible that prices go down, such as during a recession, when there is a lack of demand.

The CPI is sometimes stripped of selected components, often food and energy, and in Singapore accommodation and private road transport. The rest is then called the core inflation. That is done exactly so as to make the index less influenced by those volatile factors, as they often contract temporarily.

In the United States, the Federal Reserve Board often refers to an index similar to the CPI, the personal consumption expenditures price index (PCE). The PCE tends to grow a bit slower than the CPI, and there is a whole school of thought among contrarians that the official inflation numbers are manipulated by government and kept too low.[3]

Inflation usually doesn't happen evenly across the economy. We often see spurts of inflationary pressure in isolated sectors. During the period of massive expansion of the money supply (QE) conducted by central banks after the Great Recession of 2008–09, we saw significant asset inflation but very little wage inflation. In other words, the new money went into buying property, bonds and existing stock in companies; little ended up in the pockets of workers, and overall inflation remained low. We will deal with that in more detail later.

It is the stated goal of central banks to keep inflation at a moderate rate, usually around 2% (Europe and the United States), and for China 3% per annum. This will encourage spending and reduce the debt burden of debtors, thus stimulating growth. Governments don't want deflation (negative inflation, i.e. falling prices), as this will encourage consumers to delay spending in anticipation of lower prices and thereby slow down the economy. However, they also don't want too high inflation, as this is part of an overheating economy and an unsustainable expansion of the money supply. Extreme inflation can lead to total financial and economic collapse. Singapore had hyperinflation during the Japanese Occupation, and more recently (2009) we have seen hyperinflation in Zimbabwe.

My grandfather (my mother's father), Henrik Henriksen, was born in 1896 and as a passionate Danish nationalist he moved south of the border to Flensborg in Germany to teach at a school for the Danish-speaking minority there in 1920. He lived through the Weimar Republic hyperinflation, probably the most notorious case of monetary mismanagement and collapse of all time. When I was a child, my grandfather showed me a shoe box he had kept full of banknotes; the denominations were astronomical, billions and billions of marks. They were of course all worthless by then.

The event took place during 1922–23 when Germany was trying to pay off war damages after the First World War. The Germans let the printing presses go wild. The highest denomination was 100 trillion marks, but even that was only about US\$25, and the inflation rate was some 3,000,000% per month. There is not enough room here to tell the whole story, fascinating as it might be. (In *When Money Dies*, Adam Fergusson does a much better job at that than I ever could anyway.) However, my grandfather would tell about how they used a wheelbarrow to carry the money when they went to the bakery to buy bread. They burned stacks of banknotes at home to keep warm; it was cheaper than buying firewood. When they went to a café they would pay for the meal immediately, in case prices went up before they left.

Now that is inflation! Savers with money in the bank got totally wiped out, but others benefited. If you owned real stuff such as property, things or shares in companies you were OK. And indebted farmers benefited the most; a story has it that a farmer went to town, sold off a few eggs at the market and paid off the mortgage to his entire property with the money.

The experience with hyperinflation left deep scars on the German psyche, visible today when Germany preaches responsible monetary and fiscal management to the other Euro group members.

**GDP:** Probably the most important of all macroeconomic concepts, GDP (Gross Domestic Product) is a measurement of the total output in an economy. It is usually calculated for a national entity, a country, and usually for a year. GDP being a measurement of the value of all goods and services flowing through the national economy, there are two ways to measure the flows: as consumption, and as income. The two variables will be equal, as what is an expense for one person will be an income for someone else.

On the expense side, GDP is calculated using the formula **GDP = C + G + I + (X – M)**, where C is private consumption, G is government spending, I is capital investment, X is exports and M is imports. As such, a trade surplus will add to GDP, a trade deficit will reduce it. On the income side, the National Income (NI) is calculated by adding up all incomes like this: **NI = W (wages) + R (rental income) + I (interest) + PR (profits)**. Although NI is less often used, it can be interesting to look at the composition of the national income; we will get back to that later.

You sometimes see the terms NNP and GNP used. NNP is what Samuelson mainly referred to when I went to school. It is Nett National Product, i.e. Gross National Product minus

depreciation. It has gone out of fashion to deduct the depreciation – today the numbers are usually expressed gross. Personally I
think that is wrong, but then, no one asked me when it was imple-
mented! GNP is similar to GDP, except it is calculated on a national
basis, such that citizens owning factories abroad will add to the
GNP but not to the GDP of their country of nationality. This way,
very open economies with a lot of foreign-owned investments (like
Singapore) will tend to have a higher GDP than GNP; for a country
like Japan the GNP tends to exceed the GDP.[4]

You can play around with the GDP and calculate "real GDP",
which is nominal GDP adjusted for inflation, and "GDP per capita",
which of course is GDP divided by the population size. GDP can
also be based on PPP (Purchasing Power Parity), which allows
for different levels of prices across countries. Countries with low
prices are often poor (their lower productivity causes lower wages
and lower prices overall), but they tend to have a relatively higher
GDP measured by PPP than high-income industrialised countries.

In the end it might not be so important which method you
use, GDP, GNP or PPP. What is mainly of interest is the change
over time. Are things getting better or worse for us? That is why
you see the changes in GDP from year to year and even quarter to
quarter always making headline news. Two consecutive quarters
of negative GDP growth is considered a technical recession, i.e. an
economic decline. In the accepted public spin of GDP numbers,
more is always better. In this view, the GDP is like your report card
in school: +4% is better than +2% is better than 0% growth.

However, there is more to GDP than that. I was watching
CNBC one evening not too long ago, and the focus was on the
bush fires in California razing thousands of hectares of land and
hundreds of homes to the ground. The pretty blonde in the studio
had a bright idea; she said: "This might actually be good for the
Californian economy. When all the houses have to be rebuilt it
will be good for growth!" This is economic growth turned on its

head. In this view, a traffic accident is good for growth. Doesn't it generate lots of activity for the car workshop fixing the wrecked cars? And also the ambulance services bringing the victims to hospital, the fortunes spent on treatment and rehabilitation of the injured; funeral services for the dead; the higher insurance premiums for the insurance companies? Lots of GDP growth, everyone is a winner, right? Of course not. There is a hidden contradiction here, which has been described as the "broken window fallacy" – something the CNBC journalist either had not heard of or forgot to consider. Herman Daly coined the phrase "uneconomic growth" to account for this type of GDP increase. There are a number of other issues with regard to the GDP and the way it does or does not capture progress; we shall look at them in more detail in chapter 10.

**Economic indicators:** These are important events in the economy that investors should be familiar with. There are three kinds of indicators. *Leading indicators* usually have their peaks or bottoms before corresponding peaks or bottoms in the economy as a whole. Important leading indicators are new orders, money supply, stock prices, new business formation, wholesale price index, unit labour cost. Industrial production and personal income are *coincident indicators*, while average duration of unemployment and bank interest rates are *lagging indicators* that peak or bottom out after those of the aggregate economy (IBF, 2013a).

Economic indicators in general are extensively covered on such sites as Investopedia.com. All countries have governmental departments that produce statistical analysis and forecasting using economic data. In Singapore, you can get current data from the websites of the Ministry of Trade and Industry (MTI) and the Department of Statistics. MTI compiles an index comprising nine leading indicators, the Composite Leading Index (CLI). Even if you suffer from data overload in your investment work, it is a useful tool to check once in a while; updates are published online quarterly.[5]

My statistics teacher at Aarhus University said that statistics are like a lady's bikini: They reveal a lot, but hide the most important parts. Statistics will not tell you exactly what will happen in the future, but they are worth investigating and considering so that you can form your own informed opinions.

**Fiscal policy:** As we saw under monetary policy, this is the main government tool for managing the economy. It refers to the government's use of taxation and spending to control aggregate supply and demand. By increasing taxes and reducing spending, the government will cool the economy and reduce the demand. Likewise, if the government reduces taxes and spends more, this will stimulate demand and economic growth.

Fiscal policy works best if the government actually has some resources to manage. If the government keeps pumping up the economy by spending more than it collects in taxes, i.e. by running a budget deficit, eventually it will run out of options to borrow and then finally out of economic options period. This happened in many European countries after the 2009 recession. Greece was the poster child of economic mismanagement, but many other so-called "Club Med" countries were not far behind.

In a country like Singapore with prudent economic management, fiscal policy remains a pillar of economic strategy. The recession in 1985–86, as is usually the case with downturns, was caused by a combination of reasons, mainly external factors like falling oil prices and international trade volumes, but also local business costs and in particular wages having risen too fast. This event was countered by the government in classic fashion with fiscal policies that included reducing the savings rate (the CPF contributions), slashing corporate tax rates, privatising government-linked companies like Singapore Airlines and later SingTel, and undertaking public works projects such as the expansion of the MRT system.[6] On the private side, union workers came out in support. I remember the demonstrations at the time, workers with placards saying, "Reduce our wages!" It was a complete culture shock for me. I never saw a worker in Europe demanding anything other than more time off and free money. But it worked! The economy recovered remarkably quickly in 1987 – a case of fiscal policy in action.

So what has all this got to do with you, today? Well, all these concepts play a role in your life, whether you like it or not. The reason we have economics in the first place is that resources are limited. If there were plenty of everything we would never have to economise, right? But there isn't. Economists would like to see economics as a science, and of course it is in a way. The mathematics behind it can be as complicated as rocket science. But it is also an art, and at the final hurdle a guessing game where everyone's guess regarding the future is as good as everyone else's.

How you interpret the macroeconomic landscape and events will have a direct bearing on whether you should buy gold, DBS corporate bonds or stock in Apple Inc. tomorrow. Somewhere out there in the masses of historical and macroeconomic data available might be the answer. Of course, there is something called microeconomics as well – it is the twin brother of macroeconomics. Microeconomics deal with the role of businesses and consumers in the economy, as well as with the price elasticity of supply and demand. We will look at this later, when we consider the price formation of commodities in chapter 5. For now it is time to move on and consider each of the asset classes mentioned in chapter 2.

# Derivatives

*"Derivatives are financial
weapons of mass destruction."*
— WARREN BUFFETT

## What are they?

As you can see above, we know what Warren Buffett thinks of
derivatives. And for what it's worth, I agree with him. That is why
I cover derivatives first among the asset classes in this book, to
get them out of the way. I would stick my neck out and urge you:
Do not play with derivatives. I will tell you why not in a minute.

To young investors, the prospect of growing one's wealth in a
patient, organic manner can seem tedious and slow. So they turn
to derivatives; they gear (borrow) to multiply their stakes. Yes,
that way you can win big. But you can also lose big. I will show you
that if you keep playing in a zero-sum game, you will always lose all
your money. Instead of rich quick, you end up poor quick.

Derivatives are not something of value in themselves; they
derive their "value" from being linked to an asset, like a share of
a company or a currency. However, derivatives are surrounded by
this mystique. Since ordinary people don't really understand them,
they presume that they are brilliantly complex devices that make
financial whiz kids enormously rich. So let's consider derivatives
very briefly, and then move on to other asset classes that you can
easily access to grow your wealth in a more predictable manner.

There are tons of sources available in books and online to explain derivatives. I will take my cue from the original, official text, the Capital Markets and Financial Advisory Services Examination Study Guide, "Module 6A: Securities & Futures Product Knowledge". This text is published by the IBF (Institute of Banking and Finance in Singapore); they conduct examinations on behalf of the Monetary Authority of Singapore to ensure the competency level of workers in the local financial industry.

According to IBF, there are three basic derivatives products: futures, options and warrants. I add CFDs (contracts for difference) here because they have become popular among retail investors.

**Futures:** The idea behind a futures contract is that you set the price of a product some time in advance. Say you are a farmer; you might want the certainty of selling your corn harvest now at a price decided on today; later when the crop is in the barn you can deliver the goods. While a forward contract will do the same thing, a futures contract is a standardised product that is arranged through a clearing institution such as the Chicago Mercantile Exchange or an affiliated exchange such as the Singapore Exchange (SGX).

Futures contracts are used for all tangible commodities such as agricultural produce, petroleum products and metals. But the futures tool has been expanded to cover virtually any financial product, including shares, real estate, foreign exchange, interest rates, credit default swaps and even the weather! The contracts are settled on the last day of trading by cash settlement or through physical delivery of the actual product.

However, we don't all need 5,000 bushels of wheat or 1,000 barrels of West Texas Intermediate light sweet crude oil delivered to our doorstep. As mentioned, the futures contract is standardised and specific in terms of volume, delivery date and minimum change in price. The beauty of that is that both the farmer and his wholesale customer, or the driller and the refinery, can trade the futures contract any time they want. This gives the middleman – the futures trader – an opportunity to participate in the trade by taking a position and benefiting from a change in price that might be in his favour. The futures exchange is where the orders are collected, executed and settled; the exchange also provides a safe framework for buyers and sellers to conduct business and settle possible disputes.

**Options**: Like the word says, an option offers a choice. It gives the person who buys the option the right but not the obligation to exercise it. For instance, if you are shopping for a new apartment, you might buy an option from the developer for a small amount, and then exercise it later, whereupon you settle in full. Financial transactions are often done like this, directly between the two parties, but since the 1970s the options trade has expanded into standardised contracts that can be traded on a derivatives exchange. Options are now in place for a range of financial instruments like stocks, indexes, currencies, interest rates and commodities. Using an exchange like this and standardised terms means that anyone with a trading account can buy and sell options, thus providing liquidity to the options market.

A *call option* gives the holder the right to purchase an underlying asset at a specified price – the *strike price* – for a certain period of time. Investors buy calls when they think the share price of the underlying security will rise.

The option to sell a stock is called a *put option*; in trading jargon this is going "short" on the stock. A put gives the holder the right to receive the strike price of the underlying stock on or before the expiry date. If you buy a put option with a strike price of $10, you can now collect $10 even if the share has gone down to $8 at the time of expiry. In other words, you would buy a put option if you believe the market is bearish (meaning it is turning down).

If the market confirms your opinion, your profit in either case – call or put – is virtually unlimited. Your loss is limited to the cost of the option, i.e. the premium paid and the interest costs.

Options are usually traded on margin, meaning the trading platform will just require a portion of the value as a downpayment. This is OK as long as the option is in-the-money, meaning it can be closed at a profit. If the market moves against you, the option will go out-of-the-money, and the exchange platform might issue a margin call and require you to top up your account.

There is much more to option trading than this, obviously, but this explains the main concept. There is a time value to an option, which drops gradually towards expiry; the total value of an option is **intrinsic value + time value**, with time value becoming zero at expiry. There are many different strategies for trading options, such as combining calls and puts, "covered" as well as "naked", in a virtually unlimited number of ways.

**Warrants**: A warrant is a kind of option to buy or sell an underlying asset at a specified exercise price. Unlike options, however, warrants are issued by a company rather than an investor, and are offered to holders of company bonds and preferred stock. They are like a little bonus to shareholders and usually valid for several years. Holders can keep them and convert them into new shares at the *exercise price*, which of course should be lower than the current share price. Alternatively, the warrants can be traded on the exchange.

Structured warrants are issued by a third-party financial institution. A *call warrant* gives the holder the right to buy the underlying asset, while a *put warrant* gives the holder the right to sell the underlying asset. Structured warrants in Singapore are always so-called European-style options, meaning they can only be exercised on the expiry date. In options trading, so-called American options can be exercised anytime before or at expiry, and because of that they are usually traded at a slight premium.

**CFDs**: In the last few years, with the popularity of online trading platforms, CFDs have become popular among traders. These are contracts for difference, a kind of futures contract where settlement is done in cash only. There is no expiry date, so you can hold the CFD as long as you want (though there is a cost to this as the trading platform will charge some interest on the financing). If you think a listed company is about to rally, you could buy a CFD for say $10 and sell it again when the stock reaches $15, and pocket the difference, $5. You never actually own the stock. Why would you not just buy the stock? You could, but with a CFD, the trading platform will allow you to trade on a margin, so with a 10:1 margin, you only put down $1 to own a $10 share, but you still pocket $5 profit. Of course, if the market moves against you and the share drops to $5, you lose $5 on a $1 investment plus the interest you paid on the instrument. With a CFD you can also sell a share or an index you don't have, i.e. go short on the market, if you are bearish and believe the market will drop in the near future.

## Use of derivatives

As we saw under futures trading, there is a legitimate use for derivatives in the real economy. An airline might buy jet fuel futures a few months in advance to lock in a price they consider favourable; this way they are able to budget and set ticket prices well in advance. A copper mine operator can secure a price for his production before the metal is out of the ground; again this enables him to budget safely.

This is considered hedging, a strategy for reducing your risk. If you own a portfolio of blue-chip stocks, but you fear that the market is about to go down, you can hedge your position by buying a put option to sell the stocks (or an index of similar stocks) at a decent price on a future date. If the market does go tumbling down, you exercise the option; if the market goes up instead, you just let the option expire. Your portfolio will increase in value and you are pretty safe either way, except for the cost of the hedge.

Derivatives are used to enhance the return on investment products in something called "structured products". They can be structured notes, funds or even synthetic ETFs; we will look at ETFs (exchange traded funds) in more detail in chapter 9, when we consider how to put together a safe and profitable portfolio of diversified investments. Barrier options, callable bull/bear contracts, extended settlement contracts, swaps ... the list goes on an on. These are instruments developed by the financial industry in what they like to call "financial innovation", and they all use derivatives. There are even derivatives of derivatives, I am not kidding, you can buy options on futures!

Obviously derivatives can enhance an investment product's return. But use of derivatives also carries risks. If the market moves against you, a derivative can magnify your loss. That is why Warren Buffett said in 2002: "In my view, derivatives are financial weapons of mass destruction, carrying dangers that, while now latent, are potentially lethal."[1]

I had an older colleague in the oil business who told me on the rigs: "Don't do as I do, do as I say." In a similar manner, observers have pointed out that Buffett actually has been known to use derivatives in his investment work. Just like how he, the biggest stock picker of all, usually gives this advice to other people: "Buy a low-cost index fund."[2] We will look at this again later, in chapters 7 and 9.

So, financial products using derivatives can be dangerous. That is why financial regulars only recommend them to so-called "accredited investors". In Singapore, an accredited investor under the Securities and Futures Act is someone with net personal assets exceeding S$2 million, or an annual income exceeding S$300,000. Only accredited investors and/or members of the financial community who have passed a financial competency test are allowed to trade in derivatives, and the institutions and trading platforms offering these trading services are supposed to screen their clients.

In more general terms, an accredited investor is described in the financial business as a high-net-worth individual, which is basically a millionaire, i.e. someone with more than $1 million in investable assets (not counting home, car, etc). Someone with between $1 million and $100,000 in the bank is labelled "affluent". What if you have less than that? That is just too bad; the hedge funds are not really interested in you anyway.

Hedge funds differ from ordinary mutual funds precisely in their use of derivatives. In a contradiction of terms, hedge funds don't actually hedge. They usually take a firm position by either going short or long in the market, depending on their outlook. Hedge fund deposits typically start at $200,000 and the funds are also generally illiquid; they can be hard to exit from on short notice. Ordinary mutual funds only invest long, they don't short the market and they don't use leverage, i.e. gear up their positions with borrowed funds; they usually redeem their certificates from one day to the next.

Many observers have been sceptical of this era of financial innovation. The economist Paul Krugman, for one, has accused the financial industry of adding very little to the actual economy, while churning over huge monetary amounts and just skimming a bit off the top. The numbers are staggering. At the end of 2010, the total outstanding over-the-counter derivatives market was more than $600 trillion (IBF, 2013b). Most of that, $465 trillion, was interest rate contracts, with foreign exchange contracts and credit default swaps second and third, respectively.

For those who make a living in the financial services industry, this is great. Banking, investment services, wealth management and other financial services together with the insurance industry contribute some 12% to the Singapore national income every year, and the industry has the highest value-added factor among the services.[3] There is nothing wrong with that. Just make sure you are on the right side of this trade. You should be benefiting from this, not donating to the industry and losing out in the process.

## Derivative trading is zero-sum

Here is where alarm bells go off in my head: Derivatives trading is a zero-sum game. That is not me saying it: On page 90 of the official study guide on futures product knowledge (IBF, 2013b), you can read: "the options market is a **zero-sum game** because the buyer's gains are the seller's losses, and vice versa." The bold font is from the text. There you have it, I suspected that much: The derivatives market is a casino.

Before SGX was formed in 1999, there was the Stock Exchange of Singapore (SES) and the Singapore International Monetary Exchange (SIMEX). During the 1990s, a number of my former oil-field colleagues tried their luck at SIMEX. For a fee you could buy a trading seat and buy and sell forex and derivative products on the exchange using your own or other people's money. The place was down opposite Sentosa in what is now VivoCity. I visited one of my friends there a few times. The traders wore colourful jackets and traded the old-fashioned way by outcry.

Three out of three of my friends at SIMEX left after a while. "I am not making", one said. That was all I needed to know. They went back to the oil business, working for Schlumberger, Halliburton and Expro respectively for several decades after that, although they have started to retire now one by one. I see them now and then. They all still manage their savings and investments, of course, but I don't think they trade in derivatives any longer. One of my friends trades the MSCI Singapore Index futures for fun during the day (it's pretty much identical to the STI). I think he knows this doesn't pay the bills; his monthly annuity payments do that. He simply enjoys the excitement of it.

## Gambler's ruin

Let's say you have some dollars. You play a 50–50 game with an opponent who has an unlimited number of dollars. Did you know that if you keep on playing, you will always lose all your money? If you didn't know that, maybe you shouldn't trade derivatives.

The theorem is called "gambler's ruin", and it is not hard to understand. If you flip a coin, the chance of head or tail is 50–50 or 50% for each toss. Let's say you play a game with an opponent where you win a dollar from him for guessing the toss correctly, and vice versa, and the game ends when one of you goes bankrupt. If you and your opponent both have the same number of dollars to begin with, there is equal probability of either of you becoming bankrupt.

Now, what if your opponent had more money coming into the game? Say you started with five dollar coins, and your opponent with fifteen. Who is more likely to lose all his money? You are. In mathematical terms, the probability of you going broke is calculated by $N2/(N1 + N2)$, i.e. your opponent's dollars ($N2$) divided by the sum of your dollars ($N1$) and his ($N2$). In this case, this means the probability of you going broke is now $15/(5 + 15) = 75\%$. A much poorer proposition than if you both started with the same amount: $5/(5+5) = 50\%$. That said, you still have an OK chance (25%) of winning all your opponent's money. However, the way the formula is constructed, if $N2 > N1$, your chance of winning will always be less than 50%; your chance of losing is always greater.

So what happens if your opponent has a lot more money than you, say one hundred dollars? The probability of you ending up bankrupt is now $100/(5 + 100) = 95\%$! The more your opponent has than you to start with, the higher the probability that it is you who will end up losing all your money, with the probability approaching closer and closer to 100%. Playing against an opponent with infinite dollars, that probability becomes 100%, i.e. it is *certain* that the game will end with you going broke.[4]

This is what you're up against when you gamble at a casino. Since casinos effectively have unlimited funds, you can play all night till the cows come home, you will always lose all your money in the end.

I told you earlier that I once went to a casino with a colleague who wanted to try his luck. I cannot remember how he did now, but I do remember that there was a roulette wheel and it looked something like this: There are 36 slots for the ball to drop into with each spin – 18 are red, 18 are black. There is another slot, a green zero, but let us leave that aside for now and presume that the chance of red and black is ½ or 50–50 at each spin.

There are gamblers out there who think that if black comes out 3, 4 or 5 times in a row, the chance of the next spin landing on red is somehow bigger than 50%. This is wrong. A famous event in gambling history took place at the Monte Carlo Casino in 1913 and is still talked about today. The roulette wheel kept landing on black, and after some 10 repeats gamblers starting piling money onto red. As it turned out, black came up 29 times in a row (some sources say 26 but that doesn't really matter). One mathematician calculated the probability of that happening to be 1 in 136,823,184.[5] Nevertheless, it did happen, and the event gave its name to the Monte Carlo fallacy – more generally the "gambler's fallacy" – which teaches that past random events do not influence future equally random events. On any given spin, the chances remain at 50–50.

You think you can influence the outcome of your casino visit by wearing your lucky tie or betting on the number that is also your car registration number? Numbers don't work like that. Sure, we all know some lucky uncle somewhere who once won the lottery, and we think it could happen to us. But the fact is that if you keep gambling in a 50–50 game you will always lose all your money.

But what about those "professional gamblers" you hear about? How do they do it? In general I think that professional gamblers are a myth – except for maybe poker players. But that is because poker players do not play against the house, they play against each other, and in an honest poker game there is an element of skill involved. Each player can influence the outcome, like in a game of tennis or badminton. If I play badminton against Lin Dan he is more likely to win. That's because he is a better player. It is different from a game of chance like spinning a roulette wheel or pulling the handle on a slot machine.

## Are you gambling or investing?

I have dwelled a bit here on some elements of gambling and probability. That is because for many the finance world appears like one big gamble. The actor George Clooney said (quoted from memory): "I prefer to invest in houses. The stock market is like Las Vegas, but without the fun bits like the showgirls." And yes, even some participants in the finance industry have a hard time distinguishing between gambling and investing. The two activities seem to attract some of the same crowd.

I was at an investment seminar not too long ago, and got talking to a young man who told me that he was there to get rich quick. I can understand that. It is hard to wait when you are young, you want everything here and now. He told me that a lot of his friends gambled, especially on football games. That, however, I cannot understand. Football gambling is of course not a 50–50 game. When Manchester United from the Premier League meet Port Vale from League One in the FA Cup, their chance of winning would be better than even. But odds make up for that; the bookmakers calculate the odds in their favour, to make sure they always come out on top. In the long run, the house always wins.

Remember the roulette wheel, with its green zero? When the ball falls there, the house clears the table. Not even 50–50 is enough for the casino – they have a safety valve built into the wheel, an additional 1/37 (2.7%) margin for themselves. During the second quarter of 2015, the win percentage of Marina Bay Sands in Singapore was 2.78%. That was down from 3.34% during the first quarter.[6] Marina Bay Sands is owned by Las Vegas Sands in the US. This win percentage, or "hold rate" as they call it in the gambling business, seems to be fairly typical of the industry. The turnover is so enormous that with just a 3% hold rate they make hundreds of millions of dollars each quarter.

And the options trading that the Institute of Banking and Finance describes as a zero-sum game? It is also not quite 50–50. There are expenses to be paid to the exchange as well as to the company providing the trading platform. In Singapore, SGX makes more money from derivative trading fees than it does from trading in "real" securities. All this has to be paid for by the participants, the traders. The charges might appear small, maybe $15 or $20 for each trade, but they add up, and eat into your profits. In chapter 8 we will look a bit more closely at how you can execute your trades in practice.

I have friends who believe in derivative trading. They sell options to hedge their portfolios and increase their cash flow during quiet periods when the markets don't move much. Good for them. But I have also been told by finance insiders that amateur day-traders, i.e. freelance traders working from a home computer and closing each trade at the end of the day, rarely do well. They warn me about the companies out there peddling trading training courses and analysis software, sometimes running ads implying that you will be a millionaire in no time. Part-time investor Melvin Fu said to the *Straits Times*: "I lost in forex. I lost $5,000 in three months. I might have lost more if I hadn't closed the account. I can tell you – 10 out of 10 people will lose money in that, especially during their first six months to a year."[7] This is confirmed by other media reports, that most of the clients opening a trading account with Saxo Bank – a Danish bank specialising in online trading – lose all their money within the first six months.

I am not picking on Saxo Bank – in fact I have a trading account there myself. I am just saying, ask yourself before you start trading derivatives: Do you really think you can beat the professional traders in this game, given that the numbers are already stacked against you? Investing is many things, but it is first and foremost a numbers game. You cannot control the mathematics; you have to understand and respect how it works.

Once you respect the numbers, you can start to interpret them. And you can consider the wider economic environment in your investment decisions, as well as your own subjective outlook and values.

Luckily, not all investing is a 50–50 toss of a coin. There are instruments out there that generate reliable value. Let us look at some of these alternatives now, first of all the world of *stuff*, generally referred to as commodities.

# Investing in Stuff

*"We live by the Golden Rule.*
*Those who have the gold*
*make the rules."*

— BUZZIE BAVASI

## Commodities trading

We touched briefly on commodities in the previous chapter. That is because commodities are heavily traded using derivatives such as futures and options. Commodities are really just stuff; the term "goods" is used in the trade, but unlike consumer goods, which differ in design and quality, commodities are uniform goods. A barrel of crude oil or a bushel of wheat is basically the same all over the world.

As we saw previously, there are different types of commodities, and for convenience they are often lumped into some categories. In his Rogers International Commodity Index, the creator Jim Rogers operates with three sub-indexes: agriculture (35%), energy (44%) and metals (21%).[1] The percentages are the weight in the main index of each sub-segment, and they give an idea of the volume, liquidity and open interest of each. Metals are typically subdivided into two groups: base metals (or industrial metals) such as copper, iron, lead and nickel, and precious metals like gold, silver and platinum.

Even if not directly invested in any specific commodity, the average investor would do well by at least watching the market now and then. That is because prices and supply and demand for commodities will tell you a lot about the state of the wider economy. There are analysts who specifically watch the price of copper, for instance, as a sort of leading indicator (Fig. 2). True enough, the price headed down gradually after 2012, and that was followed by a slowdown in the Chinese economy, where much of the copper went, to be used in wiring and piping for the expansion of homes and factories. Observers would have been wise to heed these pricing signals as a forewarning of the stock market contraction that ·came later in 2015.

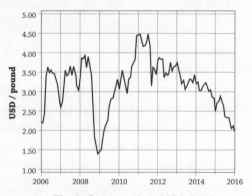

**Fig. 2: Copper prices 2006–2016**

In the commodity space, inventories are watched closely as well. An increase in inventory will often indicate a situation of oversupply and precede a drop in price. So when new statistics released show an increase in inventory, traders will take this as a signal to sell.

Although often referred to collectively, each commodity market is different. Very often the price of commodities such as sugar is driven by supply – not so much by demand. That is linked to the phenomenon that the demand for necessities such as sugar and petroleum products tends to be very "inelastic", whereas for other commodities such as gold, the demand tends to be relatively "elastic".

## Some microeconomics

To understand that, we need to take a brief look at the basics of microeconomics. As we saw in chapter 3, while macroeconomics deals with the big picture, microeconomics is the branch of economics that deals with the smaller parts, such as businesses and consumers, supply and demand, and price formation.

Everyone knows intuitively that as you lower the price of a good the demand will go up, right? However, how much will that increase be, that is the question, and it is not always so easy to resolve. This is where the concept of elasticity comes in.

Yes, there are certain goods where demand responds in a perverse manner to a decrease in price, i.e. demand drops! Luxury goods with a significant "snob value", for instance. If Rolls-Royce Motors drop the price of their limousine, maybe fewer rich Arabs would want to buy one!? That aside, it is safe to say that demand will go *up* when the price comes down, and vice versa.

Let us call the demand (quantity) for a good Q, and price P. The total revenue is then **P × Q**. (See Fig. 3.) When a cut in P increases Q so much that PQ goes up, the demand is said to be elastic, i.e. the elasticity coefficient (E) is bigger than 1. That is because $E = (\Delta Q/Q)/(\Delta P/P)$, where $\Delta Q$ is the change in demand, and $\Delta P$ is the change in price. Or you can use the percentage change %Q as numerator, %P as denominator. If the price goes down 10% but the demand then increases by 20%, **E = 2** and PQ will be bigger than before, so the demand is said to be elastic. With the demand curve sloping to the right, the elasticity would actually be a negative number, but often this is ignored and the numerical value alone is used.

Note that the elasticity is not the slope of the demand curve. Because the E coefficient is the ratio of percentage change,

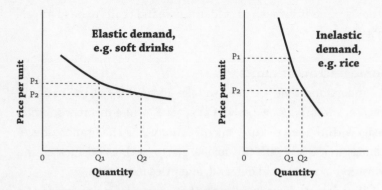

**Fig. 3: Price elasticity of demand**
The graph on the left shows elastic demand. As the price per unit of the good comes down, total revenue goes up (the area of box $P_2 \times Q_2$ is bigger than $P_1 \times Q_1$). On the other hand, in the graph on the right, when demand is inelastic (e.g. for goods as such rice and crude oil), as the price comes down, total revenue ($P \times Q$) gets *smaller*.

elasticity will vary across the demand curve. If the demand curve is a straight line, E will be 1 at the midpoint, above 1 (indicating elastic demand) above the midpoint, but below 1 to the right of and below the midpoint. So for lower prices the demand tends to be inelastic.

The price elasticity of demand has been calculated for a number of consumer goods, and it was found that necessities (or perceived necessities in the case of tobacco) generally had **E < 1** while luxury goods had **E > 1**.[2] It is interesting to see that in the US, first-class travel had **E = –0.3** while tourist travel (not so important apparently) had **E = –1.5**. (As mentioned above, you can ignore the negative sign in all these values.) In the US, rice had **E = –0.55** but in Japan rice had **E = –0.25**! Coca-cola had **E = –3.8**; that means that if the price goes up 10% the demand drops by 38%; let's face it, you don't really need all those soft drinks!

Just as there is a concept of price elasticity of demand, there is a price elasticity of supply (Fig. 4). It measures the relative change in supply to a relative change in price. With price on the vertical

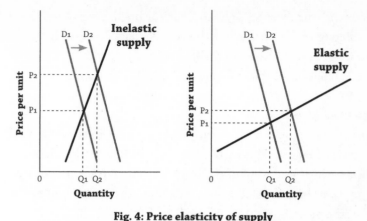

**Fig. 4: Price elasticity of supply**

Supply curves have a positive slope. If demand increases as indicated here (D1 to D2), supply quantity will also increase (Q1 to Q2), but it will increase *more* relative to the price change if the supply is elastic, as in the graph on the right.

axis and quantity supplied on the horizontal axis, this curve will tend to slope upwards, i.e. with an increase in price, producers will tend to increase production, and hence the supply. While demand usually responds quickly to a change in price, supply tends to respond more slowly, and economists operate with a short-run and a long-run equilibrium when they calculate where the demand and supply curves relative to price will cross.

We can now plot the demand and supply curves into the same graph. They will cross at some point, indicating the equilibrium – the optimal balance of supply and demand. After that, the possibilities are endless; you can shift the curves up and down, left and right, in an infinite number of ways, calculating hypothetical price, supply and demand scenarios. Microeconomists love this kind of thing. And macroeconomists do too, because when considering, say, government intervention in the form of sales taxes, you'd want to know how it would affect revenues. It could be that raising the sales tax rate might actually decrease rather than increase the total amount of taxes collected, right? This could happen for goods with highly elastic demand, such as holiday travel and Coke!

Enough for now; much of this info is available on the internet; and those readers who are really interested should get a copy of Paul Samuelson's book – no one explains this better than he does.

## The case of oil

Now that we have a basic grasp of microeconomics, let us look at a couple of case studies within the commodities world. Then you will see why the concept of elasticity is not just dry math but vital if you want to understand what goes on in the investment arena. First, the most important commodity of them all: Oil.

Why is oil the most important? It's because petroleum basically has been the driving force (excuse the pun) behind virtually all human progress since it was first put to use. Its importance really cannot be overstated. As we saw in chapter 3, the Industrial Revolution started in Europe around 1760. But there were really two revolutions. The first was driven by the energy of wood and coal converted into steam; it lasted until around 1850. The second Industrial Revolution took over from there; it was characterised by the refining of pig iron into steel, mass production of consumer goods, the rise of the chemical industry ... and it was all powered by oil. Towards the end of that century (the 1800s), petroleum was converted into electricity on a grand scale, and human mobility exploded with cars, trucks, diesel trains, diesel ships and air planes.

The power and portability of crude oil and its products are astonishing. Have you ever tried to push a car uphill? I have, and it is not easy. Just one litre of gas will make it shoot up that hill and another 20 km after that, with five people and their luggage inside.

Because oil is so important to us, it is also the main commodity to watch. It has been of tremendous benefit to mankind, but it has also been the cause of major financial and social upheavals.

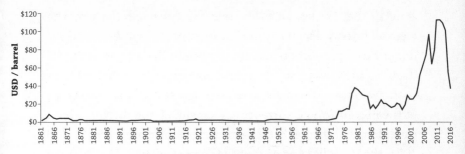

**Fig. 5: Historical oil prices, 1861–2016**
Brent Crude (nominal prices)

When I got my driver's licence in 1970, crude oil was about $3.30 per barrel. It had hovered fairly steadily around that price since before I was born, and we never thought it would be any different. We got our oil from the Middle East, where they just stuck a straw into the sand, and all the cheap oil came running up to the surface. American companies would collect it and process it and sell the refined products to us, no worries.

There were no speed limits on the roads in Denmark then, probably not in most other countries either. In towns there were limits, but between towns you just adjusted your speed to the road conditions. My mother's car couldn't go very fast anyway, so the top speed was never much of an issue for us, and there were not that many other cars on the roads that you could bump into.

All that changed in 1973 with the Yom Kippur War. In October that year, Egypt and Syria mounted a surprise attack on Israel to get back territory they lost in a previous war in 1967. Initially Israel was taken by surprise and prepared their nuclear weapons for use. But with new conventional weapon supplies from the United States, they quickly turned the situation on the battlefield around, and the war came to a stalemate after a couple of weeks of fierce fighting.

To punish the United States for giving help to Israel, the Arab countries proclaimed an oil embargo against the US as well as some of the US's key allies like the UK, Japan and Canada, who were all heavily dependent on cheap imported oil. At that time, domestic oil production had already begun to drop off in the US itself, so there was a shortage of supply to begin with. On top of that, there was a financial crisis in progress with the breakdown of the Bretton Woods currency agreements. From Bretton Woods (mentioned in chapter 3, those meetings took place in 1944) until 1971, the US dollar was pegged to the price of gold. That peg was abandoned by the US Nixon administration; the US was simply running out of gold and could no longer continue to exchange each ounce of gold with just $35. After that the dollar was allowed to float freely and dropped in value, hurting oil exporters pricing crude oil in US$.

With the embargo working and the lower US dollar, the price of crude oil quickly increased from $3+ to over $12 by the beginning of 1974. The event is referred to as the "oil shock", and it is safe to say that the Western world would never be quite the same after that. We never really knew how much we depended on that cheap energy from the deserts of the Middle East up until that point. Bottlenecks developed in the refining and supply chain, queues started to form at gas stations, panic mode set in. I was in Canada at the time, and road signs started appearing along the highways urging people to save gas. "Was this trip really necessary?" I liked that one; they should have left those signs permanently along all roads.

But people's memories are short. The oil embargo was lifted in March 1974, and although the price never dropped below $12 per barrel after that, the market soon adjusted.

That is, until the "second oil shock" came along in 1979 and the price tripled again. That crisis was caused by the fall of the Shah in Iran and the subsequent reduction of supply from that important producer. Then came the Iran-Iraq war, which kept supply in the oil market tight and prices high until the mid 1980s.

The drop in supply in 1979 was not significant, maybe only around 4%. But to understand how this can have such profound effects, we need to apply our newly acquired understanding of price elasticity of both demand and supply; both are very low for crude oil. If we look at the survey mentioned earlier covering a number of goods, in that reference oil had a demand elasticity of −0.4, i.e. well below 1. Even more noteworthy, the refined product, gasoline (or petrol) had **E = −0.09** for the short run and **E = −0.31** for the long run. This corresponds quite well with other studies.[3] Astonishingly, if the price of gas drops by 20%, we initially only use 2% more of it and over time just 6% more. This works the other way around too. That is why gas is such a great item to tax separately; we keep driving and burning it up, no matter how much the price goes up.

On the supply side, the response to price changes in oil is even more sluggish. One observer calculated the price elasticity of supply for the world oil market as just 0.02 for the period 2006–10.[4] What that means is that if the price for oil drops, it has to drop a lot before the supply will respond and vice versa. And if the steep demand curve moves a bit to the right on the price/quantity graph, it will cross the supply curve at a much higher price point.

That is why we have such enormous price swings in oil. In the 1970s the price increases were caused by relatively small cuts in supply. Recently the price collapsed as soon as there was a drop in demand. If you watched the oil drop off steeply starting in 2008 (see Fig. 6), you would have done well to prepare for the severity of the 2008–09 recession that had just started then.

Likewise, after July 2014 the price of oil suddenly came off sharply again from over $100/barrel to below $50/barrel half a year later. Like in 2008, this was caused mainly by a demand-side issue. The total world production of crude oil has been increasing steady over the decades, matching consumption quite well for a

**Fig. 6: Recent oil price developments, 1987–2016**
Brent Crude (nominal prices)

few years after 2010. In Q4 2014 it had increased to 95 million barrels/day, but that quarter demand dropped off to 93 million barrels/day due to slow economic growth in China and elsewhere; and this small disconnect caused the price to drop by over 50%![5]

Looking back I don't recall a single financial analyst foreseeing this momentous shift in the beginning of 2014, but there were plenty of talking heads willing to explain why it happened after the fact! Sooner or later, usually later, supply will drop off, and unless we find really viable alternatives to oil and gas, we will have a new mismatch between supply and demand and a new energy crisis.

For the observer confused by the two prices regularly quoted for crude oil, Brent Crude is from the North Sea and basically the price of oil in Europe, while WTI (West Texas Intermediate) quoted on NYMEX (New York Mercantile Exchange) is the benchmark product used in the US and generally a few dollars cheaper per barrel due to storage and transportation issues.

So by now we have all gotten used to the havoc played on us recurrently by the crude oil market. This is something we have to live with and get used to. We will never see $3 oil again, and we will forever have speed limits on all our roads (except in Germany maybe). Today I live in Singapore, and the car we have will go from 0 to 100 km/h in 10.4 seconds. But you are not allowed to go that fast anywhere in the country, so what is the point of that? And the traffic is such that you average less than 30 km/h in the city, about the speed of a bicycle.[6] Towards the end of the book, in chapter 10, we will consider the additional influence that the energy business has on the environment and how this impacts finance and our economy in general.

## And the case of gold

The other commodity worth singling out is gold. Why is gold special? Well, it is a mineral, a non-organic part of the Earth. It is also a chemical element, a pure substance consisting of only one type of atoms. A metal is a chemical element good at conducting heat and electricity, and gold is a metal. Although not the heaviest of metals, it has a very high density. Gold is considered a precious (or noble) metal because it is rare, and because it does not oxidise and corrode like base metals such as iron and copper. In fact, it does not react with water and air at all; gold coins dug out from a ship at the bottom of the ocean after 400 years look like new. Gold is also the most malleable and ductile of all metals, i.e. the atoms stick together. Incredibly, just one gram of gold can be beaten into a plate one square meter large or drawn into a thin wire 2.5 km long!

So much for all the facts. We all know what really makes gold special: It is beautiful! There is nothing like the colour of pure gold, the allure of that rich orange-yellow hue. That colour of course varies according to application, as gold is used in a variety of alloys. Like most people know, 99.99% pure gold is 24 karat, 75% is 18 karat, etc. Gold can be mixed with, say, 10% copper to make it more reddish, or 10% nickel or palladium to make white gold.

People have known of gold for thousands of years and mined it long before our calendar started. It was used for both decorations and as a store of value; but as mentioned before in chapter 3, it was really only with the rise of mercantilism some 500 years ago that gold really came into importance in monetary terms.

## Gold in finance

So, should you invest in gold? As you might know, gold was used as money for a number of years, especially so during the "gold standard" instigated at various stages throughout the 19th century. I have in my collection some gold coins from Denmark; they have the value of 10 kroner and 20 kroner, and you can still buy them online from the Danish central bank. The Nationalbanken got stuck with millions of these coins when they had to leave the gold standard in 1913 at the beginning of World War I. It was simply not feasible any longer to exchange a 10-kroner paper note with a 10-kroner gold coin containing 4.03 grams of pure gold. It is a good thing they did – today you cannot even buy a newspaper or a bus ticket in Denmark for DKK10, and the 10-kroner coin sells at the bank currently for 1,400 kroner (about US$211)! Had your great-grandfather left such a coin for you under his mattress for those past 100 years, you would have made an annualised compounded return of 7.5% p.a. – not bad!

The last attempt to impose a sort of gold standard was during the Bretton Woods agreements in 1944, but this came apart for the same reason that all the other gold standards failed: Central banks needed to expand the money supply far beyond what the gold market could handle. Until 1971, US dollars were exchangeable with gold at a fixed rate of $35 per oz. So the dollar was pegged to gold, and other currencies were pegged to the dollar. On paper this system looked great, but it unravelled when other countries started to exchange their dollars for gold, notably Switzerland and France, while the US got deeper into debt due to unemployment, inflation, the Vietnam War and other mismanagement. The US tried to cling to the gold standard a little while longer by devaluing the dollar to $42.22 to an ounce of gold in 1973, but this was

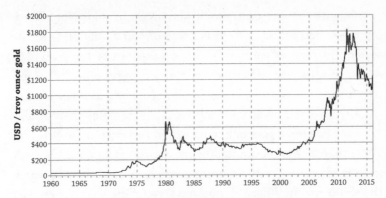

**Fig. 7: Historical gold prices, 1960–2016**
(Nominal prices)

not nearly enough. The next year gold was allowed to find its own price, and it quickly went to $160; that was how much the dollar had been overvalued before! After 1976 all reference to the gold standard was removed from US law, and gold hasn't been below $200/oz since.

Gold will never again be the monetary standard. There simply isn't enough of it around. Someone calculated that the current price of gold should be around $10,000/oz to match our supply of fiat currencies. This conversion does not make any sense and will never happen.

However, central banks around the world still hold gold as part of their reserves; it is still considered a store of value. The US has by far the most gold, some 8,000 tonnes, although other countries like China and Russia have been adding to their reserves lately. For safety reasons other countries keep much of their gold in the US, where it is stored in two places, under the Federal Reserve Bank of New York in Manhattan and at the Fort Knox facility in Kentucky. However, Germany has been trying for years to get their gold back, while the US government doesn't even want them to inspect it, so this has given rise to the usual conspiracy theories, like … is it even there?

Back to the question, should you invest in gold? Not according to Warren Buffett. "Gold is a way of going long on fear", he says in his own folksy way. "Gold gets dug out of the ground in Africa, or someplace. Then we melt it down, dig another hole, bury it again and pay people to stand around guarding it. It has no utility. Anyone watching from Mars would be scratching their head."[7]

Paul Krugman goes one step further. He wrote in the *New York Times* that we should simply stop mining out more gold. We don't need it, there is plenty around already, it is basically not worth the environmental hazard involved. Try telling that to Freeport McMoRan, Barrick Gold or the miners in the Brooks Range, Alaska.

If you have an ounce of gold and you put it on the table, 100 years from now you will still have an ounce of gold – so the argument goes against gold investment. To that Peter Schiff (who happens to own among other companies one that sells gold bullion!) would argue: Yes, but it would be worth a lot more. Schiff and others like him see gold as a store of value, a protection against inflation and the devaluation of fiat money.

My own personal opinion, for what it is worth, is: Have some gold for fun. Keep it because it is a beautiful mineral with historic, and yes, maybe some intrinsic value. There is a risk out there of a complete decoupling of fiat currencies from reality. It is small, but it is there.

You can invest in gold by buying into a gold ETF (exchange traded fund); in Singapore the UOB main branch in UOB Plaza offers a wide choice of gold and silver savings accounts and certificates, as well as sale and buy-back of physical gold. There are smaller private operators in the market as well, or you can buy gold jewellery. By all means, keep 2%, 3%, maybe 5% of your assets in gold as a hedge, as an "end-of-the-world" trade, as the gold trade has been called. I don't really believe in insurance, but I will make an exception in this case. Buy an insurance against hyperinflation! Don't expect a great return, just treat gold as an alternative investment.

## Alternative investments

This term is often used to cover any investment that is not stocks, bonds or cash. Please note that "cash" in investment jargon is used for banknotes and coins of course, but also for cash equivalents such as liquid bank deposits, corporate commercial paper as well as other money market products, including government bonds of under one year duration.

In this book, however, we pay special attention to property, which we lump together with bonds because the bond market is so closely linked to property financing. We also look at derivatives and commodities in more detail separately. So for alternative investments, that just leaves a number of asset classes that do not fall into any of these convenient categories. Let us look at the most important groups, which you might want to consider investing in as an alternative, to diversify your exposure.

**Art:** When rich people want something to put on their walls, they buy a Picasso or a Monet for a few million dollars at a Sotheby's auction. Some time later, when they calculate their net worth, the paintings have gone up in value. That is how the rich get richer. The rest of us buy a nice painting in a local art shop, and when we move house, we realise that it doesn't really have any intrinsic value, and we end up giving it away to the moving guys!

That said, please remember that as is often the case in investment circles, people will be happy to tell you all their success stories. The spectacular art auctions and mega valuations make the news; the failures and the flops and the dubious dealings behind the curtain don't. Unless you really have millions to burn, I would agree with Shane Ferro's view, as she wrote for Business Insider in 2015: "Buying art is gambling in an illiquid and shady realm dominated by a handful of players who are almost guaranteed to know more than you. The downside risks are much more prevalent than anyone in the industry wants to let on."[8] Not only is the price determination dodgy and untransparent, you also pay much more than the list price itself for the transaction. There is the mark-up by the dealer, the fee to the auction house (usually 15–25%) as well as transportation and insurance costs.

**Collectibles:** My wife collects postage stamps and banknotes, but I cannot recommend this to anyone who wants a good return on their investments. Like other commodities, collectibles do not actually produce any value; you are depending on other people for some reason wanting to own them more than you. We like wild birds and animals in our family, so my wife has a beautiful uncirculated S$1,000 note with a Brahminy Kite motif. There is one listed for sale on eBay at the moment for S$1,999. The real price is probably lower, but let us say someone would actually pay this. Then the S$1,000 would have grown since the banknote was issued in 1978 until today (2016) with a compounded annual interest rate of 1.84%. If my wife could only get S$1,400 for the note today (a more realistic price), the compounded return would be only 0.89% p.a. Although better than a kick in the head, the return on a collectible like this is not really that impressive, is it?

Like art, collectibles are something you should collect ... if you are interested. If you like fancy watches, rare coins, first edition books, fine wines, sports memorabilia, etc, by all means, have fun collecting them. As stores of value they are quite likely better than shoes, handbags, tech gadgets and most other mass-produced consumer items – just don't buy them solely to make money. You are unlikely to make a return that will beat a government-issued bond.

**Bitcoin:** A new digital financial tool favoured by some traders and investors. Bitcoin is in fact just one of many different cryptocurrencies, although the largest in terms of transactions and total market capitalisation. The jury is still out regarding the future of something like Bitcoin. Will it gain widespread acceptance as a tool for payments and as storage of value, as some patrons expect? Or will it crash and burn as others predict? Personally I don't own any Bitcoins, I simply don't know what they should be worth; but by all means look into this complex issue if you believe that digital currencies might be the future.

**Carbon credits:** What happened to the carbon credit market? In 2007 a trader with Barclays Capital in London, Louis Redshaw, said to the *New York Times*: "Carbon will be the world's biggest commodity market, and it could become the world's biggest market overall."[9] We are still waiting for that to happen.

Carbon credits are a novel idea. By putting a price on carbon mixed with air (such as carbon dioxide, $CO_2$), the plan is to lower emissions by making them more expensive for the polluters. The carbon credits are traded in tonnes of $CO_2$ or $CO_2$ equivalents, with the price being quoted in Euros (unlike the oil and the gold market, where prices are in US$). The trade can be done OTC (over-the-counter) or via a regulated exchange such as the NASDAQ or the European Energy Exchange.

The seller could be a business reducing its carbon footprint by switching to renewable energy or capturing and recycling

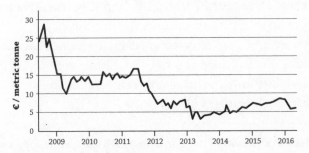

Fig. 8: EU Emissions Trading System (ETS) carbon prices

emissions, while the buyer's market falls into two categories: A polluting business such as a coal-fired power plant that has been forced through regulation to offset its carbon emissions; this is the so-called compliance market and is mainly in Europe where strict rules are in place to follow the Kyoto Protocol and subsequent follow-up legislation. The other buyers of credits would be volunteers, i.e. companies, societies or well-meaning individuals who want to offset their "carbon footprint". Maybe you have been on a long plane ride, and you want to make "amends" by buying carbon credits to offset the jet fuel gases you just caused. You can do this by donating some money (through your carbon credit purchase) to a project in the Third World planting more forest trees.

For a while, carbon credits were hailed as the next big thing in financial innovation. I remember receiving a number of enthusiastic phone calls from a smooth-talking guy in Tokyo with an impeccable English accent. This was around 2011. He told me how the carbon price was about to go through the roof; I would double my money in no time if I would only invest US$50,000 in his group. I did look into it and asked around to find out what it was all about. If you can make a buck and do good at the same time, why not? However, at the end of the day, I was strongly advised not to get into it, and I didn't invest. The carbon price collapsed shortly afterwards, from €16/tonne to €8/tonne (Fig. 8). The Japan-based outfit that called me most likely does not exist anymore. Which makes this statement by Donald Trump ring true: "Sometimes your best investments are the ones you don't make."

However, if you are interested in the somewhat complex world of climate change negotiations, carbon control legislation and associated investment opportunities, there might be some upside to catch in this field.

**Rainforests:** Buying land for investment is a concept as old as capitalism itself. Many of the gold miners in the 1848 California gold rush actually became quite successful, unlike most miners in subsequent events such as the Yukon gold rush later in 1896. And a lot of them used their gold to buy up nearby land. In 1846 San Francisco had only some 200 residents, but the city grew rapidly after gold was discovered in the hills northeast of there, and by 1870 it had over 150,000 residents. Those miners that converted their gold into land did very well and founded family dynasties and business empires that live on to this day in the Bay Area.

Obviously not all land investments pan out like that. But in today's age, what we are really short of is rainforests that can preserve biodiversity and capture carbon from the atmosphere. At the moment it is not quite clear how we can monetise rainforest conservation and profit from these issues, but I believe it is possible. We will look at the issue of SRI (sustainable and responsible investing) later in chapter 11.

## Should you or shouldn't you?

There are some investors who swear by commodities. Contrarians like Jim Rogers seem to have a knack for them. Contrarians look way into the future. They are not concerned about daily, weekly or even monthly asset prices. They are prepared to take a position and hold it for as long as five years, as Marc Faber said in an interview in 2015 with Channel NewsAsia. They believe that fundamentals will eventually prove them right. Jim Rogers thinks we are heading towards an era of food shortages; he says that in the United States there is even a shortage of farmers! It may well be so, as we shall see later. We certainly seem to be running low on quality land to farm. However, from an investment point of view, this shortage could take years to play out and manifest itself in higher food prices.

As always in investing, you look at the facts out there, and then you take a position you think will work out for you. There are funds that allow you to invest in farmland; there are ETFs (exchange traded funds) that enable you to own a piece of the pie in virtually any commodity you can think of. Later we will look in more detail at how exchange traded funds differ from ordinary mutual funds. For now just consider that ETFs will track any asset class. There are even reverse ETFs, which go up when the underlying goes down. This way you can short a commodity you think will drop in value soon.

However, before you jump in, you might want to listen to Warren Buffett again, the most quoted of all investors. He is on record as saying that when you buy something like a work of art or a collectible or any other commodity, you are essentially depending on someone else out there wanting to pay more for this in the future than you paid. He says in one of the many Buffett videos available on YouTube: "There are two types of investments: Those that produce income, and those you hope someone else will pay more for in the future. I don't know how to judge the value of such an investment."

In other words, the price of commodities and other stuff is somewhat subjective and unpredictable. The item itself, the good, does not produce any organic value as long as you hold it. That is why again and again you hear Buffett repeat in his interviews and annual letters to shareholders that his advice is to invest in a listed company, a farm or a building. In one interview he puts it like this: "Don't buy or sell on news, just own a wonderful business, or a farm or a rental building"[10] – all of which can generate real productive value and cash flow for their owners. We will look at investing in buildings next.

# 6

# Bonds and Property

*"People are living longer than ever before,
a phenomenon undoubtedly made necessary
by the 30-year mortgage."*

— DOUG LARSON

## The fixed income market

Remember in the last chapter, I quoted Warren Buffett saying that you should own one of three things to do well in investment: a wonderful business, a farm or a rental building. This is because any of those three things can make your money grow – literally, in the case of the farm. But since owning a farm is not really feasible or practical for most people, let us forget about that option.

That leaves us with (1) a wonderful business, and (2) real estate. And indeed, Buffett has suggested that if you have some money to invest, but you don't want to spend all your time analysing various companies and their performances, you should put 90% of your capital into a fund tracking the US S&P 500 stock market index, and the rest of it into bonds. Whether this is always the optimal allocation ratio is something we can discuss later; and also you might want to buy into a fund that tracks your local stock market rather than the American market if that makes more sense to you. But in general, Buffett is right on the money: This is the way to protect your wealth, grow your savings and eventually achieve financial freedom.

We will consider how to invest in stocks and companies in more detail in the next chapter. For now, let us just look at how you invest in the bond market and in real estate.

## Bonds – the basics

So how do bonds and shares differ as investment vehicles? I referred to Stacy Johnson earlier on and his useful little book, *Life Or Debt*. Since he is a financial journalist and not an academic, Johnson likes to present his topics in a nice and simple manner. He cuts through the whole bonds-versus-stock investment issue by saying that as an investor you are either a loaner or an owner: As a bond investor you lend money to someone else; as a stock investor you take part ownership of a business.

This is an important distinction. One implication is that bonds are issued against collateral such as a building, inventory or other assets; should the borrower be unable to pay, you as the lender have security for the loan. On the other hand, as a business owner or a stock investor, you don't have that security. Should the business you invested in go belly-up, any bond holders will be paid first, usually after employees and suppliers; stockholders are paid last and might not be paid at all.

The Institute of Banking and Finance (IBF, 2013a) says: "A bond is a debt instrument requiring the issuer to make specified payments to the bondholder [i.e. you] on specified dates." Often the payments are semi-annual, typically on 1 June and 1 December, but for simplicity's sake let's presume here that payments are annual. This is called a *coupon payment*. The principal is the original value of the bond, the so-called *par value*. On maturity the bond is redeemed with its full amount, i.e. you receive your loan back at par value.

There are really three types of bonds. The first are money market instruments with short-term maturity of one year or less. For these bonds, annual coupon payments don't really make sense, so the bonds are simply sold at a discount. A $100 bond might be sold at $98, providing you with a $2 profit at maturity. Your yield, i.e. your return on investment, would be **2/100 = 2.00% p.a.** It is *not* 2/98 (2.04%) because you have to hold the bond to maturity to get the return. In more general terms, the yield on a discount bond is:

$$\text{Yield} = (D/F) \times 360/T$$

D is the discount, i.e. par value minus the price the investor has to pay; F is for face value (or par value); T is the number of days remaining until maturity. This way, if there are 180 days left on the bond, the bond should be bought at $99 to yield a return of 2% p.a.:

$$(100 - 99)/100 \times 360/180 = 1/100 \times 2/1 = 0.02 \text{ or } 2\%$$

The other two types of bonds are medium-term bonds, which have maturities of more than one year but less than 10, and long-term bonds, which have maturities of 10 years or more, usually 20 or 30. We will look at how to calculate the price and yield of coupon bonds in a moment.

As such, bonds provide regular payments to the investor, and they are called fixed income securities; the market for them is the fixed income market. The contractual obligation behind a bond is called a bond indenture and as mentioned, a bondholder has a claim on the income and the assets of the issuer. Secured bonds are backed by a legal claim to assets, usually property, such as a mortgage bond. Subordinate debentures have a claim that is subordinate to other debt; usually such bonds sell at a lower price, i.e. a higher yield. As always in investment, the higher the risk, the higher the expected yield.

## The power of compounding

Before we look at the bond yield, here is one thing you should consider as an investor: the time value of money and the power of exponential growth, such as compounded interest. We looked at that briefly in chapter 3 during the discussion of interest rates. If you are one of those whose eyes glaze over as soon as you see a formula where numbers are replaced by letters, don't fret. You can easily become an accomplished investor without the use of complicated algebra and calculus mathematics. In fact, consider this famous quote by Warren Buffett: "Beware of geeks bearing formulas."[1]

However, you will do better if you just memorise one simple relationship:

$$FV(n) = PV \times (1 + k)^n$$

FV = Future Value of your investment in year n
PV = Present Value (the amount you invested in the first year)
k = Annual interest rate

Say you top up your CPF Special Account with $1,000 extra. The interest rate on this account is 4% p.a. compounded yearly. After 10 years, your investment will be worth:

$$FV(10) = \$1000 \times (1 + 0.04)^{10} = \$1000 \times 1.48 = \$1480$$

Very useful, right? You will need a scientific or a financial calculator to find $(1 + k)^n$; alternatively you can use one of the calculators available online.

Furthermore, once you master this, you can see how the formula can also be used to find PV or k. Rewriting the equation, you get:

$$PV = FV(n)/(1 + k)^n$$

$$k = \sqrt[n]{FV(n)/PV} - 1$$

So, if your goal is to have $1,480 extra in your CPF account in 10 years' time, and the interest is 0.04 (4% p.a.), you want to know how much you need to invest today (PV). You simply divide 1480 by $(1 + 0.04)^{10}$, thus determining a $1,000 investment.

And if after 10 years you find that your $1,000 grew to $1,480, you might want to know how much the compounded return on that investment was. To calculate that, you would take (1,480/1,000) to the power of (1/n), minus 1, which would give you 4%.

In finance, this simple equation for calculating the future value of an investment (and the discount rate calculated backwards) is the backbone of economic assessment and decision-making. Most financial books will stress the power of compounded interest. With these simple tools you can always check for yourself.

And I think you will agree that the feature of compounding is potent indeed. You will realise how important the prevailing interest rate is on your returns. Had you left your $1,000 in your CPF Ordinary Account, where the return is 2.5%, you would only have $1,280 after those 10 years. The $200 extra you made by transferring the money with the click of a button on your keyboard was a pretty easy profit.

## A bit about yield

I mention yield here because the future value of money formula is used in bond valuation work, and also (as we will see later) in valuating a stock using the dividend discount model. I will not go into too much detail on this; there are others out there much more qualified than me, financial academics with years of teaching experience behind them. And this is a book for ordinary investors, not professional bond traders.

Basically, the value of a bond (and as such the price you should pay for it) equals the present value of its expected cash flows. That is, it is the sum of each of the future coupon payments calculated at its present value, plus the final payment (the maturity value), also discounted to today's value. Like this:

$$P = C_1/(1+k) + C_2/(1+k)^2 + \ldots + C_n/(1+k)^n + M/(1+k)^n$$

P = Present value today
C = Coupon payments for each year: year 1 to year n
n = Years to maturity
M = Maturity value
k = Required rate of return

As you can see, to find the present value, you will need a "k" value – an interest rate that you should use. For that, you have to use somewhat subjective discretion and determine a so-called "required rate of return". This is the rate of return that you would like to make on your investment, or at least the minimum you would make by just keeping the money in the bank.

Say a bond is paid back at par $1,000 five years from now. You expect 5% per annum return on this investment to make it worth the risk. Using our new skills, you should then pay $1,000/(1 + 0.05)^5$ for the bond, i.e. **1,000/1.28 = $781**. This corresponds to the last element in the formula above, $M/(1 + k)^n$. On top of that you should add any coupon payments in the future years, each discounted to the present just like the final payment. Say the coupon payments are $40 per year for five years, the total value of your payments at current present-day value would be (in even dollars) **$38 + $36 + $35 + $33 + $31 = $173**. Notice how the present value of the future payments drop a bit; of course they will drop more if you use a higher "k" than 0.05. This should be added to the discounted par value: **$173 + $781 = $954**. The conclusion is that $954 is the most you would pay for this $1,000 par value 4% bond today to make it worth the risk.

The current yield is fairly easily calculated. It is simply your coupon rate divided by the price you pay for the bond. Just like any other venture, it is your return over your investment. Say your coupon rate on the $1,000 bond is $40 per year and you get it at a good price of $800; your yield is **40/800 = 0.05 or 5%**.

Notice two things. First, the yield of the bond has an inverse relationship to the price. The higher the price of the bond, the lower is your yield, and vice versa. Second, the price is very sensitive to small movements in the interest rate. If you look at the example above again and imagine that the market interest is 4%, investors would pay par or $1,000 for that 4% bond. Should market rates increase by just 1% to 5%, the value of the bond would drop to $800 and the bondholder just took a paper loss of $200 or 20%! That is why the fixed income market is nervous and tends to drop in value during economic conditions where interest rates go up.

During normal economic conditions, long-maturity bonds should have a higher yield than short maturity ones. That makes sense according to the price of money theory: The longer you have to wait for your money back, the more you expect to get rewarded. This way the yield curve should look like this:

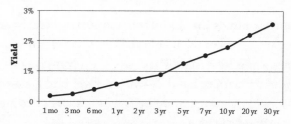

**Fig. 9: US Treasury yield curve rates (2016)**

In a high-interest environment, where the market expects lower future rates, this curve could also be dropping, or it could be humped in various ways. However, that is somewhat abnormal. If you check the yields as published on the financial news channels, it should be higher for the 10-year bond than for the two-year and higher still for the 30-year.

## Fixed income products

Of course, the bond market is not quite as simple as described above. That is the thing about money management; it is both wonderfully simple and intriguingly complex. You can always count on the people driving "financial innovation" to complicate matters. It is great for them, the people working in the financial industry; but to me personally, it is often more doubtful how much this innovation actually benefits the ordinary investor.

Special features of bonds can include a *call* feature. A callable bond is one that gives the issuer the right to retire the debt and pay the bond back in full before the maturity. A *sinking fund* provision is a partial call feature.

*Put* provisions are the opposite, they give you the right to sell the bond back to the issuer at par on specified dates before maturity.

*Floating rate* bonds, *step-up* bonds and *inflation-indexed* bonds have their coupon rates reset at certain intervals following predetermined benchmarks, which of course affects the price of the bond.

*Convertible* bonds are an interesting instrument issued by listed companies, where the bond can be converted into common stock within a specified time. They have the advantage of a fixed income product with limited downside risk, but have upside potential should the company do well and the share price increase before maturity of the loan.

That's not all. To further complicate matters, bonds can be issued outside the jurisdiction of a single country in a different currency – so-called Eurobonds. In the bond market, it is important to distinguish between government bonds and corporate bonds. The former are debts issued by a sovereign country, state or regional municipality and backed by that public entity. The latter are issued by a private company and backed only by the company's assets and future income. A large part of the bond market is backed by real estate. Some bonds are linked to one particular building, using this building as collateral until maturity. More complicated products involve a large pool of pass-through mortgage bonds bundled together in CMOs (collateralised mortgage obligations). CMOs can be sold to large institutional investors who might prefer the convenience of not having to deal with individual mortgages and bonds. They gave the bond market a bad name during the financial crisis of 2008–09 when they were pushed onto unsuspecting retail investors, and it then turned out that hidden among the bundles of mortgages were many that could never be repaid. Many investors lost money on these products; some lost everything they had.

## Bond ratings and risks

This leads us to another issue: the ratings of bonds. The three largest rating agencies out there at the moment, all recognised for use by the US government, are Moody's Investors Service, Fitch Ratings and Standard & Poor's (S&P) Financial Services. They use a system of four investment-grade ratings: AAA, AA, A and BBB, in declining order of quality. Anything rated BB and below until D (for "default"!) is considered non-investment grade, or "junk", to use this charming financial term.

For countries, having their sovereign bonds rated investment grade is important, as this allows institutional investors to buy them – many institutions such as other governments and large pension funds are not allowed to buy junk bonds. The higher the rating, the lower the interest burden will usually be for the issuer. Much of the private sector debt is rated junk, but that doesn't mean there is no market for it at all. Many investors are willing to take the risk and buy junk bonds, as the yield is typically significantly better. In a fund of junk bonds a few bonds might default, but the higher yield of the rest might still produce a better return in total.

Though in general investing in fixed income products is considered safer than investing in equities, it is not without risks. There is a *credit risk* as we just saw – the issuer of the bond can go belly-up and default before maturity.

*Political risk* occurs when even sovereign debt drops in value. Although governments rarely default on their debt, we have seen some nations do so. Sometimes it is more politely called "debt restructuring". Either way, the creditors don't get all their money back. Recent events in Russia (1998), Venezuela (2004), Greece (2010), Argentina (2014) and Ukraine (2015) come to mind.

For Eurobonds issued in a currency other than the one of your country, there might be *currency risk*.

Then there is the *interest rate risk* that we touched on. As interest rates rise, bond prices fall. This will give a paper loss to your bond portfolio, although if held to maturity and with no defaults, yield should be as calculated from the start of the loan. With rising interest rates, bond funds that reinvest the coupon payments yearly should be able to buy new bonds at a lower price, and over the long term this might help the bond fund to recover in value.

## Investing in bonds

So how do you navigate the fixed income market as an ordinary investor? Like I said, personally I love finance that is simple. And here is a scheme that is wonderfully simple: You borrow low and invest high.

I dropped out of college after two years, but during those two years I could borrow from the Danish government. There was no grant or allowance then, but we could borrow interest-free from the state. After graduation, interest would start to accumulate on the loan, and of course you were expected to get a job and start paying it back. Many countries have a similar scheme with state-funded or state-guaranteed student loans.

I did take out the full amount of the interest-free loan each year, but I didn't spend it. I invested it. Remember I studied economics! I didn't know much about the stock market, and anyway I didn't believe in capitalism at the time, so I bought mortgage-linked bonds at my bank and collected the interest. In those days we actually had real physical coupons. I was given each bond on a fancy piece of paper that I kept at home. Then twice a year I had to cut out the coupons with the right date on them and take them down to the bank to exchange them for cash. I did that every year on 11 June and 11 December; those dates were two of the highlights of my year! In those days you could buy 5% bonds way below par, maybe at 80/100 or even lower, so your yield was 5/80 or higher, i.e. well above 6% p.a.

I made ends meet during my studies by working part-time, writing books; my mother helped me out a bit; the coupon payments helped too. After I dropped out, the first thing I did was to sell the bonds and give the state its principal back. I never borrowed money again, except to finance property later.

This brings us to a classic financial concept: good debt versus bad debt. In chapter 2 I told you never to borrow. That is, never borrow for consumption. That is bad debt. It will ruin your life and imprison you in a tangled web of financial worry and misery. All you do with bad debt is feed the banks and the moneylenders, when you should in fact be feeding yourself and enjoying a life of freedom.

However, there is a case for good debt. I just mentioned one example: You borrow at 0% and invest at 6%, you cannot lose! Not all good debt arrangements are that simple, but the general principle is the same: You apply leverage, but in a safe manner. If done right, it can help you gain your freedom sooner.

I also told you earlier on never to gamble. That is because the numbers are stacked against you. Look at them and you will agree. Using your wife's birth date to bet or wearing your lucky tie when you do so is not going to change that. You cannot beat the numbers; the house always wins in the end. If you keep gambling, you will always lose all your money – it is that simple, and I proved it mathematically.

But that doesn't mean you should never take on risk. Calculated risk is different from gambling, because you are in control and you can select numbers that are likely to work in your favour. Each venture has to be evaluated on its own merits. We will look at that again in chapter 9, when we consider portfolio management. In general, though, borrowing to finance a secure and fixed asset like property, which will quite likely generate more income in rent and appreciation than you pay for your loan, would be considered good debt.

## Bonds then and now

For many years after I left school, I invested mainly in fixed income products. Gradually I started to appreciate the benefits of capitalism, and along that line I bought and sold a few shares in listed corporations now and then, mainly in oil-related companies; but I never did well. It taught me that investing in the stock market only really pays off if you are prepared to do the homework. I wasn't at that time. I was too busy with my day job on the rigs and just the business of being young.

Also, fixed income really worked in those years. Interest rates differ somewhat from country to country, across currencies and fixed income products. However, as a general guideline, look at the amazing chart in Fig. 10 showing the American federal funds rate from 1954 until today:

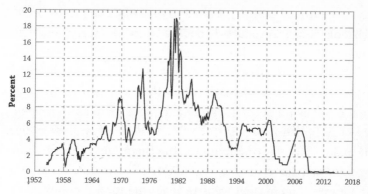

**Fig. 10: US federal funds rate (effective)**

Look at the rates in the 1970s and 1980s. Yes, inflation was higher as well then, but with the right products you could do well. Low risk, high net returns. I bought callable mortgage-backed bonds in Danish kroner that paid 20–22% p.a.; none of them ever defaulted. By 1986 I had sold off all my shares and invested only in bonds. This is not the right way to invest; you have to spread your risk over various asset classes (don't do as I do, do as I say!). But I didn't care about that then. My bond portfolio paid on average 15–16% per annum. I was laughing all the way to the bank. I retired from my oilfield career, and when the stock markets worldwide crashed shortly afterwards in October 1987, I couldn't care less, I didn't own a single share.

Thirty years ago you could make good money in fixed income. And there were two reasons for this: the low costs, and the high level of interest rates in the wider economy. I mentioned that I bought my bonds directly from the issuer – that way the transactions were low-cost. When I lived in the UK, I would buy government bonds denominated in pounds sterling at the local post office or by mail order; there were no commissions or expenses to pay. Even in the 1990s the Danish state would sell their bonds at the post office with no commission; there were no financial middlemen to feed. As interest rates started coming down, there was an additional capital gain tied to the bond market. Investors with long maturity products had locked in good returns, and their bonds appreciated in value.

This wasn't to last. Governments started marketing their debt through financial institutions that skimmed money off the top. While products got more and more complex and expensive in administrative costs, the financial industry grew in size but mainly by collecting more for the financial intermediation. For the American economy, Ben Landy calculated in a paper on the Century Foundation website that "the total economic cost of financial intermediation grew from ... 5 percent in 1980 ... during the deregulatory years of the Reagan administration ... to almost 9 percent of GDP in 2010". That is about US$1.4 trillion that the financial industry charges yearly for their services in the US. "What does society get in return?" Landy asked. "Or, in other words, what does the finance industry produce? The short answer is that Wall Street, for the last thirty years or so, has been skimming prodigiously from the top."[2]

I am sure something similar would be true if you studied any other developed country. So the finance industry is a great place to work, but a bad place to be a customer.

## How to buy

How do you avoid paying all these fees? You can't avoid them entirely, you just have to do your best to keep expenses low. These days, single bonds are sold from financial internet platforms and investment banks for the international market at fairly low cost. However, they typically require some quarter of a million dollars to invest, and they might not be liquid, i.e. you must be prepared to accept a haircut if the bond is sold off before maturity.

There are many mutual funds and ETFs that invest in the bond market. Government debt and corporate investment-grade as well as junk bond funds are all available. With funds the benefit to you is that you spread your risk by investing in a basket of various bonds. But yes, you do pay for all the people managing the fund for you, and they charge handsomely for their services. Later on in chapter 9 we will see how you can find a not-too-expensive fund when you construct your portfolio.

In local markets, bonds in smaller tranches are often available. In Denmark it is easy to buy mortgage-backed bonds from the local banks in small denominations, although the bank will of course charge you a commission on the transaction as well as custodial fees. In Singapore, some large corporations issue bonds to finance their operations, and they can be bought through the banks directly at a fairly low cost, usually in units starting as low as S$1,000. OCBC, Hyflux, City Developments, Singapore Airlines and others offer these. The yield is around 3–6% p.a., depending on the issue. They are worth looking at as an alternative to buying shares in the company. The upside is limited, but so is the downside risk compared to stocks.

And finally, in September 2015, the Singapore government went full circle, going back to the practice of European governments years ago: They bypassed the big institutional investors and started selling government debt directly to consumers. Under the SSB (Singapore Savings Bonds) scheme, you can now buy Singapore bonds directly from the government through an ATM. The interest on the bonds is tax-exempt, and the yield will be 2.4% p.a. if held to maturity (10 years), a bit lower if redeemed before that. However, the investment is liquid – the government will buy back the bonds anytime. No secondary market and no exchange operators to feed. You don't have to cut off coupons with a pair of scissors and bring them in; in fact you never see the bond! Your investment is stored electronically in your CDP (Central Depository) account and interest payments are credited directly into your bank account. You can invest as little as S$500, paying only S$2 in fees per transaction. 2.4% per year might not be enough to retire on, but it is a 100% safe way to park some of your funds at a low overhead.

## Financing a home

As mentioned, the bond market is closely tied to the market for property. To finance a major fixed asset like a house, an apartment building, an office block or a factory, the developer will issue bonds with the building as collateral. The bonds are bought by investors with excess capital, the bondholders, sometimes bundled together as described above.

For private home ownership, each country does the financing a little bit differently. In Europe there are building societies facilitating this trade; in the UK, for example, the largest of these, the Nationwide Building Society, now has some £200 billion worth of assets. Young people will open a savings account in a building society and hope that by the time they are ready to move out they will qualify for a mortgage of their own – provided house prices haven't exploded out of their reach, which often happens in a country with a perpetual housing shortage.

In the US, mortgages used to be available from savings and loan associations, but this type of financial institution more or less died a quiet death. The whole mortgage industry was basically nationalised after the financial crisis in 2008–09. Bizarrely, in the land of free market capitalism, virtually the whole business of home financing is now operated by the federal government through two mortgage companies known as Fannie Mae and Freddy Mac. Of course the government does make a buck from this. They print money at no cost and lend it to the home owners at 3% p.a. – a pretty sweet deal, right? But the private sector is shut out from this game.

In Singapore, the local banks provide home loans; additional capital is generated through the compulsory savings scheme, the CPF. Bank home loans are generally tied to the so-called

SIBOR interest rate, which is set by the banks but closely follow the American federal funds rate due to the open nature of the Singapore economy. SIBOR stands for Singapore Interbank Offered Rate. DBS for instance (the biggest bank in Singapore and government-linked) offers a SGD home loan at SIBOR + 1.38%. For an HDB (public housing) home, the rate will be capped for 10 years at the CPF Ordinary Account deposit rate, which is currently 2.5%. You might sometimes see SOR brought up; that is the Singapore Swap Offer Rate; it is calculated in relation to the SGD exchange rate versus the USD, more volatile and therefore not so suitable for long-term arrangements like a home loan. There is a boat-load of information about all this on the internet, and each bank will offer you slightly different terms, but this is the situation in a nutshell.

## (Almost) always own your home

For most people, buying a home will be the most important financial venture they will ever undertake. This is not the place to go into the finer details of home ownership; there are plenty of specialised sources out there. Let me just add my voice to the choir: Do it, own your own home! I have met hundreds of people who purchased their own home; I have never met anyone who regretted it, not once. In some cities like New York and London, it is considered normal for working professionals to pay as much as 50% of their salary on rent. Surely this is money straight down the drain.

In 1976 I was working on the oil rigs in the Norwegian sector of the North Sea, but I kept getting letters from the Danish armed forces to go and do my compulsory national service. I didn't want to postpone it any more – I was not getting any younger – so I travelled to Aarhus, Denmark, a few weeks before I was supposed to report and started looking for a place to live. I bought the first little apartment I viewed.

It wasn't much, it was old, in the middle of the city, and there was just one bedroom. But it was OK for a single guy. The owner wanted 110,000 Danish kroner for it, I offered 100,000, and we signed the papers at the agent's office that afternoon. DKK15,000 cash down, DKK85,000 on a mortgage, most of it a callable bond with security in the property.

After I completed my national service, I kept the apartment as an investment and rented it out for a few years, but it was cumbersome to deal with. I couldn't find good tenants who would pay on time. So when I moved to Singapore in 1980, I sold it off. The price by then was 280,000 kroner. I don't know what the place would go for today, maybe a million. I stayed in Denmark for free and I even made a buck in the end. Now you know why I believe in home ownership.

I did the same thing when I moved to Scotland. There was a chronic shortage of housing in Aberdeen at the time (1977–78). The place was buzzing. For my first weeks in the city I shared a small room under the roof in some bed and breakfast with two other working guys. I slept on a fold-out bed in the middle. We could hardly move around there. I didn't make much money then, so that was all I could afford. To this day I have respect for the foreign workers who endure this kind of life to improve their lot. This time the financing took a bit longer, but after a few months I secured my own small place in Jamaica Street. I eventually sold that apartment as well at a small profit. Again I stayed virtually for free in a high-rent boomtown.

Over the years I have owned four apartments and one house in various places, and I have always come out ahead. Regarding the house, when it was sold off my ex-wife "forgot" to give me my share of the sale proceeds, so I didn't make anything on that one, but you get the general idea. I think all home owners would agree with me that buying your home is something you will never regret.

## A second property?

The rule is not necessarily true, however, for all property invest-ments. You might think that if owning your own home is so great, why not buy another one and lease it out to collect the rent?

Here is why not: There are serious expenses involved when buying and selling property, especially when you sell. First of all, the place has to look presentable; there are repairs and cleaning to be done. Then most estate agents charge some 2% commission on the sale; there are lawyer fees on top of that; as well as stamp duties to the government. Some countries charge capital gains tax on any profit you make within a certain number of years. In a busi-ness-friendly place like Singapore, these charges are manageable, but they still eat significantly into your profits, maybe as much as 5%. When my mother sold her second home shortly before her death in 2012, she ended up paying 12% on the sale in repairs and expenses. That is doing business in Europe for you!

For home ownership, usually a three-year minimum holding period is recommended just to break even compared to renting. Although you cannot be 100% sure that your house will go up in value, in most places houses do in the long term, and over time your home acts like a hedge against inflation and rent increases. By the time you retire, the plan is to have your mortgage paid off, and you live rent-free, apart from some property taxes and a bit of maintenance. This usually works well.

But if you speculate in property and buy houses to flip them quickly for a profit, this is a different matter. Prices can drop, and historically they have done so indeed. If that happens, you might find yourself "under water", i.e. your mortgage is higher than the value of the place, as millions of Americans did after 2008. If a good tenant is suddenly hard to come by, your cash cow becomes a vacuum cleaner sucking you dry.

Also, the property market is not totally free. This limits the upside potential. Especially in Singapore, the government takes on a very active role and has explicitly expressed that they do not want housing prices to increase over time by more than the general economic growth rate. Which is not much at the moment, maybe 2% p.a. They do not want to see a situation like in London, where the local working people are virtually barred from living in their own city due to exorbitant home prices and rents.

In Singapore, housing prices started to go up quickly after the crisis in 2009, when interest rates dropped to almost 0% and QE by the central banks around the world vastly increased the money supply. This "hot" money floated around the world looking for a return; it pushed up property prices rapidly in most cities and some ended up in Singapore. However, the government wanted none of that. When ordinary people started struggling to own a home, the government's "cooling measures" reversed the trend, and from Q3 2013 to Q3 2015 housing prices in Singapore dropped some 8.2%, according to the all-residential index calculated by DBS Group Research. The cooling measures included a large increase in stamp duty on both buyers and sellers, especially for foreigners, as well as lower permitted loan-to-value ratios and TDSR (Total Debt Servicing Ratio), with total debt payments to housing as well as car and consumer loans not allowed to exceed 60% of income.[3]

Not that anyone asked me, but personally I find this very reasonable. Maybe people's homes should not be chips in some roulette game for institutional investors with too much cheap money. Housing price bubbles rarely play out well, the grotesque events in Japan up to the market crash in 1991 being a case in point.[4] Situations like that should be avoided.

As an investor, you should ask yourself if the housing market is then really the place to get the best return on your savings. I mean, when government policies explicitly aim to limit your upside potential? There is no such upside limit to the value of a good business. Nobody tells Apple Inc. that they are making too much money and should lower their profits, except if they breach the rules of fair competition.

## REITs

To circumvent the tight governmental controls on the property market in Singapore, local investors increasingly are tempted to invest in properties overseas: in Malaysia, Australia, the UK, the US. Virtually every day, foreign developers advertise their projects in the Singapore media and promise great returns. (Funnily enough, the requirements regarding transparency and accuracy on overseas investment advertising are less stringent than those that apply to domestic developers, although the MAS is looking into levelling the playing field in this regard.)

In my opinion, I would be wary of pouring my hard-earned cash into a property in a country that I don't know too well. What are the conditions there, what is the quality of the work, is there a bubble forming? I know it works for some – I see investors who are very happy owning houses or apartments in various countries and collecting rent from them. Personally I find that very tedious and not very profitable. The overheads, the administration, the risks are just not worth it.

If you want exposure to the property market and live the easy life of a rent collector, why not invest in REITs? A REIT is a Real Estate Investment Trust, i.e. a company that owns and operates real estate. For a REIT listed on the stock exchange, you can buy a share of the company and benefit from the business as a shareholder. In Singapore, REITs are a fairly new addition to the investment scene, the first one only incorporated and listed in 2002. Today there are some 36 REITs listed in Singapore, and virtually every other national stock exchange will offer this investment vehicle.

I like REITs. Hey, wait a minute, didn't I just say that you should try to cut out the middleman when investing? Buy the bond instead of a managed bond fund, etc? Yes, but I also wrote that I don't quite know how to do that, avoid all fees. If anyone can show me, I would be happy to find out how, but until then it seems to me that some fees are unavoidable. As with REITs. They offer you the convenience of not having to worry about changing lightbulbs and leaking taps in your rental unit; you pay others to do that. Yes, that cuts into your return at the end of the day, but you sleep better at night.

As an asset class, REITs are under a lot of regulation and restrictions from financial oversight agencies such as the US Securities and Exchange Commission in the USA and MAS in Singapore. REITs are limited in how they can be structured and what they can and cannot do. You have to check the conditions in each jurisdiction to understand the product. In general, however, REITs must have most of their assets in real estate; they must be jointly owned as a collective investment scheme (in the US by a minimum of 100 persons); they can only borrow on (or gear) their holdings up to a certain amount (in Singapore 35%); their properties must be valued yearly. And, most important to you, they must pay out 90% of their income from rents and capital gains to shareholders as dividend.

All these statutes work to protect you, the investor. REITs offer you exposure to the property market if you think it is about to take off big-time. In more quiet times, there is the steady flow of rental income and high dividend yield to look forward to. You spread your risk by owning a share in several properties, and your investment is liquid – you can sell your shares from one day to the next should you need your money for something else.

That said, REITs are not risk-free investments, far from it. REITs usually specialise in one sector within the property market, such as residential, office, industrial or health care. You have to form your own opinion about which sector you like, want to support and think is profitable. The dividend might look good now, but what about in future? Will the management always be able to find tenants and keep operating costs down? Like all listed companies, REITs have to publish detailed quarterly and annual accounts. Study them closely. However, they will only tell you so much; they will not tell you about the quality of the management and the future prospects of the business.

That is why it is important that you do your own homework. If you are in Singapore, check out the Moneysense.gov.sg website, which offers decent and easy-to-understand financial advice. In fact, even if you are not here, check it out: It has the integrity of a clean administration behind it. There is a good chapter on REITs and how they work, with plenty of warnings about the risks as well as the opportunities.[5] When you understand how REITs are structured and how they are different from ordinary listed property companies, you can look into each listing in turn. Try to identify the prospects of the business; how is this likely to play out in the future? If you think there is a glut of office buildings in your area, maybe look into a REIT running hospitals, hotels or one operating computer server warehouses.

I own a few REITs nominated in USD and SGD, and so far they have done alright for me. They go up and down in value a bit, but the dividends are nice. I suggest you include some property in your investment portfolio, as we shall see later in chapter 9. For now let us look at the final asset class, what Warren Buffett says you should always own: a wonderful business.

# Shares

*"I hate weekends because there
is no stock market."*
— RENE RIVKIN

### A share of what?

Shares, stocks, equities – they are all terms for the same thing: ownership of a business. In most countries there are typically two ways to register a business. In a *sole proprietorship firm*, the owner, or a few owners in partnership, own the business; they are liable for all the firm's activities with all their capital, including personal assets. In a *limited company*, a corporation, shares are issued and each shareholder is liable with only his share of the company. The most he can lose should the company go belly-up is his share of the capital; he will not be asked to inject new money to cover debt.

Many corporations are private, i.e. they are owned by a few shareholders who often know each other or are family members. In Singapore, the suffix "Pte Ltd" is added to the company's name; in the US "Corp" or "Inc" (they are the same!); in the UK "Plc"; in Germany "AG", etc. If the owners decide to list the company on a stock exchange, this is called an IPO, an Initial Public Offering. After the IPO, the company is listed, i.e. the public can buy and own and sell shares during stock trading; the company is now "Ltd" (not Pte Ltd). The old owners get a lot of new capital into the company to be used for expansion, but they also lose some control of the ownership of the company, and they have to comply with more stringent regulations imposed on them by the stock exchange where they are listed and public financial regulators.

## In business we trust

As we saw in the last chapter, when we considered investing in bonds and properties, a somewhat special business formation is a business trust. A REIT is a trust, while a property company is an ordinary corporation. The difference is that a set of special rules apply to business trusts. In Singapore the rules are set out in the Business Trust Act of 2004, available on the MAS website, which also has a list of local business trusts (apart from REITs); they currently number 22.

The business trust model is structured so that a single company, the trustee-manager, holds and operates the business for the investors, the unit holders. So, investors do not have operational control or shareholders' rights, but they benefit from owning a stable company; most business trusts are involved in infrastructure, utilities and other activities with long-term contracts and steady income streams.

While a business trust is not legislated to pay out a certain dividend ratio (REITs must pay out 90% of earnings to maintain their tax status), they often do pay high dividends, typically around 75% of earnings. Although this means less upside to the stock price (as less capital is retained for expansion), investors benefit from a steady flow of income and the yield (dividend over unit price) for a business trust is typically 5–7% p.a.

## Now you are an owner

When you buy shares, you are an owner. You participate in the company and share its fortunes. If the shares are registered in your name, you will be invited to a yearly AGM (Annual General Meeting), which all corporations are required by law to hold.

Large shareholders can be either passive owners or more activist owners; they might pull their weight during the AGM and dictate who should be members of the board of directors. The directors will appoint a CEO, a Chief Executive Officer, to take charge of the daily running of the business.

As an investor you should know that shares are considered a somewhat risky asset class. In the worst-case scenario, you might lose all your money, and believe me you can. It has happened to me personally more than once. I have seen my shares go to zero, and it is not a pleasant experience. However, the upside of owning a good company is virtually unlimited. This is not some 50–50 gamble where the house always wins. A company is real people making real stuff or providing real services of real value. Owning a part of a well-managed company providing the right product at the right time in the right place is a goldmine. Remember Warren Buffett advised you to put 90% of your capital in the stock market? That was how he got rich himself.

The problem is finding that goldmine. Bear in mind, you are not the only investor out there. There are thousands of other people who want to get rich quick. So identifying a good company at the right price is a skill. The good news, though, is that it is a skill that can be acquired. Even some basic knowledge will give you a leg up in the market place.

And another piece of good news: Since this game is not zero-sum, we can all be winners. A rising tide will lift all boats. If you are not sure which company to invest in, "buy the index", as Buffett says. Historically and collectively, over time stocks always go up. As regards whether you should buy the index or pick stocks your-self, we will cover this in more detail in the next chapter. In this chapter, I want to show you the tools you need to be familiar with if you want to DIY in the stock market.

There are countless professionals out there in the financial world who are specialist stock pickers. Brokers and fund managers all go to basically the same school and learn a set of instruments that help them valuate a company and make recommendations on the stock to clients. The question is: Can they beat the market? Each fund manager will measure himself against a benchmark, like a stock index comprising a basket of equities. If his stocks perform better than the index, he has beaten the market – but often he cannot. We will look at that in more detail in the next two chapters.

For now, even if you don't think you can beat the market consistently – i.e. have a better return than an ETF tracking your favourite index – you might still want to try your hand at picking stocks. Maybe there is a business you'd like to own a part of. Maybe you love Apple gadgets and wish to be associated with the company and share in its success. Or you simply have a hunch that a certain market segment or a specific company is about to do well.

Let us look at some of the metrics you need to be familiar with when analysing a company.

## How to find a wonderful business

Why don't we look at an actual example? You are interested in the infrastructure and environmental industry in Southeast Asia. You think there will be a future need for improving conditions and the environment for the millions of people in the region. There are a number of companies involved in this listed on the SGX, the stock exchange of Singapore.

You decide you want to put your money to work in one of these two companies: Sembcorp Industries Ltd or Hyflux Ltd. You do a quick check on one of the financial websites, e.g. Bloomberg, Google Finance. I am sure there are many others – they pretty much do the same thing – but let us try Yahoo Finance, I find it easy to navigate.

It says that Sembcorp Industries is an investment holding company, engaged in utilities, marine, and urban development businesses worldwide. The utilities segment provides energy, water, on-site logistics and solid waste management services to industrial and municipal customers. The company's activities in the energy sector include power generation and retail, and process steam production and supply, as well as natural gas import, supply, and retail; the water sectors comprise wastewater treatment and the production and supply of reclaimed, desalinated, and potable water.

Then you check Hyflux and find that this company is also an investment holding company. It provides integrated water management and environmental solutions worldwide. It operates through two segments, municipal and industrial. The municipal segment supplies a range of water and fluid treatment solutions to municipalities and governments; the industrial segment offers liquid separation applications for the manufacturing sector. The company is also involved in membrane-based desalination of seawater, purification of raw water, cleaning of wastewater, recycling and reclamation of water. In addition, it provides home consumer filtration and purification products, and engages in the design, construction and sale of water treatment plants and seawater desalination plants. Further, the company designs, constructs and operates power plants, as well as trades in the electricity markets.

Hmmm, in general Sembcorp seems to be a bit heavy in the marine and oil and gas industries. It doesn't say on Yahoo, but in fact they also build a lot of coal-fired power plants, while Hyflux mainly cleans water. That might be a consideration for you, but let us leave the ethical aspect aside for now and just look at which company would make the best use of your capital. For that, pretty words are not enough; we have to look at the numbers. We quickly compare some key statistics before we go any further, again from Yahoo (the data is from the last year available, but will serve us perfectly well for understanding what the key statistics mean):

| Metric | Sembcorp | Hyflux |
|---|---|---|
| Shares outstanding (million) | 1,790 | 804 |
| Market capitalisation (million $) | 6,410 | 571 |
| Share price ($) | 3.58 | 0.71 |
| 52-week high/low ($) | 5.23 / 3.00 | 1.12 / 0.60 |
| Revenue (million $) | 10,460 | 308 |
| Gross profit (million $) | 1,420 | 156 |
| Net income (million $) | 790 | −79 |
| Diluted EPS ($) | 0.44 | −0.10 |
| Forward P/E ratio | 9 | 24 |
| Price-to-book ratio | 0.97 | 0.43 |
| Price-to-sales ratio | 0.60 | 1.84 |
| Dividend yield (% p.a.) | 4.60 | 3.30 |
| Analyst mean target price ($) | 4.17 | 0.91 |

Now we know roughly what we are dealing with. Market capitalisation is simply shares outstanding times the share price. Sembcorp is obviously much bigger than Hyflux, in terms of revenue as well.

What about profitability? From this source, Sembcorp appears much more profitable. After all its gross profit is S$1,420 million versus S$156 million for Hyflux, which in fact has negative net income. If you divide net income by the number of shares, you get EPS, earnings per share, in this case the *diluted* EPS, which means that allowance has been made for any warrants and other convertible shares that the company might have outstanding, so diluted EPS tends to be a bit smaller than EPS; that doesn't really matter as long as we compare the same metric.

Yahoo also provides some basic financial ratios that are commonly used in fundamental financial analysis. In this case they include the P/E ratio (price/earnings ratio). This is simply the share price over the latest earnings per share. Keep in mind that the denominator is not the dividend the company pays out, it is the earnings before dividends are paid (we will get to that later). In this case, Yahoo provides the *forward* P/E, which is good since with negative earnings for this period the P/E for Hyflux would not really make sense. The trailing (i.e. past) P/E for Sembcorp appears to be 3.58/0.44 = 8.14.

As a financial metric, the P/E ratio is probably the most used. It is referred to as the multiple of the company, i.e. roughly the number of years it would take for the company to make back the price of its stock. But it is important to note a few things. The trailing P/E is based on facts, i.e. the reported earnings as published by the company. As the company share price changes from day to day, the numerator changes as well, so the ratio will always be in flux. The forward P/E is based on future earnings, either those provided by the company as a guidance to the market or those estimated by the analyst himself. So by definition the forward P/E ratio is somewhat subjective.

In our case study, Sembcorp has a much lower P/E than Hyflux; this is typical for a mature company with solid income and earnings. However, if you look at the price-to-book ratio, this picture becomes less clear. The current price per share divided by the net assets (or the equity) per share is close to 1 for Sembcorp, but less than 0.5 for Hyflux. Usually you would associate a low price-to-book with an undervalued company, so we will have to look at that in more detail later. Price-to-sales is market cap divided by sales (revenue); it indicates how many times the market is willing to pay for the company's revenue. A low ratio, like the one for Sembcorp (0.60), could be an indicator that the company is undervalued, while a high ratio, like Hyflux's (1.84) could be a warning sign that the stock is too expensive.

The dividend yield is important, especially for value investors who are looking for regular income from their stock portfolio. It is simply the dividend divided by the share price, and like the P/E it will vary slightly from day to day. Say Sembcorp paid 16.50 cents per share dividend, the current yield would be **0.165/3.58 = 0.0461** or 4.61%. One thing would strike you now looking at this. If Hyflux loses money, how can they have a dividend yield of 3.30%? With this share price they should pay out more than 2 cent per share in dividend, when if fact they lose 10 cents per share at the moment; it doesn't add up. So we have to investigate this in more detail.

This snapshot from Yahoo Finance tells us something about the two companies. But it also raises a few questions. Is Hyflux really losing money? Why is the price-to-book so low? Is this dividend policy sustainable? We cannot invest based on this alone; we need to find out more.

## Checking the annual report

There is nothing like going to the primary source. In fact, like everybody else, those fancy stock analysts out there get most of their information from the company itself. Then they rehash that and work out a few more ratios and add their own opinion to charge for their services. Some big shareholders can do a bit better than that, like visit the company and talk to the management to get a better take on the company's prospects. The rest of us have to form an opinion based mainly on the annual report. All listed companies have to file an annual report to shareholders and potential investors, as well as quarterly updates.

It has been suggested that quarterly reports are a bit of an overkill, and personally I tend to agree with that. The rule was scrapped in the UK in 2015; in Singapore large listed companies with a market cap above S$75 million are still required to report quarterly by the exchange.[1] Quarterly reporting gives a lot of work to accountants and other bean counters in the company and its external auditors, but is also a waste of resources. Maybe the company would be better off putting that time and money into doing their core business, and then just report to the public once a year? Anyway, until further notice we have to live with the quarterly reporting and the associated "earning seasons" (i.e. the beginning of each quarter) and all the busy noise and soul-searching this generates in finance.

It used to be that when you wanted to know more about a listed company, you wrote a letter to the HQ and asked for an annual report. It would arrive a few weeks later in the mail. Now of course everything is available online. Make sure you use this to your advantage.

Let us have a look at the annual report for each of the two companies we are interested in. To do that, you go to the company's website and find the investor information link.

Sembcorp's report for 2014 is an impressive 355-page affair. It gives a good idea about what the company does and how it would like investors to view it. The 135-page report from Hyflux by comparison is less elaborate but it quickly provides you with all the information you need. It turns out that while Yahoo Finance reported a loss, this loss was calculated "ttm" (trailing twelve months) until 30 June 2015, while the company actually made a profit after tax for the full year of 2014 of $59 million and had EPS of 1.66 cents (not –10 cents). This way, using multiple sources is useful for getting a better picture.

However, there might be some problems with Hyflux. From the annual reports we can piece together a picture of how the two companies fared over the past 5 years, and see what trends there are. While the revenue, profit and earnings per share of Hyflux have been erratic and so far down over the last five years, the numbers for Sembcorp appear rock-solid. The NAV or net asset value per share is the number used to calculate the price-to-book (or price-to-NAV) ratio that we saw earlier; should the share price for Sembcorp drop to S$3.15, the price-to-book would then be 1, which is considered good. A price-to-book of 1 or less is typical

| Metric | | 2010 | 2011 | 2012 | 2013 | 2014 |
|---|---|---|---|---|---|---|
| Revenue (million $) | Hyflux | 562 | 460 | 655 | 536 | 321 |
| | Sembcorp | 8,762 | 9,047 | 10,189 | 10,798 | 10,895 |
| Net profit (million $) | Hyflux | 89 | 56 | 65 | 43 | 59 |
| | Sembcorp | 793 | 809 | 753 | 820 | 801 |
| Earnings per share (cents) | Hyflux | 10.5 | 4.3 | 4.4 | 2.4 | 1.7 |
| | Sembcorp | 44.4 | 45.3 | 42.2 | 45.7 | 44.3 |
| NAV per share ($) | Hyflux | 0.59 | 0.61 | 0.56 | 0.58 | 0.57 |
| | Sembcorp | 2.13 | 2.31 | 2.52 | 2.93 | 3.15 |
| Return on equity (%) | Hyflux | 17.6 | 7.1 | 8 | 4.1 | 3.0 |
| | Sembcorp | 22.2 | 20.4 | 17.5 | 17.1 | 15.2 |
| Dividend per share (cents) | Hyflux | 4.17 | 2.77 | 3.20 | 2.30 | 2.30 |
| | Sembcorp | 17 | 17 | 15 | 17 | 16 |

for a well-consolidated business with plenty of capital or real stuff at hand, such as a bank or a manufacturing conglomerate, while a high price-to-book might be accepted for a business with mainly "soft" intellectual property or good growth prospects. For Hyflux, at 71 cents per share, the price-to-book would be around **71/57 = 1.25**, not 0.43 as Yahoo stated. As we suspected above, the figure from Yahoo was simply too low, i.e. wrong. So again it pays to check the primary source of information.

And what about those Hyflux dividends? An important aspect of evaluating the future prospects of your return is to see how much of the earnings are paid out as dividends to shareholders. What is not paid out will be retained in the company; the funds will be added to the equity in the company, where they can either be invested in more projects or returned to shareholders at a later time. This is reflected in the dividend payout ratio, which is the dividend divided by the earnings per share. For Sembcorp in 2014 this was **16/44.3 = 0.36**. In other words, almost two-thirds of the earnings were retained in the company. A prudent company might pay out only half of its earnings to the shareholders; Sembcorp pays less than that. What did Hyflux pay in 2014? **2.3/1.7 = 1.35**, i.e. they paid out more than they made! If a company keeps doing that, it will run out of equity.

Return on equity (ROE) is another important variable. It is simply net income divided by the equity in the company or the book value, i.e. assets minus liabilities. It is similar to when you calculate the yield on your investment: You take the net return over the invested capital. Hyflux has quite a lot of equity in the company, but they have not been able to get a very good return and worse still, the ROE is dropping year over year. Sembcorp has a better return but is also struggling to keep up profitability.

We found out all this just by looking at the financial group highlights in each of the annual reports. If you want to peel off one more layer of this onion, you go in and find the full financial statements. Here the analysis gets a bit more tedious. Just like a musician can pick up a sheet of music and hear the symphony play in his head while he reads the score, a good accountant can pick up a financial statement and comprehend the workings of the company from the numbers. But not all of us have the experience or the skill to do that.

The financial statements consist of three parts: the income statement (or P&L, profit and loss statement), the balance sheet, and the cash flow statement. From the income statement you find out in more detail where the revenue that the company reports is coming from and you look for extraordinary items. While the income statement reports for the whole financial year, the balance sheet is a snapshot taken on a certain date, in this case the last day of 2014; it shows the assets the company owns against its liabilities.

There are a number of financial ratios that you can derive from the statements. To gauge the company's liquidity position, you can calculate the *current ratio*, i.e. current assets over current liabilities. For Hyflux it is $839 million over $391 million = 2.15; it was 1.72 the previous year, so this is encouraging. For Sembcorp the current ratio is 1.14. Both companies have over twice the amount of non-current assets as current and appear well consolidated. However, financing debt is a large portion of the liabilities; so when we look at the ratio of total debt to total capital, we find out that it is 1.05 for Hyflux and 1.38 for Sembcorp. Both companies seem to carry quite a lot of debt. The *debt-to-capital ratio* should be lower, preferably around 0.5.

Before you close off each annual report, quick-read through it and ask yourself: Do you trust this company? What are the management up to, what are their plans? Would you like to be associated with it, to own a part of it?

One thing I always like to do is to see who owns most of the company. In the case of Hyflux, you find that one person, the founder, executive chairman and CEO Olivia Lum owns 33% of the ordinary shares. Most of the other large investors are Singapore-based banks and institutions, with 20 entities owning 74% of the ordinary shares. There are some 17,000 shareholders altogether. Sembcorp is obviously a so-called government-linked company because Temasek Holdings Pte Ltd (a Singapore government investment company) owns 49% of the ordinary shares. DBS (another government-linked company) owns 13%. The 20 largest shareholders own 89% of the company, and altogether there are some 31,000 shareholders.

Keep in mind when you look at the ownership of shares that there are two ways the shareholders are registered. One is the depository register and the other is the register of substantial shareholders. The two could differ if the "real" owners have put their shares in deposit somewhere else to finance a take-over maybe, or to place their shares in trust with a financial institution acting as the trustee. In that case, the register of substantial shareholders would more accurately reflect corporate ownership.

## Digging a bit deeper

We found out a lot from all this. There are some further ratios that we could calculate based on the full financial statements.

Looking at liquidity, the *quick ratio* is current assets minus inventories over current liabilities; by taking out less-liquid assets from the equation, it gives you a better idea of the company's ability to cover immediate liabilities. The *cash ratio* is simply cash plus short-term investments only over current liabilities; this is the most conservative of the liquidity ratios and will tell you if the company is able to pay its bills on time.

Regarding debt, the ratio we used earlier can also be modified. By placing total debt over total shareholder equity (not total capital), you get a slightly higher ratio to consider. You might also want to know how much the company is weighted down by interest payments, so you can place operating profit over interest expense to get the *interest coverage ratio* – obviously the higher the better. Value investors in particular will be concerned if the debt and interest expenses in the company are too high, while growth investors might accept more debt in the belief that future rapid growth will shave the debt down.

At this point you might want to consider getting some help. Until now we have looked at publicly available data that anyone can find fairly easily and which is totally free. So our research has cost us nothing thus far, but if you are willing to pay, much more is available. It is somewhat tedious to calculate these ratios yourself, especially if you are looking at many companies. Your time might be too valuable for this, or you are simply not interested in doing all the searching and calculating yourself.

There is plenty of help out there, lots of financial analysis services eager to help you – for a fee of course. If you use an online trading platform for your investing, most likely this company will provide you with analysis services; you pay for it already through your trading fees. VectorVest often advertises in Singapore, and they have some pretty impressive software packages that allow you to screen the stocks you consider and track them according to the criteria that are important for you. You might consider this service if you invest worldwide. If you are mainly into the local Singapore market, a lot of information about the listed companies can simply be found on the SGX site itself. The big Singapore media company SPH operates Shareinvestor.com; I find it very useful and easy to use. There is plenty of information readily available for the public.

Let us look at what happens if you sign on, pay, and consider Hyflux and Sembcorp as in our case study. Now you are in a site that is like Yahoo on steroids. What we have done thus far, looking at the annual report and the financial statements to gauge the value and prospects of the company, is called fundamental

| Metric | Sembcorp | Hyflux |
| --- | --- | --- |
| Price over revenue (adjusted) | 0.58 | 1.74 |
| Price over revenue (historical) | 0.85 | 2.84 |
| Price over earnings (historical) | 12 | 67 |
| Price to book (historical) | 1.7 | 1.92 |
| Dividend yield (%, historical) | 3.10 | 2.06 |
| Gross profit over revenue (%) | 13 | 49 |
| Net profit over revenue (%) | 7.3 | 4.3 |
| Dividend payout ratio (historical) | 0.36 | 1.39 |
| Net earnings over total assets (%) | 4.6 | 0.5 |
| Return on equity (%) | 14.6 | 2.9 |
| Cashflow over equity (%) | 27.3 | 0.9 |
| Profit over interest ratio | 18.5 | 2.4 |
| Total debt over equity ratio | 0.9 | 2.4 |
| Total debt to total assets ratio | 0.28 | 0.41 |
| Total assets over equity ratio | 3.2 | 5.8 |
| Analyst mean target price | 4.01 | 0.87 |

analysis. Shareinvestor has page after page of this for each company. It includes all the ratios we have looked at up until now and a few others. Many of the numbers are from the annual report we looked at, but some are calculated historically over a number of years, and there are more current tables and graphs on the site based on the most recent quarterly reports published.

By paying for this additional information, you also get access to data and statistics that are not so obvious in the public domain. Shareinvestor provides a detailed analysis of the company's dividend policy, going back much further than the most recent annual report. This is obviously important to all investors, but especially so to value and income investors who mainly look for rock-solid enterprises that can grow their dividend payment year over year.

Many investors also watch how insiders trade the stock. This is a grey area because outright insider trading is illegal. The MAS and regulators in other countries view it as a serious offence if directors and officers of a company trade their stock on information not yet released to the public. Say, for instance, that Olivia Lum with Hyflux has just finalised a new mega sale of a desalination plant to a country in the Middle East. She cannot go back to her hotel and buy Hyflux shares knowing very well that the price will shoot up the next day when the news is announced to the public. She may be unlikely to do that, but what about her secretary who has a cousin who has a friend who is a stock broker? Any "funny" movements in a listed company's share price are closely watched by the exchange and by public regulators, and the company itself might apply for a temporary trading halt while the dust settles regarding major news releases, take-over rumours and that sort of thing. As an added protection for ordinary shareholders, directors trading the stock have to make their dealings public. Shareinvestor.com publishes these filings, and they might be of interest to the public; if a director suddenly sells out of his holdings big-time, this could be bearish for the stock, and vice versa.

Shareinvestor also lists company buyback schemes. A listed company might buy back its own shares for two reasons usually: to have shares available to honour employee stock option commitments, or simply to invest in themselves! If they have excess cash on their books, management might buy back shares as this will improve the ROE (return on equity) ratio (by reducing the denominator in this ratio). This could be bullish for the stock.

For day-traders, Shareinvestor also accounts for minute-to-minute trades in the stock you are watching, although your online trading platform would probably provide the same information. Traders also watch outstanding shorts in the market; a company might come under attack from short sellers or hedge funds that borrow shares and sell them in the hope of buying back later at a lower price. This could be bearish for the stock; at some point, however, so many shorts could be outstanding that you would expect the stock to bounce back soon, when the speculators surrender and buy back during a so-called "short squeeze". But then, this is short-term trading and speculating and should not distract long-term value investors.

So what do the new numbers in the table tell us? The gross margin (gross profit, i.e. revenue minus cost of sales, over revenue) does not really make sense for Hyflux during this reporting period, but if we also take out operating expenses and interest payments and taxes we get net profit over revenue and it is clearly better for Sembcorp, as is historical P/E and virtually every other metric available. From all this it would be pretty safe to say that Sembcorp has made better use of its capital until now.

## Which stock to buy

Looking at all the data here, there is little doubt that a value investor would buy shares in Sembcorp Ltd. It is exactly the kind of company that value investors like Warren Buffett and his many followers look for.

That said, the statistics and graphs provided by financial analysis services are not the be-all and end-all of investing. Yes, they can be very useful and powerful, the software is amazing, and the amount of data that's available is truly mind-boggling. You can analyse, screen and compare virtually hundreds if not thousands of listed companies to assist you in your decision-making. But personally I find that they can be so overwhelming and clinically automated that you lose sight of what is important. I like to just read through the information in the company annual report and go through the financial statements carefully. Here you see what the company is actually doing and how it does it.

Furthermore, the financial ratios, graphs and statistics cannot always tell you if what you're looking at is a well-managed company with a future. Growth investors look for small-capitalisation companies that might do well in the future. Who knows, while Hyflux has been struggling a bit on and off lately, maybe they have a rosy future ahead of them, and the stock could go back to $3 as it once was. If you trust the management and the business concept and put your money where your heart is, you might do well; then the current dividend payments or lack thereof might not matter so much.

There are many cases where value investors got trapped by looking at all the past data and projecting it forward into the future, ruler-across-the-chart style. I mentioned the unexpected drop in oil price in 2014; that event took down a lot of "rock-solid" oil production and service companies and all their junk bonds with them. Kodak Eastman was a nice dividend-paying index stock for many years, founded in 1892, but they didn't see the digital age coming and had to declare bankruptcy in 2012. "Past performance is no guarantee of future results" – this bedrock disclaimer of the financial world is so true!

In fact, the old methodology of looking at P/E and price-to-book values to gauge a company is being re-evaluated. Those who applied mainly these techniques would have missed out on the phenomenal rise of new companies like Google (now listed as Alphabet Inc), Amazon, Alibaba Group and Facebook. How in the world did Facebook manage to outcompete Myspace, which was owned by News Corporation between 2005 and 2009, when that huge corporation couldn't make Myspace work and sold it at a loss of over half a billion dollars? I don't know the answer to that, and I cannot explain why Facebook is now a US$300 billion company when it only has US$5.4 billion worth of fixed assets and a staff of just 10,000 people.[2] In traditional analysis this doesn't make sense. But many investors are now scratching their heads over this, and they wonder whether this time it is really different, i.e. whether the "weightless" tech companies are really rewriting the laws of investment. Or will the old fundamentals eventually catch up? Is this just another asset bubble waiting to burst? Only time will tell.

## The bigger picture

A comparison like the one we performed above can be done for any stocks or groups of stocks. It is important that in fundamental analysis investing you consider three things: the macroeconomic environment, the sector or industry, and the company itself.

**The macroeconomic environment:** We covered this in chapter 3. Is this a good time to be in the stock market at all? Are interest rates rising or falling? When interest rates rise, it is usually bad for stocks, but if the economy is otherwise strong and production and wages growing, stocks might go up anyway. Some investors read the news carefully every day and look out for macroeconomic or even political events like civil unrest that might influence the market. They swear that following events and pre-empting market reactions is the key to good returns.

On one hand, some analysts advise that you try to exit when the market is at a historic peak, or at least reduce your holdings.

Then buy back during a recession, when the stock market is in a bear market. In market jargon, a 10% drop from the peak is a technical correction, a 20% drop from peak is a bear market. In a cliché-filled business environment, this Buffett quote is maybe more repeated than any other: "Be fearful when others are greedy and greedy when others are fearful."[3]

However, it is easier said than done. And there is the opposite cliché: "It is not the market timing that matters; it is the time in the market." I cannot remember who first said that, but it is the mantra of many value investors. My late friend Iain Ewing (mentioned in chapter 1) subscribed to this school of thought. One year I got a funny refund from the tax department – I had overpaid my property taxes over a number of years and suddenly got some S$10,000 back. It was a bit of a windfall so I wanted to stash it away and invest for the long term. I asked Iain for advice and he said: "Buy OCBC." I said: "But what if it goes down? Banking stocks are awfully expensive at the moment." He said: "It doesn't matter, just hold your nose and buy." And he was right, the stock came down for a while after I bought, but the company is well-managed and recovered the next year, and in the end it didn't really matter.

**The sector:** You have to consider which sector of the economy you are involved in; this is called industry analysis. In Singapore, the SGX operates with 12 different sectors (plus shares in foreign currencies). In terms of trading value, the finance sector is the largest, followed by transport and communications, properties and services. The other sectors are smaller, with just double-digit million-dollar daily turnover value. In the US, the Dow Jones publishes indexes for 10 different broad industries and a larger number of subsectors.

So if for instance you want to invest in a banking stock, you must consider the industry as a whole. When you compare the quality and performance of "your" company, you should first of all compare it with other banks or financial institutions. How will rising (or falling) interest rates affect this industry as a whole? How about government regulation or other events specific to the sector?

You often hear financial commentators talk about "growth industries". Preferably your investment should be in that category; it could be pharmaceuticals, mobile technology or clean energy. The other side of the coin are the "sunset industries", maybe anything related to coal or out-of-date technologies. Technological developments, government legislation and consumer preferences keep the economy in constant flux and as an investor you should keep that in mind.

During periods of stagnation or slow growth, investors try to seek shelter by shifting capital into "defensive" industries. This does not refer to armament manufacturing, but means recession-proof sectors like food, public utilities and health care – people will spend their money here no matter what. "Cyclical" industries, producing stuff like cars and other durable goods such as television sets and refrigerators, usually suffer during recessions – consumers simply just wait a few years to upgrade. However, they might boom after the recession is over, together with sectors like luxury hotel chains and upmarket jewellery companies.

**The company:** If you look at the case study above, our starting point was that we considered this the right time to invest in a certain sector: multi-industry with an emphasis on environmental services and water treatment. We then looked at two companies, comparing them closely and concluding that one (Sembcorp) might appeal to a value investor and the other (Hyflux) was more of an uncertain entity, but it might appeal to a growth investor willing to hold the stock and trust it would land more contracts in the future.

## What's a good price?

So this is the million-dollar question: How much should we pay for the stock? This is the question everyone is seeking an answer to all the time. We went to great lengths to look at some of the metrics that stock analysts use to gauge the fair value of the stock. One we didn't cover is the dividend discount method.

This is somewhat similar to the method we used in the previous chapter to calculate the value of a bond: We discounted all the future dividend payments to present-day value as well as the par value, also discounted. Calculated this way, the price of a stock today (year 0) should be:

$$P(0) = D(1)/(1+k) + D(2)/(1+k)^2 + ... + D(n)/(1+k)^n + P(n)/(1+k)^n$$

P(0) is the maximum market price we are willing to pay
    today (if the current quote is lower, so much the better)
D(n) is the dividend in year n
P(n) is the selling price of the stock in year n
k is our required rate of return, the discount rate

Like with the bond calculation, "k" is somewhat subjective; it could be the yield on our alternative safe investment, at minimum the local bank deposit rate. If our alternative safe investment is keeping the money at home under the mattress **k = 0** and all the denominators are 1. But the higher the k, the lower P(0) would be, i.e. we would need to secure the stock cheaper to make the investment worth our while.

But there is one more problem with this now. A bond is called "fixed income" for a reason. The income is fixed! With a stock we have no certainty that the dividend will continue in the future. We also don't know what the "maturity" of the investment is – how long will the company be in business? What will our eventual selling price be? Analysts who use this method have to do a lot of guesswork. Even then, I think you should try it. It forces you to consider some of your conceptions about the company and its future as well as the alternative interest environment; in the end it might help you to "guesstimate" a fair value.

## More tools

When evaluating a business sector and the role of a company within the sector, I find the "industry life cycle" concept useful. Maybe it is because I have seen some inventions catch on and many others die a quiet death – or maybe not so quiet in the case of Concorde. When I was young in the 1970s, supersonic passenger transport was the latest and greatest. Everyone talked about how you could now fly from London to New York in 3½ hours. But Concorde never caught on. It was expensive and noisy, and after a fatal crash in 2000 the programme was discontinued in 2003. On the other hand, there is the story of a certain college dropout who started a software company with a friend in his small office in New Mexico while I was working on the oil rigs in the North Sea in 1975. He ended up as the richest man in the world. Had I bought shares in his company (Microsoft Corporation) when it listed in 1986, I would have done alright. His name is of course Bill Gates.

Witnessing events like these gives you a sense of respect for the industry life cycle. The concept, developed by Michael Porter of Harvard University, teaches that an industry goes through five different stages – development, introduction, growth, maturity and decline – corresponding to a rise and eventual fall in total industry revenue. Understanding this trajectory allows you to situate a company or an industry within a larger timeframe.

Porter seems to be fond of five-bullet explanations, because he has another analysis methodology relating to the competitive nature of an industry. He believes there are five basic competitive forces that ultimately determine the industry's ability to sustain above-average rates of return on equity: rivalry among existing competitors; threat of new entrants; threat of substitute products; bargaining power of buyers; and bargaining power of suppliers.

A company's competitive advantage could be that it has a product that is difficult to substitute, or the barriers to entry are very high, i.e. it is difficult and costly for new start-up companies to break into the business. Microsoft, for instance, enjoyed this competitive advantage for many years, sometimes walking a thin line across a minefield of government regulations designed to maintain fair competition and reduce monopolistic tendencies in the capitalist economy. They had to pay a few fines in Europe when they wavered off the line – I will get back to that in chapter 12. Overall the shareholders were quite happy though![4]

Now if you look at Sembcorp and Hyflux again, ask yourself, how does Porter's work relate to them? Where are these two companies within the industry life cycle? What is their competitive advantage?

## Is technical analysis mumbo jumbo?

There is one thing we actually never checked in the case study above: the charts! Probably one of the first things you would do when considering Sembcorp and Hyflux would be to look at their stock charts. Let's look at how the two companies did in the last five years (Fig. 11 and 12).

Sembcorp Industries Ltd is a holding company; they own fully or partly a large number of smaller companies. Many of these, such as listed Sembcorp Marine Ltd, are heavily exposed to the petroleum industry, so with the fall in crude oil prices in 2014, SembCorp took a big hit as well. Hyflux is just Hyflux, somewhat erratic and down at the time of writing, but who knows what will happen in the future.

This is the thing about charts: They tell us what has happened, but they don't tell us what will happen. However, technical analysts are out to fix that. They believe that by studying past chart

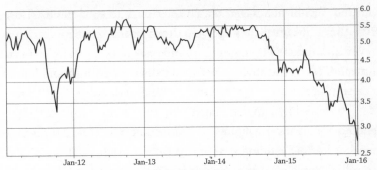

**Fig. 11: Sembcorp Industries recent share price (S$)**

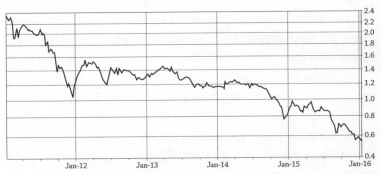

**Fig. 12: Hyflux Ltd recent share price (S$)**

patterns they can predict with some certainty how the stock will perform in the future. Most investment companies and mutual funds employ some analysts specialising in this, chartists, who use a very different set of tools. These analysts are not concerned about the fair value of a stock derived from fundamental analysis. In fact, they are doubtful about this; they believe that stock prices are driven mainly by market sentiment and speculative (somewhat irrational) forces of supply and demand. They study charts and trading statistics because they believe that chart trends tend to repeat themselves, and as such can be predicted.

I am certainly no expert on this, but I did go through the technical analysis material to qualify as a fund manager, and I have (patiently) sat through various seminars by men in suits lecturing on this. Technical analysts watch the charts to spot trends. They ride the trend until they spot a pattern in the chart indicating a reversal. Gradually rising support and resistance levels indicate an uptrend; when the stock penetrates below the rising trend line it is a trend reversal. High volume uptrend with a dip ("left shoulder") followed by a higher "head" and then a smaller peak ("right shoulder") on lower volume is an important indicator that the bull market has peaked and is about to turn bearish, so it is a signal to sell. Reverse head and shoulders indicate a market bottom and is a signal to buy. Consolidation rectangles form when the stock chart moves sideways in a narrow band. Chartists watch for "flags" where the stock moves out of its usual trading range under heavy volume and they buy and sell accordingly.

Trading volume is an important indicator for technicians; the breakout from the trend is only significant if it happens on large volume. Most charts on financial service sites also indicate volume to assist with this assessment. As mentioned earlier, the outstanding short-interest volume is viewed by technicians in a contrarian manner; thus a high outstanding short-interest volume is regarded as a bullish sign; the stock is expected to bottom out and reverse up when the shorts have to be bought back.

The moving average lines are of especial interest. They smooth out the erratic day-to-day trades and make the trends clearer. The 200-day moving average is simply the average stock price over 200 days. Each day the oldest day is removed and the newest added to make the average "move". Chartists watch the 200-day moving average (the long-term trend) and plot it with the 30-day shorter-term trend. In a downward-trending market, the 200-day moving average would normally run above the short-term one, so when the short-term line moves up and crosses the long-term line from below this is taken as a sign to buy. In a bull market with rising prices, the short-term line will run above the 200-day line; so when it drops and crosses the 200-day line this is a signal to sell out, especially so if it happens under heavy volume.

I would urge you to look into this in more detail yourself if you are interested. There are plenty of experts out there who would love to teach you more, for a fee; with their trading methods you are sure to beat all the other traders out there and get rich quick – so they claim.

But then there are others in the financial industry who out-right reject technical analysis as voodoo finance. I have one good friend in the business, Saurabh Singal, who taught me a lot. He categorically told me not to waste any time with this. I tend to agree. The seminars on this that I attended never impressed me. It is easy for the chartists to select the case studies that prove their point. They love to project up fancy candle charts of past events to show that "This is when I bought" (low) and "This is when I sold" (high of course). Right, what about all the times this didn't work for you?

The trend is your friend, I can understand that. You ride a stock up as demand pushes it up. But your indicators for spotting a reversal in the trend only seem to become obvious after the trend has changed, so they may not be of much use. I consider myself a numbers person, and I just cannot see the numbers work in your favour in technical trading. If all the traders use these signals, won't the trades cancel each other out? With all those profession-als doing computerised high-frequency trading stacked against me, I just cannot see myself winning in this stressful game.

However, in general I do believe that it is worthwhile gauging the sentiment in the market, i.e. the public perception, to consider supply and demand factors. These factors could help you deter-mine a good time to enter the market or to "take money off the table", as industry jargon puts it, in another tasteless reference to the casino business. There are times when a good stock appears oversold due to illogical reasons, unreasonable fear and mass hys-teria among investors. And there are other times when "irrational exuberance", to use a famous phrase by Alan Greenspan, drives up asset prices to ridiculous levels and it might be time to sell out.[5] But then, in my view, you need solid fundamental analysis to establish what a fair value is to begin with, before you can decide what unfair value is.

Up to now we have looked at various financial concepts, tools and investment vehicles. In the next two chapters we will apply these concepts in practice and determine how you can mix up the various products at your disposal, with the ultimate goal of maximising the value of your total investment portfolio.

# Getting Started

*"Behold the turtle. He makes progress
only when he sticks his neck out."*

— JAMES CONANT

## Shares – the way to go

So, you know all your investment options now and you want to
invest. My advice is to buy shares in good companies and build up
a portfolio based mainly on equities. As we saw in the last chapter,
it is possible to identify solid dividend-paying companies with a
competitive advantage. The problem of course is that thousands of
other investors have the same idea, so those companies are often
highly valued already. However, look at the fundamentals, develop
your own opinion about the future, and if you feel confident, hold
your nose like Iain Ewing said, and just buy the stock.

Sure, the stock market is volatile – I know that better than
anyone else, because I started buying and selling shares in 1975.
More recently, the first decade of this century was pretty slow;
most likely you would not have made much capital gain on your
portfolio during those ten years, but the dividends would still have
come in and if reinvested at a compounded rate would have given
you a decent yield (decent meaning beating inflation plus another
percent or two).

For macroeconomic reasons that we have covered, mainly the
tremendous expansion of the money supply since 1980, stocks

tend to be on an upward trajectory. Look at this amazing chart of the US S&P 500 stock market index:

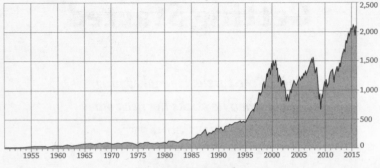

**Fig. 13: S&P 500 index**

Within the last decade or so, a trend has emerged of large investors simply bypassing the stock markets altogether. Private equity funds often do not invest in listed companies; they simply buy the company outright and keep it private. They may even take a listed company private or lump several together in mergers and acquisitions, as has happened with increased frequency on the NYSE in the US. In Singapore, there has been a serious drop in IPOs on the stock exchange in recent years. When queried about this, the CEO of SGX Loh Boon Chye said: "The presence of more sources of capital, including venture capital and private equity which have been active investors in start-ups and growth companies, has drawn away potential IPOs."[1] So there you have it, what many investors suspected, from the horse's mouth. All this reduces the choice available to retail investors. But unless you want to own and run your own business, which is a lot of work, investing in listed shares is still the way to go in my book.

## Start your portfolio

How you compose your stock portfolio depends on your age and your appetite for risk. In general, the younger you are, the more risk you can accept. This is simply because when you are in your

20s and 30s you will have more time to make new money should you lose it all. Even in your 40s and 50s, your future earning prospects might have declined a bit, but you still have time to wait out a bear market should your portfolio be under water for a few years, as bear markets rarely last longer than that. Once you are in your 60s and 70s, well, you should play it safe and watch your portfolio carefully. Get rid of the speculative, small-cap stocks and keep only the safe bets, those with low P/E and high dividend payouts to provide you with a stream of passive income. Tweak the mix in your portfolio to include more fixed income products, such as low-risk government bonds.

Study your stocks; even high-dividend-paying companies are not always safe, as we saw in the last chapter. Check the dividend pay-out ratio; it should be below 1 and preferably below 0.5. And remember the business life cycle analysis in the previous chapter? Consider where your industry and your companies fit into this concept. Ask yourself: Will this corporation still be relevant 10 years from now?

If you really want to play it safe, stick to index stocks – in Singapore those that are part of the STI, in the US the Dow Jones Industrial Average index. These shares have already been scrutinised for selection by the index provider, so by definition they are solid companies with high daily turnover, i.e. they are liquid and easy to get in and out of. Furthermore, there is a natural requirement for the stock from all those ETFs tracking the index; this keeps demand and prices up. Notice how a company's shares inevitably fall if it is kicked out of the index. This happens once in a while, as the index owner tweaks the composition to maintain market relevance.

Remember the price-to-book ratio we covered in the previous chapter? Looking at this ratio before buying an individual stock will help to tell you if the stock is over-valued or under-valued relative to the estimated net value of the company itself. Likewise there is a similar ratio for the market as a whole, called the Tobin Q ratio. That is basically the total market value of all the firms over their combined assets/replacement values. As you can imagine, the ratio should be 1 or close to 1 if the companies are correctly priced by the market. Professional fund managers watch the Tobin Q chart, and during periods when it is much over 1, they may be reluctant to enter the market, while a low Q (**Q < 1**) could be a signal to buy.

## Executing the trade

You can buy shares through any of the big banks. They all have associated brokerage firms. Your shares will be registered in your name, and if you are based in Singapore they will be deposited electronically in your CDP (Central Depository) account. It just takes 20 minutes to open an account like that. You have to go in person with your IC of course, but typical for Singapore, the process is a breeze.

When I started trading shares many moons ago, the stock broker commission was around 1% of the transaction. We, the customers, didn't think much of that, such was the going rate. And of course, we all hoped to double our money within a few months. You expect that when you are in your 20s. Your broker always had a hot tip for you when he called you up – "This one is about to go through the roof for sure!" – so what is a percentage or two among friends, right? Then after a while you realise that the world doesn't work quite like that. And the cost of the whole investment business becomes more important to you. In fact, surveys have shown that transaction costs are very important to your long-term return.

Long live computers. With computerised online trading, the cost of each transaction has come down to around 0.2% or even less. You don't really need to talk to a person anymore, unless you really value the personal contact highly. The trading fee varies a bit from platform to platform and also depends on which exchange, which country, and which currency you are trading in. And there is of course also a minimum charge for each trade, maybe some $15–20.

On the platform, you place your order to buy or sell. There will be a bid price by a potential buyer (low) and an ask price (a bit higher) by a potential seller. If the share is moving quickly and you just want to grab it, you select "market" and the transaction will be done immediately at the prevailing ask price. If you want to buy but feel the ask price is still a bit high, you can key in a new bid price, lower than the prevailing one, set a time limit (maybe a day or a week) and wait until the ask price drops to your bid price.

In the past, you had to buy stocks in Singapore in minimum lots of 1,000 shares. This was changed in 2015, and the minimum lot size is now 100. Ideally there should be no minimum, so that you can trade any number of shares you want, including so-called "odd-lots" (i.e. lots less that 100), which might appear in your portfolio from share splits and bonus issues.

How often you should trade is up to you. It depends on whether you consider yourself a trader or an investor. If you are a trader, good for you; then that is what you do. If you are a long-term investor, then make sure you don't just feed the service provider by jumping in and out of the market too often.

If the stock you just bought is a short-term speculative purchase and you don't really intend to own the company for the long term, you should consider setting a *stop-loss* on the stock. Traders do that; should the stock move contrary to their expectations it is important that they get out quickly before they lose too much and then try something else. You can set a stop-loss at say 10% below your price, if that is where you plan to cut your losses.

Or, perhaps you really love this company. You did your fundamental analysis thoroughly, and you are convinced that this great organisation is trading at a ridiculous price way below fair value. In that case don't set a stop-loss. In fact you should consider buying more of the stock if it drops further to build up your holdings.

So basically, get rid quickly of the ventures that didn't work out and hold on to the good stuff. Sounds easy, right? Except that when it comes to economic decisions, you are often your own worst enemy.

There is a branch of economics, behavioural economics, that deals with human psychological and cognitive patterns, and examines how these traits influence people's economic choices and as such the larger forces of aggregate supply and demand in the economy. In finance, studies show time and again that people do exactly the opposite of what they should: They buy when the market is high, and they sell out when the market crashes. They sell their winning stocks as soon as they go up a bit, and hold on to their losers, hoping in vain they will turn around one day. If you can do the reverse, you are already one step ahead. If your dentist or the housewife next door starts telling you how much money they just made by buying gold, it's probably time to get out of that asset class.

Maybe now you can see a contradiction: On one hand, analysts advise you to ride the trend. In a bull market, hold on to the stocks and enjoy all the capital gains, even if they are just paper gains. But they also tell you not to follow the market herd mentality! What to do?

I find the advice from David Kuo of the Motley Fool quite sensible. In one of his presentations in Singapore, Dr Kuo compared a stock portfolio to a pyramid. You know, like the food pyramid we learned about in primary school, with plenty of rice, bread and healthy vegetables at the base, some meat in the middle, and a little bit of ice-cream at the top. Likewise you should have, Dr Kuo says, plenty of solid companies at the base – the value companies with their impressive fundamental ratios and dependable dividend policy. You hold on to these through thick and thin. In the middle, buy some newer companies – companies that are doing well but still early in the industry cycle and with growth potential. Review these once in a while; take out the laggards and research for new potential winners. At the top of the pyramid, by all means keep a few "fun" stocks and trade these more often. They could be new start-ups trading at a few pennies per share; they don't pay any dividend, they may even be running at a loss, but who knows, they may suddenly pop up in value due to a corporate take-over or a new patent paying off. Just make sure these risky stocks are less than 10% of your portfolio. Don't build your pyramid upside down.

## A bit about risk

One financial metric we didn't cover in the last chapter is *beta value* (represented in financial formulas by the Greek letter $\beta$). I find it useful when considering the composition of your portfolio and risk management. I didn't include it earlier because Yahoo Finance does not provide a beta for either Sembcorp Industries or Hyflux, but you can find it from other sources. The SGX calculates a beta for Sembcorp over five years of 1.28, while for Hyflux it is 0.74.

The beta indicates how much the stock price deviates over a period of time from the market as whole. A beta of 1 means that the share moves in exact tandem with the market. A beta of 1.2 means that it is 20% more volatile as compared to the market as a whole. If the market moves up 10 points, the stock will move up 12; if the market is down 10, the stock is down 12. A beta of 0.8 means that the stock moves less than the market, 8 versus 10 points up or down. A high beta stock ($\beta > 1$) is considered a risky stock; a low beta stock ($\beta < 1$) is less risky.

For a risky stock, you as an investor would require a higher rate of return to make it worth the risk of holding it; for a low beta stock, the required rate could be lower. The beta of a totally risk-free investment, such as cash in the bank supported by government deposit insurance, will have a beta of zero. Otherwise, beta will always be more than zero (although for inverse products such as inverse ETFs designed to short the market the beta will be negative, i.e. as the index moves up, the short product will move down).

Analysts use the beta value to plot a security market line graph, which is the expected return plotted against the beta. I will not go into it here, interesting as it might be for some. Visit Investopedia.com and key in "CAPM" (the capital asset pricing model) and you'll find a good explanation there.

Professional fund managers use these tools because they must. As mentioned before, they are expected to "beat the market", so they need a uniform quantifiable method to gauge if they do or if they don't. This is how they get promoted or fired and how their fund companies attract new customers or lose capital due to poor returns and withdrawals.

As a private investor, just managing your own savings, you might not have the time or the interest to get into this. But even then, you can fairly easily estimate the expected risk of your stock investment simply by studying how "your" company has fared compared to the index. Go back to your favourite service provider and plot the graph of the company five years back, then click in the relevant index. How do they correlate? If "your" company is all over the place compared to the index, the beta risk is higher. In that case you should only invest in it if you feel confident from other metrics that it will do better than the market as a whole in the future. If "your" stock gyrates up and down much less than the index graph, your risk premium (the extra risk you need on top of the bank deposit rate) can be smaller.

It is important to consider that investors face in general two types of risk.

**Systematic risk** is the market risk. It is caused by macro-economic conditions and events beyond your control, such as government fiscal (taxation) and monetary (interest rate) policies. Political, environmental and social events are systematic risks; when war breaks out the market might crash and there is little we can do about it. It won't really matter what kind of shares we own.

**Unsystematic risk** is associated with a particular industry or business. Microeconomic events can cause demand to shift, new technological innovations or management issues can cause returns to drop off. Because it is specific to a certain sector of the economy, unsystematic risk can be controlled and reduced through diversification. If you have just one stock in your portfolio, say an oil company, your unsystematic risk is high. What if oil goes out of fashion? However, should you have four stocks – an oil company, a windmill company, a solar panel company and a tidal wave energy company – you have reduced your unsystematic risk as the other energy companies are likely to grow should the demand for oil and your return from that company come down.

When you mix up your portfolio to reduce unsystematic risk, it is important to consider how the stocks you select are correlated. This can be expressed with a correlation coefficient, r. A coefficient of $r = 1$ means that there is perfect correlation, i.e. if stock A moves up one point, stock B will also move up one point. This might be a stock in an oil company and another in a natural gas company. But to reduce risk, you don't want that, you want stocks with correlation less that 1. For example, $r = 0.5$ means that when stock A moves up one point, stock B will move up less, just 0.5 points. When $r = 0$, it means there is no correlation; in the case of your oil stock, it could be a stock from a totally different industry, say child care. Finally, if A moves up and B then moves down, there is negative correlation, $r < 0$. The four stocks above – an oil company, a windmill company, a solar panel company and a tidal wave energy company – would be considered negatively correlated. So if you want to reduce unsystematic risk, look for uncorrelated investments.

As mentioned, systematic risk cannot really be avoided. However, there's a way to measure how risky your portfolio is – by using standard deviation (SD). Standard deviation, represented by the Greek letter sigma ($\sigma$), is a measure of how much the return of your investment fluctuates around the mean. A high $\sigma$ indicates a volatile stock, whereas a stable blue-chip stock will have a lower $\sigma$. In finance, SD is used to calculate the risk-adjusted return of your past investments as well as in the future expected rate of return of considered investments, where various scenarios and their probability of happening are incorporated. There is a good example of how this might work out for you in practice at Investinganswers.com.[2] The calculations are a bit cumbersome, but anyone with secondary school math skills can work it out.

It should suffice here to say that the risk of your well-diversified portfolio against systematic risk in the market as a whole can be calculated using the SD of your portfolio against the $\sigma$ of the market. In the Sharpe ratio, you divide your return by the standard deviation. A high standard deviation is bad, a low one is good. This means that for two portfolios with the same return, the one with the lower $\sigma$ will have a higher Sharpe measure, and it will be considered to have a better performance.

## Spread it ... your risk

Now you know a little bit about controlling your risk. That doesn't mean that you should always avoid risk altogether. It just means that you should be aware of it. Frank Scully said: "Why not go out on a limb? Isn't that where the fruit is?" In chapter 6 I touched on the issue that most investments carry risk, but hopefully it is different from the risk you take on when gambling. If you don't want any risk at all, you look at the ratios above and you make sure that your beta is always 1, your variance close to 0 and your correlation always perfectly negative ($-1$). Great, but then your return is always k, i.e. the risk-free rate of return you get in the bank!

If you want to do better than k, you need to go out on a limb – how far is up to you, and it will reflect your so-called risk appetite. You may load up on a bunch of oil stocks if you are a contrarian and you think fossil fuels will rebound as soon as inventories run low (which they obviously will one day). But then your correlation coefficient is in positive territory, your β is probably higher and your σ will most likely creep up. You could be rewarded, or you could be punished, for taking on this risk.

It might be a cliché, but I think most advisers would agree with me when I say that controlling your risk is a matter of adhering to the old saying that you don't put all your eggs in one basket. Even going from one stock to just two or three would help spread your risk significantly, especially if the companies are negatively correlated as we saw above.

Here is a story from the real life. When my kids were born, I opened a Danish children's savings account for each of them. I chose a small regional bank, Morsø Bank; they offered a slightly better savings rate than the bigger banks. That was in the beginning of the 1990s and the saving rate was 4–5% p.a. as far as I remember, but soon it dropped below that and I decided it was not good enough. I bought securities instead and to spread my risk I bought three products, with about a third of the capital in each: a high-yield bond fund, shares in the bank itself and shares in Novo Nordisk A/S. I considered the bank safe; it had rock-solid fundamentals and paid a good dividend. Novo Nordisk ... I considered that one somewhat speculative, they mainly treat diabetics and there is a lot of competition in the pharmaceutical industry, but they also paid a good dividend, and I figured that should they go bust the bank shares would make up for it. It was the bank that went bust! Novo Nordisk went up by 300%. I lost all the money invested in Morsø Bank in 2009 when it turned out that the little local bank's apparently nice balance sheet was loaded with toxic debt in worthless property developments in Spain and Ireland.

They got taken over by a bigger bank later, but all the equity was lost. The bond fund did OK. Over time my mother and I put DKK36,000 into each account, and my twin sons got DKK56,000 each at the age of 21 when the scheme expired – an annualised compounded return of about 3%. My younger son got a bit more (DKK109,000, or US$15,600, compounded return of about 7%) a few years later when he turned 21, all thanks to the power of one successful Danish company! I should add that one of the twins gave the money away to charity, so that he could pass a means test and qualify for welfare; the other twin used his sensibly as a downpayment on his own apartment. The younger one dropped out of college and squandered his money on drugs. So most of the money was wasted, but at least I feel I tried!?

## Going international

Diversification is the key to investing. You should diversify across asset classes and across companies. You should also consider diversifying across countries. These days it is easy to invest in another region or country; most trading platforms make this completely effortless. You can set up a separate account in SGD, USD, EUR, JPY or any other currency you like and trade that country. I didn't really cover currency trading before – like derivatives trading, currency and interest rate speculation is basically zero-sum and as such not really investing in my view. Capital allocation should be about making things grow, not about futile trading back and forth where nothing really is accomplished.

However, there might be a case for watching currency developments in the international economy. These variations are linked to fundamental economic and financial alterations among nations; they are interesting, relevant and could have significant influence on the outcome of your investments.

When I arrived in Singapore in 1980, the Malaysian currency and the Singapore dollar were virtually at par. You could use

Malaysian coins in shops in Singapore, until enough people realised that there was an arbitrage trade to be made, exploiting the
tiny difference in the currencies of a few cents. The rest is history,
as they say. Last time I checked, one Singapore dollar was worth
some 3.07 Malaysian ringgit. In spite of all its natural resources
like oil and gas and minerals and timber and fish, over time the
fundamentals didn't work in Malaysia's favour, and gradually it
showed up in the value of their money.

The moral is that currencies matter. They move slowly
most of the time but over the years the shift can have a significant effect on your returns. In the late 1980s I had friends who
travelled to Bali to open up Indonesian rupiah accounts with the
small money-changers scattered around Kuta Beach. The deposit
interest rate was staggering, some 15–16% p.a. When large institutional investors do this it is called the *carry trade*. You borrow
in one currency at low interest and deposit in another at higher
rates. The USD/IDR was stable at around 2,000 at the time, and
my friends probably did alright on this trade for a number of
years – in 1997 the USD to rupiah rate was still only around 2,400.
Then we all know what happened, the Asian Financial Crisis hit
later that year, the rupiah collapsed, the USD/IDR rate shot up to
12,000 within weeks. If you had US$100,000 in your account one
month you suddenly only had US$20,000 the next. Today the rate
is around 13,700.

The carry trade looks good on paper, but fundamentals have a
tendency of catching up eventually. The day-to-day currency fluctuations cannot be predicted with any degree of certainty in my
opinion, in spite of a whole industry out there trying to do exactly
that. As a long-term saver, look to invest in a country with solid
fundamentals such as a current account surplus (this generates
demand for the currency), plenty of foreign reserves to fight off
speculators, and price levels and inflation under control. Countries
like Singapore, Switzerland and Norway come to mind.

The US dollar is a special case because as the world's reserve currency it seems to be able to defy fundamentals. As the least dirty shirt in the currency laundry basket of dirty shirts (the other indebted major currencies being the EUR, GBP and JPY), it is still in demand during hard times, when capital flows into the US in spite of very poor returns, simply for the perceived safety of this militarily and culturally strong nation. In 2015 Russia had to suddenly raise its interest rates to 17% p.a. to stem capital flight; something like this is unlikely to happen to the US in the foreseeable future, although there is a small school of contrarians out there who argue that it might one day.

In general, be aware of high-interest-rate currencies. The interest rates are high for a reason, most likely because the country is short of capital. Either the country is facing bankruptcy or the interest rates will come down soon. Either way, the currency is likely to drop and that will eat up your profits on the carry trade.

These days, with internet trading and the amazing software available from financial service providers at fairly low cost, it is like a smorgasbord out there for investors. I should know, because I am of Scandinavian descent and have seen a real smorgasbord! Like Alan Jackson says in his famous country song, "It's five o'clock somewhere". There is always an asset out there that you can go long or short on if you feel it is under- or over-priced respectively. So you are sure the Russian stock market is oversold? Just buy a Micex ETF. If you feel it is overbought, buy an inverse one. Mark Spitz got into investing after his swimming career, and he compared capital flows with the ocean tides: When it is low tide somewhere, it is high tide somewhere else; but there is always this liquidity sloshing around looking for yield. The secret is to find out where it will move next.

## Prediction is difficult

There's the rub: Where will the capital move next? The exact source is disputed, but it was definitely some Dane who said: "Prediction is very difficult, especially about the future."[3]

I remember reading in December 2007 a survey of 36 American financial analysts on their outlook for 2008: 35 predicted slow growth; 1 predicted a recession. By that time, December 2007, a recession had already started, data showed much later. By September 2008, after the bankruptcy of Lehman Brothers, the US entered its worst financial crisis since 1929; 8 million people lost their jobs and the economy shrank by 0.3% in 2008 and by another 2.8% in 2009.[4] Only one guy out of 36 saw it coming!

All through 2013 and 2014 we were told how the Chinese currency was undervalued. And what happened in 2015, did it go up? No, other events took place, the Yuan was devalued, everyone was apparently taken by surprise; then suddenly all the news was about the crisis in China. Financial commentators are great at giving long speeches about what has happened and why, and then extrapolating this forward. In my experience they are just not very good at predicting, and especially not about the future.

In their book *Practical Speculation*, Victor Niederhoffer and Laurel Kenner take the financial industry to task by showing how one year a financial strategist might predict market developments spot on and everyone thinks he is a genius, when in fact market data is random over time. The next year that same expert might get it wrong, and no one will ever hear about it. With a bit of irony, Niederhoffer and Kenner show that the number of baseball home runs in a season has a strong inverse correlation with the Dow Jones Industrial Average index and is in fact a better leading indicator of stock price movements than company earnings!

In 2006 Peter Schiff correctly predicted the financial crisis. Some of the videos from those days are still available online, and today it is sobering to see how most other commentators not only disagreed with Schiff but openly laughed at him for daring to suggest that the US economy and the housing market would not grow forever. The events in 2008 proved Schiff right and he was 100% vindicated. The problem is that after that he hasn't really won one for a while. His predictions in later years of imminent US dollar collapse, hyperinflation, gold going to $6,000/oz, all never really panned out – not yet anyway.

So take all the noise on financial television and on internet chat rooms with a grain of salt. And always ask yourself: Is the commentator neutral, or is he just trying to talk up the bond fund he works for? My view is that fundamentals have a way of making their way through all the short-term chatter. Bubbles burst eventually. It could take a year or it could take two or three or four, but prices eventually revert back to the historic mean determined by the fundamentals, after all the fear or exuberance and all the temporary distortions wear off. And at the end of the day you are all alone, and you have to find your own place in the investment market.

# Mix It Up

*"Money is always eager and ready to work
for anyone who is ready to employ it."*
— IDOWU KOYENIKAN

### The right mix of assets

Among the financial experts out there, the talking suits, I like Marc Faber. He tells it as he sees it. Check out his videos online. During an appearance in Singapore on 15 August 2015 he said (quoted from my notes): "As an investor you should consider global events, try to identify sectors in demand. Buying on dips like the 1987 stock market crash sounds good. Yes, it was a buying opportunity, but lots of people had no money left! Pay attention to macroeconomic events, but also watch sentiment and technical indicators. Get out of the herd mentality; pay attention to what people are *not* watching. Everyone piles into gold when it is high! The bubble in asset prices now is much bigger than in 2007. Don't use leverage; then you can take a hit and still recover. The key is to be conservative. We don't know the future. Diversify into bonds, equities, gold, properties and cash."

This is sound advice. Regarding the stock market, if you don't have the stomach, the interest or the time on your hands for all the stock-picking techniques we looked at in the previous two chapters, take Warren Buffett's advice: Buy the index! But if you remember the "Don't do like I do" joke in chapter 4, Buffett in fact doesn't always do as he says. Referring to the fact that he started out as a newspaper delivery boy, in a 2013 interview Buffett said: "Save something every month and put it into a stock index fund. Don't save what is left after spending, spend what is left after saving." But grilled by the interviewer that maybe you cannot beat the market, Buffett added: "If I subscribed to that theory I would still be delivering papers."[1] In other words, go with the index fund – most people cannot beat the market – but a few can.

## ETFs (exchange traded funds)

In my view, the part-time investor should do a bit of both. When you start making some money, invest in a stock market index ETF. The technique called "dollar-cost averaging" works for many people. The idea is that you invest a fixed amount regularly into your favourite asset class, say $500 each month into a stock index fund. When the index is up you get fewer units, when the index is down you get more. Over time you build up your position at a reasonable average price.

One stock market ETF to seriously consider would be one that tracks the S&P 500. The S&P 500 index is often used as a benchmark, as it is linked to by far the largest economy in the world and denominated in US dollars, the world's reserve currency. However, if you live in Singapore, you may want to use an ETF that tracks the STI index. If you live somewhere else, your local index will be available as well. And if you really want to diversify, there is an ETF by iShares that tracks the MSCI All-Country World Index, which in turn tracks stock markets across 23 developed markets as well as 23 emerging ones. You cannot get much more diversified in the equities space than that.

Alternatively, diversify bit by bit into the regions you believe in. When you can, buy into a combination of regional ETFs, like a Europe stock ETF or a Pacific Rim, an emerging markets or a NYSE large-cap ETF. Yes, by all means try to do like Buffett does (not as he says) and pick stocks in companies that you like, but do this last, when you have the extra means and the interest and business experience to understand what is happening. Remember David Kuo's pyramid structure; get your foundation in order first to reduce your risk.

One quick word about ETFs vs mutual funds. Mutual funds are called actively managed funds; they have a management team of analysts and managers. With a fund like that you get instant diversification – because a stock fund will own many individual stocks, a bond fund many different bonds. The exact composition of the fund should be transparent from the prospectus. You are not protected from systematic risk, however, and a fixed income fund will drop in value should interest rates rise or capital flow out of your area. Mutual funds are usually sold through banks and financial advisers. However, because of the management involved, mutual funds are also more expensive, so check out the cost of each one carefully. The spread between bid and offer price could be substantial, maybe 3–4%, so this is lost automatically as soon as you sign on the dotted line. Then there might be an annual expense ratio of maybe 1.25–1.5%. Some years you might only make 3–4% return; then these expenses dig out a substantial chunk of your profits.

ETFs, as their name implies, are traded on an exchange. As such they are traded throughout the day, unlike mutual funds, which only have their NAV (net asset value) and unit price calculated once a day at the end of trading. An ETF is an investment vehicle that can invest in anything such as shares, bonds or a commodity. A stock index ETF simply tracks the index by replicating it; it will buy and hold the shares in the index in the right proportion; this requires less active management and decision-making, so ETFs are not only more liquid (trading throughout the day), they also have lower expense ratios and smaller spreads, i.e. they are cheaper to trade and to own. According to Goh Eng Yeow with the *Straits Times*: "Most ETFs charge a management fee of 0.25% to 0.3%, compared with the 1% to 2% levied by unit trusts."[2] ETFs have become increasingly popular with investors in recent years, and especially so with day traders and other active investors who trade on their own on online platforms.

The company managing the ETF doesn't actually own the assets under management. In a stock index fund, for instance, the shares will be held in trust by a trustee financial corporation, a different legal entity. The owner is you, the investor. Should the ETF provider go broke, you will still own the assets and get your money back when they are sold. However, since the shares are not registered in your name, you will not be invited for AGMs, etc, as mentioned before. But you will receive dividends. In a stock ETF, dividends are pooled and usually paid out in tranches to investors once or twice a year; a bond ETF will most likely pay dividends monthly or at least 10 times per year. This way you can calculate your yield and your annual rate of return like with any other investment.

All ETFs are created equal, but some are more equal than others, to paraphrase George Orwell. So do your homework before clicking on the "Buy" button. *Synthetic* ETFs make use of derivatives to duplicate the underlying; they can be geared 1, 2 or 3 times and have a time decay as well, a bit like futures do. In an attempt to beat the market, *smart beta* ETFs do not track the index 100%; after analysing each component stock for quality and growth prospects, they tweak the composition and weight of each company to improve results. So be aware of the risk and make sure you know what you are getting into with these different methodologies.

That is why in Singapore only accredited investors, and people with a financial background, are allowed to trade the full spectrum of ETFs available. Currently, out of 87 ETFs listed on the SGX, 19 are classified as EIPs (excluded investment products), open to all investors. Check on the MAS website to find the funds that anyone can buy and those that are allowed under the CPF Investment Scheme; they have been cleared by the regulators because they are less complex, well diversified, have lower expense ratios, and should in theory be less risky.

The Vanguard Group has many ETFs for sale at a low cost, and there are hundreds, probably thousands, of other products available out there. iShares by Blackrock Inc and SPDR (pronounced "spider") ETFs by State Street Global Advisors are the other two big groups that will do pretty much the same thing. Just search on Google or go to a financial site such as Bloomberg or Yahoo Finance. No, I am not paid by Vanguard Group, they are simply the largest provider in the world of mutual funds and the second largest of ETFs, and their expense ratios are among the lowest in the business. They make it up on the volume, I presume.

One problem with the Vanguard funds, and most of the others mentioned here, is that they are based in the US. So, when you buy into them you are exposed to currency risk by holding USD. There is also a US withholding tax of 30% on dividend payments that you cannot get away from if you trade through an online platform and the products are not listed in your name. I am not sure how every country works, but I know that in Norway overseas investors are taxed 15% on dividends; in Denmark the rate is 27% but can be reduced to 15% if the products are in your name and you apply for a refund.

That is one thing I like about Singapore: There is no tax on dividends or capital gains. The thinking here is that companies already pay tax on their earnings (17%), so any further tax on dividends would be double-taxation. In the US, the company first pays 26% tax on its income, and then the investor pays an extra 30% on the dividend. I don't really resent paying taxes; I do believe that there is a role for the state to play in protecting society and the environment, and we should all pay our fair share. But "fair" is the key word. In Singapore the rates are fair, and we are not forced to pay for wars, illegal immigration, farm subsidies and a bloated, multi-layered bureaucracy, all of which are detrimental to our welfare.

## Gone Fishin'

As you saw above, like most other financial advisers, Marc Faber suggests holding a mix of assets. How this mix should be constituted exactly is subject to endless discussions in the industry. The conclusion must be that there is no one size that fits all.

As we also saw earlier, the mix of assets will depend mainly on your age. Some say that if you subtract your age from 100, you get the percentage you should keep in equities; the rest should be kept in investment-grade bonds and bank deposits.

But then, not everyone has the same comfort regarding risk. Some are more risk-averse than others; those who enjoy walking a tightrope across the Grand Canyon maybe also enjoy owning some more risky asset classes, such as shares in start-up internet companies. For others, the most important thing is to sleep soundly at night; they should put most of their money into a mutual fund holding only BBB-or-above-rated government securities.

The closest thing I found to a one-size-fits-all investment strategy is the Gone Fishin' Portfolio concept, such as Alexander Green describes in his excellent book by that name. The subtitle is: "Get wise, get wealthy... and get on with your life."

The Gone Fishin' asset allocation model is wonderful in its simplicity: You put 70% of your capital in stocks and 30% in bonds. This is perhaps not so groundbreakingly original, but Green is more specific than that. He advises 10 different Vanguard funds, and the proportions in which to invest in each (see Fig. 14). You can find them all on the internet and check current prices, dividend yields, expense ratios and other terms. Green calls this the Holy Grail of investing: "Not because you'll generate eye-popping returns, although that may happen from time to time ... [but]

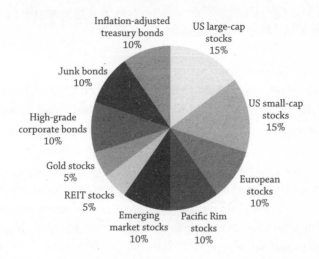

**Fig. 14: Gone Fishin' asset allocation**

because investing in this way should generate above-average returns with below-average volatility. And it will allow you to spend your time doing what you want."

You can check on this website if Green is still doing alright: Gonefishinportfolio.com. The last time I checked he was. He seems to be doing the near-impossible: beating the S&P 500! The beauty of this is that you can leave the set-up all alone. Green advises just to check once a year, and then tweak the allocation. Buy more of what came down over the year and sell out of what went up, until the new percentages match.

The beauty of it is that there is no emotion involved – it is pure math – because we know how emotions and irrational expectations often get in the way of sound judgement. There is no room for that here. After rebalancing, you just leave the portfolio be for another year. Total time spent on your investment management according to Green: 20 minutes per year! And then you go fishing for the rest of the time. Your financial adviser and all the people building online trading platforms might not like this kind of investing; they don't make much on fees. But hey, who are you trying to help, them or yourself?

## Not so sure about insurance

This is all I have to say about insurance: Don't do it! I touched on that briefly in chapter 2 and I haven't changed my mind. Well, if you feel you are in a high-risk category, perhaps you might bene-fit from insurance. Insurance is basically a gamble where you bet against yourself. If you are a reckless driver, your chance of getting a pay-back from insurance is higher than if you drive carefully. So high-risk drivers should get car insurance. Sickly people should get health insurance. People living in high-crime neighbourhoods should get theft insurance.

But like we saw in chapter 4, numbers don't lie. You have to respect them. If you consider yourself average (or above average), insurance will always be detrimental to your financial health over the long term. Yes, you might get into an accident tomorrow, but then you might live for another 40 years and never have one, you don't know that. That is why you should go with the numbers, not with your intuition. Your intuition is wrong; your fear is irrational and it will mislead you and cost you money.

Did you know that the government does not buy insurance? The government is self-insured. They have a bit of reserves, and when something goes wrong they just fix it out of their savings. It is a cheap and easy arrangement, and it saves the government a lot of money. Be like the government, be self-insured.

I know this is not for everyone. For most people, insurance is in some way part of their financial planning. I see that in all the industry chatter and all the interviews with professionals and customers that I read. I accept that. But that doesn't mean they are right. People don't always make the choices that are best for them.

What I do is I look up at the gigantic AIA building downtown and I ask: Where did all that money come from – the money to build the building and fill it with busy people? It comes from the clients, the prospects, the customers, from you. Prudential, Great Eastern, Aviva, dozen of others – they all have imposing head-quarters. I know what you will say: So do the banks! Correct, but the banks can actually make money grow, by funding real eco-nomic activity. And anyway, there is no getting around working with the banks; if you want to do business at all you need a bank account. But you don't need insurance, except if you own a car you might need a compulsory third-party insurance, or to qualify for a mortgage you might need home insurance. Apart from that, it is your own free choice whether you want to work with an insurance company. Be free; use that freedom to say no.

The reason for that is in the numbers. They are stacked against you. Insurance is zero-sum. Except it is not quite zero-sum: a cut goes to the company. Another cut goes to all the people who make bad life choices, not to mention those who outright cheat on their car accident and theft insurance. Who pays for this? The honest customers! The ones who take care of themselves, who never claim. When you buy insurance you are in effect gambling against yourself – why would you do that?

We have already established that if you keep gambling in a casino you will always lose all your money. Overall, insurance cus-tomers always lose; they donate money to the skyscraper-owners and their agents. The house – in this case the insurance company – always wins. Like casinos, insurers have mathematicians and statisticians employed to make sure that the odds are always in their favour.

But what if I get sick, you ask, don't I need health insurance? No, you don't. In Singapore, the government started providing general basic hospitalisation insurance for all residents starting November 2015 – the MediShield Life scheme. Only if you want to stay in a fancy suite in a private hospital would you top-up with a commercial insurance policy, but who needs that? You don't want to live in luxury when you are sick; you want to get it over with, get well and get out fast. In general, what you need to insure yourself is a bit of savings to see you through. Save the money you would otherwise pay the insurance agent, invest it in a low-cost Gone Fishin' portfolio and watch it grow. Yes, a bit of discipline is required, and to help you with that you can set up a monthly or yearly Giro payment or other automated debit agreement with your bank. This is just like what you do when paying insurance premiums – except you get to keep the money!

The same goes for life insurance. Don't bet against yourself. Be selfish; let your dependants take care of themselves if you die. If you really want to help them, make sure you have some savings stashed away, or a house or a gold coin collection they can inherit. You don't help them by feeding the insurance industry.

If you are tempted to buy a policy, look at it closely. The bonus investment returns they promise you – are they guaranteed? Most likely not, so forget about those. From anecdotal evidence it is unlikely that the company can beat the benchmark, especially considering the enormous overheads they carry. You are much better off leaving the money in your CPF account or buying dividend-paying index stocks. The world is full of smart insurance agents who sell complicated and expensive life insurance policies to people who don't need them, don't understand them and can't afford them.

Here is a story from the real world. Geoffrey Kung wrote this letter to the *Straits Times* in Singapore: "My 10-year endowment policy recently matured and the return received is lower than the total premium paid over the 10-year period. This is partly because there were charges for investment fund management and insurance mortality, as well as an administrative fee."[3] I rest my case.

I will mention one more aspect of insurance, and then I will leave the subject, because I know that most people will not take my advice anyway to cut it out, even though it is obviously in their best interests. I saw an interview on CNBC in 2009 while America was in a recession and millions lost their jobs. This newly unemployed man told the interviewer (quoted from memory): "Now that I don't have a job, I've also lost my comprehensive health insurance cover. So I started living more healthily. I've cut out smoking and I exercise more and eat less." The journalist thought that sounded quite reasonable, but I couldn't help thinking: Are these people even listening to themselves? What the guy is really saying is that before, while he had a health insurance, he lived like a pig. It didn't really matter if he got sick, because someone else would pay for his hospitalisation. The same goes for car insurance. It generates a strong financial incentive for you to smash into something. If you have home insurance, you only come out on top if you have plenty of burglaries, better still if your house burns down. If you have a life insurance, you only win if you die. Is that the kind of life you want, always betting against yourself?

## What should you expect in return?

So you have set up a portfolio and you expect to see it grow, to generate a return. Right, but by how much? Let us first of all establish what we mean by return. Yield, as we saw in chapter 6, is simply your numerical income divided by your investment:

$$\text{Yield} = \text{Income/purchase price}$$

To calculate return, you include your capital gain (or loss), like this:

$$\text{Return} = (\text{Income} + \text{capital gain})/\text{purchase price}$$

This is over an established period of time, of course, say one year. If you buy a stock 2nd January at \$8 and it pays a dividend of 50 cents over the year, your yield is **0.5/8 = 0.0625 = 6.25% p.a.**

If you sell the stock on 31st December at $9, your return for the first year is:

$$0.50 + (9 - 8)/8 = 1.5/8 = 0.1875 = 18.75\% \text{ p.a.}$$

What if you don't sell the stock? Your return would be the same, but in that case you would just be sitting on a paper gain; the stock might drop to $7 next year before you manage to sell it. Your actual income for that year was really only 50 cents.

Let's presume you buy more stock with your dividend payment, so that after one year, you now have a net worth of $9.50. If you can maintain 18.75% annual return on your investment, the second year you will have $9.50 times 1.1875, which is the same as $8 \times 1.1875 \times 1.1875$ or simply $8 \times 1.1875^2$. The third year, your capital will have grown to $8 \times 1.1875^3$, and so on:

Year 0: $8
Year 1: $8 \times 1.1875 = $9.5
Year 2: $9.5 \times 1.1875 = $8 \times 1.1875^2 = $11.28
Year 3: $11.28 \times 1.1875 = $8 \times 1.1875^3 = $13.40
...
Year 22: $295.39 \times 1.1875 = $8 \times 1.1875^{22} = $350.78

In general terms, your capital C after n years will be:

$$C(n) = C(0) \times (1 + R)^n$$

Where C(0) is the capital you start off with and R is your annual rate of return.

Recognise this formula? It's what we used in chapter 6 to calculate FV (future value) from PV (present value)! It is simply the classic formula for compound interest, and it is the greatest thing since sliced bread. Albert Einstein has been quoted as saying:

"Compound interest is the eighth wonder of the world. He who understands it, earns it … he who doesn't … pays it."[4] So make sure you understand it!

If you want to know how long it will take you to double your investment, there is the funny "rule of 72" in finance that says that $n \times r\% = 72$. In other words, $n = 72/r\%$. So if your return r is 18.75% p.a. it would take you about $72/18.75 \approx 4$ **years** to double your money. Alternatively you can take this cue from Frank Hubbard: "The safe way to double your money is to fold it once and put it in your pocket."

Another numerical issue you should be aware of is that with compound returns over a period, the arithmetic method doesn't work for calculating the average, the mean, return. If your portfolio is worth $1,000 year 0, $1,500 year 1 and $900 year 2, the arithmetic mean would be **(+50% − 40%)/2 = +5%**. But this is clearly not the case; the portfolio value didn't increase, it dropped! Using the geometric mean instead, the average portfolio return would be **$((1 + 0.50)(1 - 0.40))^n - 1$**, where n is the reciprocal value of number of years, here ½, so this would be −0.09 or −9%, which makes more sense.

What about those paper gains? On paper the value of your portfolio might shoot up in "good times" when asset bubbles inflate, and your returns look great. But this is not really income, unless you liquidate all your investments, which usually you wouldn't do. During other years, the value might drop a lot, when the economy goes through a recession or deflationary period, so you might have a negative return on your portfolio, even though the income stream was normal. How do you deal with that?

### Learning from the big boys

Why not look at what the big boys do? GIC is the Government of Singapore Investment Corporation Pte Ltd. Together with MAS they manage the Singapore government reserves such as budget surpluses and pension savings. By its investment policy, GIC is considered a sovereign wealth fund (SWF).

A national wealth fund (NWF), in contrast, is involved in active management of operational assets. The third public investment entity in Singapore is a NWF: Temasek Holdings. Temasek is wholly owned by the government but operates independently and invests in companies, mainly in Singapore and the rest of Asia; it does not manage pension funds and as such can take on much more risk. Unlike GIC, Temasek has a completely transparent investment policy; according to its website it owns a portfolio of S$266 billion (2015), and the annually compounded total shareholder return since inception in 1974 has been an impressive 16% p.a. Temasek invests 33% of funds in unlisted companies, 33% in large blocks (i.e. stake > 20%) of listed companies, and 34% in smaller blocks of listed companies and liquid assets.

But this is not really representative of what you might want to do as a private investor. Your approach should be more conservative, a bit like GIC's. GIC does not disclose its assets; as it works closely with the MAS, which manages the SGD exchange rate, it does not want to leave itself open to currency speculators. On the GIC website they just say that they manage well over US$100 billion, invested in 40 countries spanning six core asset classes.

One interesting detail to notice: While Temasek is heavily committed to the local Singapore economy and the near region, GIC only invests abroad. This policy has been debated in the public space, but so far GIC is sticking to its guns; it does not want to be seen propping up the local capital market; all the money is outside of Singapore in perceived safe havens in large mature economies.

According to the Sovereign Wealth Fund Institute, GIC is the world's eighth-biggest SWF, with US$344 billion of assets under management.[5] Its most important asset classes are nominal bonds and cash instruments (32%), developed market equities (29%), emerging market equities (18%), private equity (9%), real

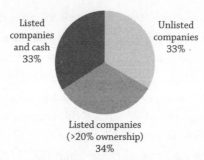

**Fig. 15: Temasek asset allocation (2015)**

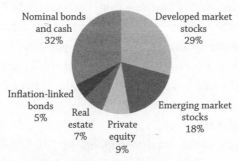

**Fig. 16: GIC asset allocation (2015)**

estate (7%) and inflation-linked bonds (5%). The return from GIC? It varies depending on which period you select, but according to their website, 20-year annualised real rate of return independent of currency was 4.9% for the financial year that ended in March 2015. This allows for inflation of 2–3% over the period. Nominal return in USD was 6.5% over five years, 6.3% over 10 years and 6.1% over 20 years.[6]

In my view, you could consider the GIC returns your benchmark. As a private investor, forget about Temasek Holdings. They are active investors owning and running both large corporations and smaller start-ups. GIC has the same conservative investment strategy that you should have: Don't lose the pension funds! GIC has the best investment managers and advisers money can buy; the Singapore Prime Minister is company chairman – it doesn't get more official than that. If you can get 6.5% annualised return on your portfolio, about 5% after inflation, you have done just fine. If you get more, you have beaten the big boys at their own game.

And what about the paper gains/losses? How do you deal with those? The Singapore government has a formula for that as well, the Net Investment Returns (NIR) framework. It allows the government to spend up to 50% of the expected total investment returns (income plus capital gains) from GIC, MAS and Temasek combined. The actual amount may vary according to circumstances, but usually NIR income contributes some S$7–8 billion to the government budget annually. The rest of the returns are reinvested to ensure sustainability. So there you have it, learn from the best: Every January you calculate your NIR for the previous year, reinvest half and spend the other half over the coming year.

## Reality kicks in

Let's consider what would have happened if GIC had simply taken Buffett's advice and bought the index. Remember, GIC's nominal return in USD over 5/10/20 years was 6.5%, 6.3% and 6.1%. The last 10 years, financial crisis and all, the S&P 500 index went up by a compounded rate of 4.8%; the average yield was 2.2% p.a. Total 10-year return in USD was 7.0% p.a. Five years compounded return with dividends reinvested was 14.0%. For 20 years (GIC's preferred period), it was 8.2%.[7] Considering that GIC has offices in 10 cities around the world and a staff of 1,200 analysts and strategists and managers and secretaries, most of them could have been let go, and a handful of accountants in the Singapore office just buying into the S&P 500 index would have yielded a significantly better result over any period you might consider!

Are other institutional investors doing much better? I doubt it. The *New York Times* wrote in 2015 that we have had "six consecutive years of underperforming by the hedge fund industry. The average hedge fund returned 3% last year." For that, investors have to pay typically 2% annual management fee and 20% of returns.[8] And here is another quote, from the *Straits Times*: "According to a recent study by research firm Dalbar, typical equity mutual fund returns over the last 20 years were about half (4.25%) of market gains (8.2%)."[9]

There is a lesson in this for the average investor. You can beat the big boys. But you must have the discipline and the patience not to get caught up in the daily financial chatter and trading and panic. Just set up a Gone Fishin' portfolio or buy an ETF tracking the stock market index and relax. You check and rebalance for an hour or two once a year. You cannot beat Temasek; but you can beat GIC and most hedge funds, insurance companies and other institutional investors that way.

Nassim Taleb is a mathematician and philosopher who has worked in finance and investing. He has come to the conclusion that financial markets and most other events in life are driven by a certain degree of randomness. In his most famous book, *Fooled by Randomness: The Hidden Role of Chance in Life and in the Markets*, one of the many interesting observations he makes is that investors in general get much more pain from experiencing a loss than they do pleasure from experiencing a gain, which is often just shrugged off without much enjoyment. Therefore, Taleb concludes, as the markets fluctuate up on down on a daily and weekly basis, you feel hurt and miserable if you check your investments too often, simply because the major feeling of anguish will overpower the feeling of happiness ... even if the markets end up over the year. Had you just checked once (at the end of the year), you would have felt only joy, and you would have avoided all the pain. So my advice is, check the value of your investments as infrequently as you can, preferably only once a year. Not every month and certainly not every day – it will just leave you feeling miserable.

But do we, the ordinary investors, really beat the big boys? We saw that all we have to do is buy and hold on to a stock index

– it doesn't really matter which one or when. Almost any index will automatically work, except one that is linked to the Japanese market, which has never fully recovered from the apocalyptic crash of 1990. Then we check once a year, and rebalance the portfolio a bit. That will leave us wealthy and content. Unfortunately, the short answer is no. In reality most people cannot do this.

I base this conclusion on analysis from the CPF Board, the Singapore pension scheme administrators. The CPFIS (CPF Investment Scheme) allows members (account holders) to invest their savings, subject to a number of conditions that I don't want to get into here (they are somewhat complex but easily available from the CPF website). The important matter here is that all products allowed, such as blue-chip stocks, low-risk mutual funds and some ETFs, have been approved by the CPF Board. This weeds out dubious products like loss-making penny stock companies, gold buy-back arrangements and that sort of thing. In spite of that, most CPF members investing their own money cannot beat the CPF Ordinary Account interest rate, currently 2.5% p.a. In 2014, 902,300 investors sold their CPFIS investments. Only 15% did better than 2.5% annual return; 45% made between 0 and 2.5%; 40% made a loss.[10] The survey did not go into how many of the 15% got more than 4% p.a. return, the interest rate you get if you transfer your CPF funds from the Ordinary into the Special Account – that would obviously be an even smaller percentage. But the conclusion in any case is that most ordinary investors are simply far better off not trying to invest themselves. Let GIC do it, at least they don't lose your money!

## What lies ahead

As Marc Faber says: We don't know the future. It's an obvious fact, but an important one to keep in mind. People who study time emphasise that there is no "now"; as soon as we reach the future it becomes the past. That is why I transferred cash funds into my wife's CPF Special Account to max it out. I hope I can do better than 4% p.a. with most of our capital. But in case I cannot, 4% compounded is not that bad; the money there is not going any-where, and at least my wife has the prospect of a decent govern-ment-administered annuity payment one day.

I have invested since 1971, and I have always read a daily newspaper from cover to back since way before then. I remember where I was the day I heard John F. Kennedy was shot. I never got ultra-rich; I think I stopped working a bit too early for that. But that was also never my intention. My intention was to be free – free to do what I want, free from financial worries, free from having to depend on government handouts – and that I am.

But today times look tough, possibly tougher than they have ever been in my lifetime. I keep looking at the numbers and they just don't add up. We are bombarded with statements by well-spo-ken men and smiling ladies in power suits; I advise you to take all the chatter with a grain of salt. However, in general, I agree with this assessment from Saxo Bank, as stated in their outlook for Q4 2015: "The expected mathematical return year-over-year for both equities and bonds remains close to or below zero for the next five years."

Why is this? I don't claim to know it all, and I don't have all the answers, but I do have some ideas why this might be the case. I will elaborate on that in the next chapter. It has to do with limits within our natural environment. It seems to me that we are finally running out of places to grow into and running out of cheap and easy-to-recover resources to use. This is a complex and highly contested subject that I cannot cover in full over a few pages. But there are experts out there who have been working on this all their lives, so I can point you to some sources where you can explore the details for yourself, if you are interested. And based on that, I can draw a few conclusions of my own; you can decide for yourself if you agree with me or not.

# It's a Finite World

*"Growth for the sake of growth
is the ideology of the cancer cell."*
— EDWARD ABBEY

**Are there limits to growth?**

When I was in my second (and last) year at university, this book came out: *The Limits to Growth*. It stirred up quite a lot of fuss. This was in 1972, and it was the first time that serious researchers questioned the Western growth model. The book examined the growth of five variables – population, industrial production, food, pollution and the depletion of finite resources – and projected them into the future. Using computer models that were just being developed at that time, the authors concluded that with "business as usual", economic growth would lead to overshoot and environmental collapse. The average quality of life would decline sometime during the 21st century. Only if immediate measures were taken to control population growth and consumption might a collapse be avoided and a sustainable world be possible.

The book ended up selling some 10 million copies. I heard about it and considered its message but didn't buy it. I was somewhat sceptical at the time of the capitalist market system, which I felt led to wasteful production, recurring economic crises, wars and unfair inequality. In spite of that, however, I didn't question the need for economic growth. Very few people did at the time

or do today for that matter. Once I left school and started working, even my scepticism regarding the market economy vanished.
Wasn't this the greatest system ever? Look at the prosperity we
had compared to the communist countries with their planned
economies. Look at the opportunities, the fast cars and computers and all the other stuff we could make. With some democratic
controls, surely the market economy could find a solution to small
issues like a few resources running a bit low.

The Limits to Growth was soon all but forgotten. The doomsday predictors were proven wrong time and time again. We always
found a way to keep growing. When I started working in the oil
business, we were told we only had oil left for the next 40 years.
Well, 40 years later we still only have oil left for the next 40
years. So what's the problem? you might ask.

In 1798, Thomas Malthus wrote his famous book, An Essay
on the Principle of Population, in which he predicted that uncontrolled population growth in Europe would outpace food production and lead to starvation, diseases, wars and eventually collapse
and population decline. That also never happened. The Industrial
Revolution, the miracle of petroleum, electricity and the seemingly
unlimited power and productivity all that gave mankind, took care
of things. When Europe ran out of resources at home, the various
countries just expanded into the colonies to get some more. As we
saw in chapter 3, neither Adam Smith before Malthus nor Marx or
Keynes after him considered the limits of our growth. The no-grow
camp has simply cried wolf so many times that we have learned
not to take them seriously. Isn't that so?

Today I am not so sure. In fact, a few years ago, I finally bought
The Limits to Growth: The 30-Year Update (2004). What a revelation. Everybody who is in business, politics or any other position
of influence should read this. It turns out that the authors never
foretold abrupt limits in their analysis from 1972, which was the
impression I had. They didn't say that one day we would wake up

and suddenly there would be no food and no oil left. The limits don't work like that. The authors Meadows, Randers and Meadows wrote instead: "The expansion of population and physical capital will gradually force humanity to divert more and more capital to cope with the problems arising from a combination of constrains." These constraints would include good land to grow food, fish in the ocean, easy-to-get-to mineral resources and what they call sinks, i.e. "the finite capacity of the Earth to absorb emissions from industry and agriculture".

The authors predicted with astonishing accuracy that with business as usual – and that is what business has pretty much been since 1972 – we would reach some 6 billion people on Earth by the turn of the millennium, and after that things would get gradually harder. "Even in the most pessimistic *Limits to Growth* scenario the material standard of living kept increasing all the way to 2015", the authors write in their update. In 1972 we had 40 years to prepare for a collapse, and we didn't do anything, or we did very little; now the collapse will be very difficult to avoid.

## Shrinking returns

The constraints on growth are starting to close in on us. Take energy, for example. Sure, there is still plenty of oil in the ground, but we are being forced to "gradually divert more and more capital" to get it out, as the authors put it. In the energy business there is a concept called EROI or EROEI – energy returned on energy invested. In the old days, drilling for shallow oil in West Texas and later in the sands of the Middle East, you could get 100 barrels of oil out by just using one barrel worth of energy. When I look at my photographs from the rigs in the North Sea in the 1970s, there was just one driller on the brake with a few analog gauges in front of him, and three roughnecks handling the drill pipe. The whole operation was simple and required little capital. The oil came gushing out on its own when you opened the valve. The

EROI at the time was about 30:1. When I look at pictures from offshore installations now, the transformation is astonishing. The complexity has increased immensely, and so has everything else that goes into the operation: the safety features, regulations, administration, technology. The only thing that hasn't increased is output per well – that variable is getting smaller.

In his book *The End of Growth*, Richard Heinberg shows that the EROI ratio for Saudi crude is still fairly good at 40:1 (cost: $20 per barrel). The global average for the petroleum industry is about 18:1 (cost: $40/bbl). As we move down the scale, these numbers become critical. For ultra-deep drilling, like in offshore Brazil and the northern Atlantic, you recover about 8 units of energy for each one invested (cost: $60+/bbl); for oil tar sands like the ones in Alberta, Canada, the EROI drops even further, to 3:1, and the cost increases to over $80/bbl. Evidence from the American hydraulic fracturing (fracking) industry applied to shale formations indicates that many projects are simply not economical. Chevron's CEO John Watson said to *Fortune* magazine: "The unique characteristic of shale is very rapid decline. You drill a well, and 12 months later that well will be producing 70% to 75% less. So you have to keep drilling."[1] In reality much of the energy industry is just running on the spot, producing very little real output.

Converting to biofuels was seen as the answer to all this a few decades back. If we grow plants and extract the ethanol (which is like the alcohol you find in a vodka bottle), our energy supply will be unlimited, right? Wrong, sorry, it just doesn't work. Don't take my word for it, here is what *National Geographic* magazine wrote a few years back: "Some studies of the energy balance of corn ethanol – the amount of fossil energy needed to make ethanol versus the energy it produces – suggest that ethanol is a loser's game, requiring more carbon-emitting fossil fuel than it displaces."[2] If you also take into consideration the climate change issue and the land clearance practised by biofuel producers, the picture is even grimmer. "Clearing land to grow biofuels emits more carbon than is cut by using the fuels" – concluded a study published in *Science* magazine in 2008.[3]

We are now in the weird situation where we actually have plenty of fossil energy resources left. Even though the days of cheap and easy-to-extract crude oil and gas are over, there is coal to last us hundreds of years. The problem is that we cannot take it out and burn it, because if we do the pollution will harm us. So going back to 1972, the main limiting factor to our growth is not only the lack of cheap resources, it is the limit of the "sink" – the capacity of the Earth to absorb our pollutants, in this case $CO_2$, $NO_x$, methane gas, particulate matter and what have you.

Other resources such as metals and other minerals are also becoming harder and harder to get to. In mining, as in oil exploration, the industry will always go for the low-hanging fruits first – the so-called "best-first" principle. Now, we are having to dig deeper and deeper for ore of lesser quality, spending more and more capital to achieve the same result.

There is a concept called "peak oil", i.e. the year after which we cannot grow global oil production anymore. In other words, even the very costly and low-EROI crude we are using now will start to run low, and after peak oil we will gradually enter a period of terminal decline. Heinberg, looking beyond oil at copper and iron as well as nickel, lead, zinc, rare earth elements, chromium, gold, indium, tin, uranium, phosphorus, etc, concludes: "Perhaps it is not too much of an exaggeration to say that humanity is in the process of achieving Peak Everything."

Yes, I know what you will say: But copper prices are down at the moment, there is plenty of it, in fact there is a lack of demand! Correct, but that is like saying that there is no global warming because we had a cold winter. That is confusing the weather with the climate, short-term market fluctuations with long-term social and economic trends.

We will get back to the current lack of demand in the economy later. It is sufficient here to conclude that our resources on the planet are finite. You cannot expand indefinitely in a finite space. So the short answer to the question earlier is: Yes, there are limits to how much we can grow. The problem is, what will these limits look like? And how do we deal with these limits, or at least adapt to them?

## The skeptics are growing in numbers

Let me first of all reiterate one important conclusion which forms the basis for the rest of this chapter: "Economic growth as we have known it is over and done with."

These are not my words; they are from Heinberg's *End of Growth*, but I have come to agree with them. The more I look at the data available to us, the more I concur. It is the only conclusion you can draw if you look objectively at the situation today and study it from all sides.

But people don't like it. And the people's elected public representatives don't like it; in fact they have to deny that it is so, because if they don't they won't stay elected for very much longer. Business people don't like it either; to stay in business or in employment by a business you have to project endless optimism. No one wants to do business with a sour-faced naysayer – that is the first thing they teach you in business school.

Luckily I don't work for anyone, and I am not running for public office, so I can call things out as I see them. And what I see is a planet that has reached its carrying capacity of people and man-made capital. And I am not alone in thinking so; many eminent academics and researchers have reached the same conclusion. The world is full. In fact, this was the expression that Herman Daly used for the title of his 2005 article in *Scientific American*, "Economics in a Full World".[4] Daly is a pioneer of the economics of sustainable development, the subject of an earlier book of his, *Beyond Growth*

(1996), in which he coined the phrase "uneconomic growth". In his paper about a full world, he went back to this idea: "Evidence suggests that the U.S. may already have entered the uneconomic growth phase." The disutility of growth now exceeds the utility.

In Daly's view, as growth progresses, the marginal utility of it becomes smaller while the marginal disutility grows. A poor person who makes 100 bucks is very happy; a millionaire does not get the same marginal benefit from an additional $100 income. So the marginal utility of growth is lower for a higher level of development. Meanwhile, the disutility gets bigger. If you take a tree and make it into a table, you convert natural capital into man-made capital, and that works out well if you really need a new table badly. But there is a disutility as well: not just the labour of the work involved, but also the loss of the ecological service of the tree in providing oxygen and shade, and its aesthetic value. As you work longer and longer hours to cut more and more trees to make them into more and more tables that pile up in a warehouse, this economic process becomes more and more futile and destructive. At some point, the disutility exceeds the utility – Daly concludes that the US is at that point.

If, on top of the disutility of resource depletion caused by industrial production, you add the pollution of the atmosphere, earth and waterways, this might be the case for most countries in the world.

## Who benefits?

It is conventional wisdom among mainstream economists that international trade is good. I will not go into the complex issues of this huge and multifaceted subject. It has been discussed since David Ricardo's time – he was the first to describe the miraculous effect of "comparative advantage", where international trade is said to benefit everybody, even the nations that cannot produce anything very efficiently.

Daly, however, doesn't buy that. He points out that the magic of comparative advantage only works in a world where capital stays within each trading nation, and we are long since past that point. In fact, Daly thinks that much of our trade today is counter-productive and bad for sustainable development because it rewards the trading partner with the lowest wages and the worst environmental record! Since wages are kept low, purchasing power will decline, resulting in insufficient demand. With more inequality and greater concentration of income, "more luxury goods will be produced and fewer basic-wage goods", Daly points out. "The further undercutting of local and national communities ... is a poor trade, even if we call it free trade."

Consider too the so-called "boomerang trade". As reported by the BBC website on 25 September 2009, and highlighted by the New Economics Foundation, the UK is said to import 22,000 tonnes of potatoes from Egypt *and* export 27,000 tonnes back the other way. While 5,000 tonnes of toilet paper heads to Germany from the UK, more than 4,000 tonnes is imported back. I don't have a quote for this, but I remember hearing that shrimp are caught in Scotland, then sent to Thailand to be peeled (due to the lower wages there presumably) and then returned to Scotland to be canned. How many more cases like that are out there in the world of free trade? It looks like uneconomic growth to me. Little is gained, while resources are wasted.

"'Free trade' is a euphemism", writes John Perkins, an economist who has worked as a consultant for the World Bank, the US Treasury Department as well as private corporations. "It prohibits others from enjoying the benefits offered to the multinationals." The North American Free Trade Agreement, for example, gave subsidised US corn-producers an unfair price advantage, putting Mexican corn farmers out of business, so that they turned to drug trafficking and other organised crime. In Somalia, the pirates operating out of the region used to be fishermen until their villages and likelihood were "devastated by illegal trawlers and waste dumping from industrialised nations". Perkins blames corporate greed, multinational companies protected by Western governments and what he calls "predatory capitalism" for the social and environmental mess we are in.

In a famous study by the World Wide Fund for Nature (WWF), the *Living Planet Report 2014*, the organisation concluded: "We need 1.5 Earths to meet the demands we currently make on nature. This means we are eating into our natural capital, making it more difficult to sustain the needs of future generations."[5] So it is not as if we don't know what is going on. There is abundant evidence out there to show exactly what is happening to our economy and our environment.

If all this information is too much for you, just consider one thing: The Americans are about 320 million people, give or take a few; this is somewhat less than 5% of the world's population. But with their lifestyle they use up some 25% of the Earth's resources. Everyone in the world wants to live like the Americans, but at the Americans' rate of consumption, at maximum the Earth can only support the US four times over – the equivalent of 20% of the world population. So what would the rest, the other 80% of people do? There would be nothing left for them? On top of that, you have to consider that not all Americans are doing so great. Conditions in large swathes of the country are not that much above Third World standards, and 46 million people are getting by on food stamps. The world economy is becoming a game of musical chairs. But there will not be chairs for everybody when the music stops.

There was a brief period in the 1950s and 1960s when we thought that one day we could all live in peace and prosperity on Earth. Today we know that is not mathematically possible. The human population has doubled since then, and the resource base is near collapse. Since I was born, some 90% of the large fish have been taken out of the oceans.[6] We have more man-made capital than ever, the fishing fleet is four times the size it needs to be, but there is not much left for all the trawlers to catch. Just building more fishing vessels is not going to help us.

## Lingering reluctance

All this is a bit depressing to deal with. You get tired of listening to all the doomsday reports of rainforests burning and animals going extinct. Most people deal with this by simply ignoring the data. Like the passengers on the Titanic, it is tempting to just enjoy the music and dance on, while the main hull below is slowly taking in water. When one passenger confronts the ship's chief engineer in the 1997 movie and says that surely this huge beautiful ship cannot possibly sink, he replies: "The ship is made out of iron, sir. I assure you that it can sink. And it will!" And as we know, the ship did not have enough lifeboats for all the passengers.

I don't believe we should ignore the facts and just dance on and consume and gobble up the Earth. But I also don't think we should panic. We should try to understand what is going on and accept the facts. Then we should adjust and position ourselves for the future, staying nimble and flexible. Because, like Marc Faber said, we don't know exactly what the future will look like, so we need to fine-tune our course as conditions change, as we learn more and as we mature.

Yet, no world leader I know of is planning or reforming our society to prepare for a shrinking economy! This despite the obvious signs that "one way or the other – whether through planning and methodical reform, or through collapse and failure – our economy is destined to shrink, not grow" (Heinberg). Instead, every single day I hear this message from leaders: We need to restore growth. That is not entirely the leaders' fault, either; that is just what everyone wants to hear them say.

Usually this is done by expanding credit. We lower interest rates, which are now below 0.5% in most developed countries or even negative. We borrow more; central banks buy up more bonds and issue more credit. But this is just a giant Ponzi scheme. It feeds on itself. Dividends are paid out from new capital expansion, not from real earnings, and the scheme will collapse if you ever stop issuing more debt. However, it does enable us to consume beyond our means for a while. So the effect is that together we are destroying the planet on credit.

Incredibly, there are irresponsible economists urging us on. Dr Keyu Jin is a professor of economics at the London School of Economics and she writes for the Project Syndicate: "In recent years, Chinese household debt amounted to about 12 percent of GDP, compared to a massive 95 percent in the US." This should be good, right? No, not according to this "expert". She continues: "China's government should pursue ... consumption-boosting policies, beginning with an easing of household borrowing constraints. Clearly, Chinese households have plenty of room for more borrowing ... the current generation is simply too fixated on saving to provide the kind of surge in consumption that is needed."[7] Needed for what? you might ask. For more destruction?

When mainstream economists and politicians talk about getting back to economic growth, there is this elephant in the room that no one seems to notice: Economic growth forever is not possible. But that doesn't mean that we cannot develop. Daly puts it this way: "We must distinguish *growth* (quantitative increase by assimilation or accretion of materials) from *development* (qualitative improvement, realisation of potential). Sustainable development is development without growth." And in the words of Heinberg: "The end of economic growth does not necessarily mean we've reached the end of qualitative improvements in human life. We can survive the end of growth, and perhaps thrive beyond it, but only if we recognise it for what it is and act accordingly."

## Not all growth is good

Were you told in school, as I constantly was, that the US came out of the economic depression in the 1930s only during the Second World War, because the war was somehow good for growth? That is simply not the case. It is a "broken window fallacy" that leads to that misunderstanding.[8]

The fallacy goes like this: A boy breaks a window. Then that provides work for the glazer who needs to repair it. The boy's father pays the glazer, who spends that money somewhere else, and the whole process jump-starts the economy, right? Wrong, the new window is a replacement cost that is wrongfully added to the GDP, when in fact society is not better off. The glazer might be, but money is diverted away from other sections of the economy, like the shoemaker who missed a sale or the tutor who should have taught the boy new useful skills. They don't get paid, because the boy's father has to spend his money on repair jobs.

Likewise, during wars productive capacity is channelled into destruction and reconstruction which uses up valuable resources. After all the devastation and rebuilding, the place is no better off than before; those resources could have been better allocated to begin with.

The US emerged stronger from the war in the 1940s exactly because they were not destroyed; their impressive factories and wealthy domestic consumers generated a unique economic boom for some three decades after that. Those of us who grew up during that period thought that was how the world would always be, but it didn't last. When the oil crisis in 1973–74 started shifting funds from the US into the oil-producing countries in the Middle East on a massive scale, rather than accept a decline in purchasing power, the Americans stuck to their lifestyle and started borrowing to finance it. In 1979 the oil price took another hike up (tripling again as we saw in chapter 5). In the second quarter of 1980, when the US economy shrank at an annual rate of 7.8%, President Jimmy

Carter encouraged Americans to live within their means. He instituted credit controls and urged people to cut their credit cards in half.[9] Of course that didn't go down well with voters, and Carter quickly became a one-term-only president. After Ronald Reagan got elected at the end of 1980, the debt culture became institutionalised, as did financial deregulation, while the real economy, the manufacturing base, started to shift across to Japan and later to China. Real wages in the US haven't really increased since then, but asset prices sure have.

So with the benefit of what we learned from the broken window fallacy, we need to reconsider how we measure and value economic growth. Many economists have worked on this. To go back to Daly, he says: "Depletion of fossil fuels, minerals, forests, and soils is capital consumption, yet such unsustainable consumption is treated no different from sustainable yield production (true income) in GNP." And: "We are building up negative capital (illth, rather than wealth). To speak so insouciantly of 'economic growth' whenever produced goods accumulate, when at the same time natural wealth is being diminished and man-made illth is increasing represents an enormous prejudgment ... that sinks are infinite." Daly recognises the sinks are finite; we cannot convert natural capital into garbage forever and still be wealthy.

To get a more appropriate measure of economic development, Daly suggests that we should subtract from the GDP all "expenditures that do not reflect any increase in the net product available for consumption without eventual impoverishment". He lists a range of what he calls "defensive expenditures": costs of environmental protection activities and damage compensation, as well as increased spatial concentration for the urban population; increased expenditures for protection against crime, accidents, sabotage; costs from traffic accidents with associated repair and medical expenses; and costs generated by drug addiction, smoking and alcohol.

Daly stresses that this list is somewhat arbitrary and by no means exhaustive. But the principle is clear: We should stop counting all growth as good. Next time you see a country triumphantly proclaim that it grew 5% last year, stop and ask: How many trees did it cut to make this number? How much of this was actually broken windows, traffic accidents, fires, gambling and crime? Where did all the garbage go? How much of the growth was uneconomic?

## Too much of a good thing

Cheap credit issued by central banks, instead of real capital consisting of deferred savings, has brought about our current situation, an abundance of supply (and a lack of demand) in the economy. We are producing like crazy and gobbling up resources to make things that we already have plenty of. Have you been in a department store lately? Each one is packed with smart TVs and smartphones and tons of other gadgets that no one buys. Next month and next year new models come out, and the old ones end up in a swamp somewhere in Africa where poor people try to make a few dollars by salvaging spare parts.

Similarly, about a third of our food is simply wasted. Two billion tonnes of food, worth $750 billion, is thrown out each year.[10] And much of what is eaten is in reality wasted too: 2.1 billion people in the world are overweight or obese, up from 857 million in 1980. We need a drop in food consumption, says Dr Klim McPherson from Oxford University, but he wonders: "Where is the international will to act decisively in the way that might restrict economic growth in a competitive world, for the public's health? ... Nowhere yet."[11] This in spite of other surveys that have found that eating less is good for fighting climate change. "When it comes to food consumption, moving about in a heavy body is like driving around in a gas guzzler", said a study from the London School of Hygiene and Tropical Medicine in 2009. That is because food production is a major source of greenhouse gases. "We need to be doing a lot more to reverse the global trend towards fatness, and recognise it as a factor in the battle to reduce (carbon) emissions and slow climate change. Staying slim is good for health and for the environment," the report concluded. But it wouldn't be good for growth, so most governments would probably prefer that the obese people keep eating more and then have expensive liposuction operations to remove excess fat once in a while; it looks better on the GDP. Treatment for obesity costs Britain's state-run health service £5.1 billion ($7.7 billion) every year[12] – but it sure keeps a lot of people busy.

Diane Coyle deals with some of these issues in her book, *The Economics of Enough* (2011). Unlike Heinberg, Coyle believes that we should grow. She writes: "Rich countries need economic growth because otherwise it won't be possible to avoid the debt trap." Doyle wants the Ponzi scheme to roll on; if we stop now, the debt is too large. She also quotes surveys to establish that even rich people gain benefit from further wealth: "There is good evidence that growth and happiness *are* linked."

This should debunk the assumption that somehow there is a saturation point for prosperity. Many countries have experimented with various measurements to show that economic growth is not the only factor generating happiness and welfare. The small Himalayan country of Bhutan became famous back in 1972 when they introduced the Gross National Happiness concept to show that well-being depended on other issues such as cultural values, environmental conservation, good governance and sustainable development, not just GDP numbers. In 1989 Daly and his associate John Cobb designed the Index of Sustainable Economic Welfare as an alternative measure to the GDP. More recently, the Happy Planet Index tried to do something similar; the Human Development Index is much used by development economists; while the Genuine Progress Indicator (GPI) seeks to provide a more comprehensive measure of development by including social conditions and environmental costs.

However, it seems to me that these alternative measurements, although somewhat interesting to the public and the media, never make it to the front page of the newspapers, where the headlines are still based on the cold, hard GDP numbers. Did we grow or did we shrink last quarter? That is what people want to know. The nature or the quality of the growth doesn't seem to matter.

Singapore Prime Minister Lee Hsien Loong, like all politicians I know of, is pro-growth in the conventional sense. He has said, as reported by the *Straits Times* 4 October 2014: "We need growth and prosperity in order to be good-hearted." Meaning, in order to help the less fortunate in society. "We most not go pell-mell for growth regardless of social, human and environmental costs, nor are we doing so. But I do worry when people say we should take it easy on growth because we are okay, and they talk airily about the more important things in life. They do not understand what our well-being depends on and I think there is a strong element of condescension and complacency in that view because essentially they are telling others: 'Well I am well-off enough, you should be satisfied with whatever you have even if you are poor'. That is not the way forward."

There is a point in that. The reality is that everyone wants growth. The poor to get out of poverty, and the rich... what about the rich? We have established before that the marginal utility of wealth drops with higher values, but does the benefit ever stop completely? Not according to Coyle; she believes that you can never be too rich. Although she advocates more comprehensive wealth measures, "in order to demonstrate the almost-certainly shocking erosion of natural capital and absence of human and social capital in very poor countries", she still believes that "growth *does* make us happier". She adds: "I argue that economic growth ... contributes to other important aspects of welfare, especially freedom."

That might be so. I am not going to dispute Dr Coyle who is so much better educated and connected than me. For me there is only one problem: She just doesn't put forward a convincing case for how this future growth will take place.

## What will the limits look like?

It seems to me that we are past the point of no return. Economic growth as we know it (meaning growth that improves our welfare) will come to a grinding halt no matter what we think about it or what we do. It probably already has. I agree with Heinberg when he says: "If the world had listened (in 1972), today we would all have much less to worry about." But we didn't listen. I certainly didn't, and no one in authority did either. In fact, during the following years the 1972 study was ridiculed for being all wrong. On the 10th-year anniversary of the book, President Ronald Reagan publicly denounced it. Another ten years later, President George H.W. Bush used the 20th-anniversary occasion to launch a scathing attack on the work of the authors. Even today, most analysts still insist that we just need to get back to growth, and everything will be fine again. Which reminds me of a famous Mahatma Gandhi quote: "First they ignore you, then they laugh at you, then they fight you, then you win." I think Dennis Meadows and Jørgen Randers (the two surviving authors from the 1972 team) can recognise that sequence, as can many early climate change activists like Al Gore today.

So if we again look at Meadows, Randers & Meadows (2004), they operate with 10 different future scenarios in their computer models. Nine of them presume that we take some sort of preventive action to avoid collapse. I think we can disregard all of those – this seems unlikely to happen. That leaves us with scenario 1, where "the world society proceeds in a traditional manner without any major deviation from the policies pursued during the twentieth century". Then this is what will happen: "Population and production increase until growth is halted by increasingly inaccessible non-renewable resources. Ever more investment is required to maintain resource flows. Finally, lack of investment funds in the other sectors of the economy leads to declining output of both industrial goods and services. As they fall, food and health services are reduced, decreasing life expectancy and raising average death rates." That is the recipe for collapse, but that is what the limits to growth will look like.

So how long have we got, according to the authors? With business as usual (as per 2002), industrial output, food production and the human welfare index will start to drop off around 2020; world population will start a forced decline around the middle of the century. Under various scenarios of more accessible non-renewable resources, pollution control technology, land yield enhancement and resource efficiency technology, the drop-off in industrial production can be postponed to around 2040–50, and the forced decline in population and human welfare can then be deferred to around 2070–80. Either way, a decline in overall living standards is inevitable.

Like I said, it seems to me that this collapse has already started to happen. But just like with the recession that began in December 2007, we might not realise the downturn until much later.

This economic decline will also not be universal. Some parts of the world will be doing fine for a long time to come, thank you very much; it is just the overall planet as an ecosystem and as a global community that has started to crack up. As in a game of musical chairs, there will be chairs for some of us, but not for all. The Global Environmental Outlook Report by Earthscan from 2002 used a phrase that might prove prophetic when it described our future as one in which there will be "islands of prosperity in an ocean of poverty and despair".[13]

So in selected parts of the world the collapse will be sudden and catastrophic. The Arab Spring started in Tunisia in December

2010 because of environmental decay and overpopulation, which manifested in high food prices that were intolerable to the poor. According to Thomas Friedman, the war in Syria started as an environmental crisis, when prolonged drought forced rural populations into the already overcrowded cities and fermented social unrest.[14] This view is confirmed by a Pentagon report that concluded that climate change has to be considered a security threat. "Droughts and crop failures can leave millions of people without any lifeline, and trigger waves of mass migration", then US Defence Secretary Chuck Hagel said at the launch of the report, somewhat prophetically as it turned out. The rise of extremist groups like the Islamic State in Iraq and Syria (ISIS) has also been attributed to environmental factors. "Climate change and water shortages may have triggered the drought that caused farmers to relocate to Syrian cities and triggered situations where youth was more susceptible to joining extremist groups," said Dr Marcus King with George Washington University in the same report.[15] The bottom line is that there are just too many people, not enough resources for them, and nothing for them to do.

When 2.3 million people in India apply for 368 low-level government jobs, as reported by the BBC in September 2015, or when millions of people from Africa, the Middle East and as far away as Pakistan and Bangladesh walk or sail illegally into Europe to escape overcrowding, poverty and associated social unrest, you don't really need a PhD in sociology to see that something is way out of balance.

Saskia Sassen has one of those – a PhD in sociology – as well as a few other degrees in economics and philosophy. In her book *Expulsions* (2014), she deals with the uneven effects of our shrinking economies. She refers to the GPI (Genuine Progress Indicator) that I mentioned earlier and observes that this measure of our development peaked in 1978 and "has been declining slowly but steadily ever since (Fig. 17). In contrast, GDP per capita has been

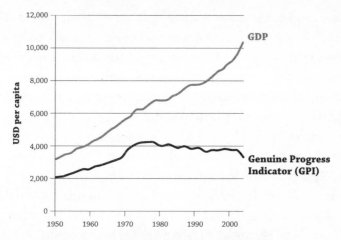

**Fig. 17: Genuine Progress Indicator (GPI) and GDP**
GPI measures economic activity, but takes into account some 20 economic and social aspects that GDP ignores. Like GDP, GPI is expressed in monetary terms, so the two are easy to compare. However, unlike GDP, GPI adds household work and volunteer work as a positive but deducts depletion of natural capital as well as elements of uneconomic growth such as crime, accidents, drug addiction and pollution control. The graph above aggregates data from 17 countries where GPI has been calculated and shows the general global trend.

rising steadily since 1978 … this signals that social and environmental negatives have outpaced the growth of monetary wealth." No wonder some people feel we were better off in the old days!

One of the negative consequences of growth that Sassen documents is the expulsion of large sections of our populations from our economic sphere. In resource-rich countries, they are expelled from their land by mining, logging and agricultural corporations; they drift into the cities, where they are also not needed. In richer countries, the expelled are those who are poorly educated, with no family wealth; they end up unemployed and under water with their mortgages; they are just not required any more, not even as consumers.

In the same way, Sassen also looks at the parts of the Earth that we have "expelled" – parts that are no longer fit to live in, rivers and other water sources that are no longer fit to drink. Chernobyl in Ukraine, the scene of a nuclear power plant melt-down in 1986, is one obvious example, but there are hundreds of other smaller "Chernobyls" around the world that don't make the news: contaminated mining areas, military test ranges, abandoned industrial sites, infertile farmlands.

In the Pacific Ocean, the Pacific trash vortex already covers an area somewhere between the size of Texas and maybe twice that of the continental United States. It is a concentration of plastic debris and chemical sludge that is continuously being accumulated. Today as much as 88% of the open ocean's surface contains plastic debris.[16] "We are being overwhelmed by our waste", Professor Jenna Jambeck, who studies this very subject for the University of Georgia, said to Bloomberg.[17] Much of it is ground into tiny pieces (microplastic) and gets absorbed into marine life forms, even the tiny stomachs of corals, which then die of starvation. How do we imagine we can fix these problems by "getting back to growth", by producing more plastic and chemicals and dumping them into our waters? Shouldn't we really be making less plastic?

While absolute poverty in the world has declined, more people are living at subsistence level and barely getting by. It is often repeated that some 500 million have been lifted out of poverty in China since market reforms and international trade were intro-duced into the economy in the 1980s. This is great, of course. But half of the people there still live on under $4 per day; in India that percentage is 91%, and it is even higher for many African countries.[18]

More growth doesn't always fix that. In Southeast Asia the Philippines has been growing well, but poverty has not come down. On paper, Bangladesh is growing 6% per year, but this is what Ziauddin Choudhury writes: "In Bangladesh, we live in a par-adoxical society. We have impressive statistics that show a grow-ing national income, steadily rising exports, and an impressive flow of foreign earnings. What these statistics do not show are the pathetic state of our rural economy, the rising unemployment of rural youth, and the growing disparity of rural and urban income."[19]

And the 500 million that have been lifted out of poverty in China? Some ended up working for Foxconn making electronic gadgets for the Western market, with some 300,000 people working in one factory alone, complete with netting installed below the windows to prevent the workers from jumping out and killing themselves in sheer despair. They work 11–13 hours per day in a polluted environment, their daily wage is about $5, and after work they sleep 24 to a room.[20]

In Singapore, working conditions are generally better of course. But I suspect many of the foreign workers in the construction industry can recognise the conditions described above. A Gallup survey found that just 9% of workers here were passionate about their firm and committed to work. "Close to two million people (in Singapore) are just showing up at work every day, doing what they need to do, but not feeling emotionally invested in their companies", the Gallup manager said.[21] All over the world, people are clamouring for jobs. But maybe working life is not everything it is cracked up to be.

## The more the merrier?

For some reason, we are being told that if we just get more people, things will be better. In Singapore, like in most countries, having children is encouraged and financially subsidised. That might make some sense if you look at a small country with virtually no unemployment in isolation. But if you look at the world as a whole, as an ecosystem, it doesn't add up. I cannot go into this complex issue in much detail here, but let me mention that like other development economists, in *Development Economics* Debraj Ray deals extensively with this issue. He says that "individuals who lack insurance and old-age security choose to invest in the future in the form of children." But he also later determines that for the society as a whole, "fertility-related externalities are typically *negative*" (his emphasis). So he concludes: "Population growth has implications for the rate of economic development. In large parts, this relationship is thought to be negative." And finally: "This summarises the consensus argument that population growth is unambiguously bad for economic development." That might be why China has done better than India lately – their one-child policy, often portrayed as terribly inhumane in the Western media, could actually have paid off.

Indonesia is one of the most beautiful countries on Earth. It is packed with stunning rainforests, high volcanic mountains, coral reefs and abundant biodiversity, and it has more endemic bird species than any other nation in the world. It could be paradise on Earth, and pockets of the country do indeed look like paradise might. But these pockets are shrinking fast; they are now islands in an ocean of destruction, mainly caused by uncontrolled population growth. And with two million people joining the workforce every year while companies are shedding jobs, social unrest is a growing threat. "If this condition is allowed to continue, what we would get is not a demographic bonus, but a demographic disaster. There could be social turmoil and higher crime rates." So says the chairman of the Indonesian employers' association to Reuters.[22]

So why are we always being told that we should have more people? Well, you have heard it a million times: We have too many old people, so we need more babies to take care of them. Next time you hear that, object! It is simply not true. If we have more babies, they in turn will need even more babies themselves for when they get old. Where does this stop? Just feeding the demographic pyramid from the bottom in an ever-expanding fashion is not just bad for development, as we have seen, it is especially bad for the planet. I say, let us old people take care of ourselves. With an active and healthy lifestyle we can stay vigorous, most of us, and keep working till we are 60, 70, 80, maybe 90 – at least part-time. You don't require much money when you are old; you already bought most of what you needed and desired; your kids have left home; the house is paid off. Let us live off our savings and die off quickly in peace as soon as we get sick. The younger generations will thank us for that. They need the space and the resources.

The Japanese do it that way, so do the Russians, and I think more and more observers are coming round to their way of handling the aging issue. Daniel Alpert is an investment banker who wrote *The Age of Oversupply* (2014). He is concerned about the debt burden and how to clear it. One solution he considers is immigration, but ultimately he rejects it. Looking at the case of Japan from a population perspective, he writes: "Curiously, though, while Japan's situation is not at all rosy from a nominal-growth perspective, it does have options that appear to be quite different from those of other countries in the advanced world. The third-largest economy in the world can slowly dissave and shrink itself into continuing affluence (from a standard of living perspective) for those who remain."

I strongly believe that we should work towards a gradually declining human population on Earth. And I am not alone in this view. David Attenborough (of BBC Natural History Unit fame) has two kids of his own, but he is also a passionate campaigner for a shrinking population. Speaking at the Royal Geographical Society in 2013, he said: "I have little doubt that if we have the capacity to limit our birth rate, then we should consider doing that. We have a finite environment – the planet. Anyone who thinks that you can have infinite growth in a finite environment is either a madman or an economist."[23] In an interview with Radio Times the same year, he put it even more starkly: "We are a plague on the Earth. It's coming home to roost over the next 50 years or so. It's not just climate change; it's sheer space, places to grow food for this enormous horde. Either we limit our population growth or the natural world will do it for us, and the natural world is doing it for us right now." Well said, Sir David!

## Meanwhile, on the islands of prosperity

For those of us on the "islands of prosperity", we are OK, but we are sensing some slowdown. This is what the limits look like for us: stagnation and deflation. There is no demand in the economy, because we have "enough", as Diane Coyle says in the title of her book. Due to inequality, those that do not have enough have no money to spend, and the society regards them as superfluous – "expelled", as Sassen puts it. Resource prices and wages are stagnating; only selected asset prices are inflated by an expanding money supply with nowhere else to go. And all that is here to stay. As Joseph Stiglitz puts it most bluntly: "The likelihood that loose monetary policies will restore global prosperity is nil."[24] This has direct implications on your ability to be free – financially and otherwise – and remain free in the future to come.

In *The Age of Oversupply*, Alpert writes that "the central challenge facing the global economy is an oversupply of labour, productive capacity, and capital relative to the demand for all three." The end of the Cold War and the subsequent globalisation increased the supply of cheap labour from the former communist bloc in Europe, the Soviet Union and China; together with general population growth, this helped keep the cost of labour and wages everywhere low. More recently, monetary expansion by central banks has made capital virtually worthless. Just making more of everything is not going to help. "More supply is not the solution when the problem is oversupply," as Alpert puts it.

Thomas Piketty became famous with his analysis in his best-selling book, *Capital in the Twenty-First Century* (2014). Like many economists, he did not only observe that the pie was not growing much, he was also concerned about how it was shared out, about economic inequality between nations and within each country. He advocated higher taxes on the financial industry and better distribution of wealth. But it is this simple formula of his that stuck in my mind: $r > g$. By that, Piketty means that the return on capital has been greater than our general economic growth rate.

This is confirmed by many sources. As our production processes have become more automated, more complex and more capital-intensive in recent decades, the return on capital has improved, but salaries for labour often have not. Blasi, Freeman and Kruse put it this way regarding the US in the *New York Times*: "The stagnation of earnings for most Americans despite rising productivity, and the shrinkage of the middle class because of soaring inequality are without precedent in US economic history. Capital's share of national income has risen, while labour's share has fallen. Sadly, since the 1970s, wages have stagnated, and the idea of profit-sharing has been largely forgotten in public debates."[25]

Lawrence Mishel writes something similar: "Between 1979 and 2014 while the GDP grew 150 percent and productivity grew 75 percent, the inflation-adjusted hourly wage of the median worker rose just 5.6 percent – less than 0.2 percent per year."[26] Presumably the rest of the productivity improvement went to pay capital. "Until the 1980s, about 70 percent of income went to labour income and 30 percent to capital", writes Dalia Marin, looking at the GDP from the income angle. "But, since then, the share of income going to labour has declined in all rich countries. It is now about 58%."[27]

So what happened to the wealth? It must have been scooped up by the capitalists – a presumption supported by Alpert, who writes: "The incomes of the top 1 percent would grow by 275 percent between 1979 and 2007."

So it is all about $r > g$. That is why I say, even if your employer "has forgotten the idea of profit-sharing" as mentioned above, be sure to get some capital of your own and enjoy the higher "r";

don't rely on a shrinking "g" and your moribund salary. Alpert drives this point home: "If ... prices remain constant ... while the input costs of labor, materials and debt capital fall on a real basis, guess who gets to keep the difference? Yes: shareholders, owners, landlords, and 'talent'. In fact, economists have a special word for that group: rentiers." So do yourself a favour: Don't waste your capital on consumption, let the others generate the aggregate supply in the economy, save your money and turn yourself into a rentier.

If you need even more reasons to do that, consider the fact that many jobs are totally disappearing. This has happened to us all the time since the Industrial Revolution of course, but this time it is different, as they say. The jobs are not coming back, observes Dalia Marin, and "increasingly intelligent machines will reduce the demand for advanced skills, and the economic advantage of having these skills will decline as a result." She concludes: "As the scarcity of human capital declines in importance, the rapid expansion of education may not be the answer to the challenges of globalisation that we hoped it would be."

In this economic environment, not even productivity is going up much now. Sam Fleming and Chris Giles write about America: "Even as US manufacturers adopt automation as part of their fightback against offshoring to Asia, productivity growth across the economy is at a near-standstill."[28] In the US, productivity increase began to ebb in 2005 and it is now only 0.6% per year. Other developed countries, including Singapore, are not that much different.

Economist Lim Say Boon sums up Singapore's situation this way: "The world is set for a period of deflation. Emerging markets, including China, cannot be expected to power the global economy. There is excess supply and inadequate demand, and economies ... dependant on supplying to the world will be hit."[29] Personally I think we are simply reaching our limits to growth, economic or uneconomic. Should demand in the economy somehow return, what would happen is that resource prices would start to creep up again, oil would go back to $140/bbl, etc, so inflation would simply eat up the benefit of any economic expansion. That is what "economics in a full world" looks like, to borrow Herman Daly's phrase.

## But technology will save us, right?

I don't think I have to go on and on making this case, that the end of growth is already here and that overpopulation, the depletion of finite resources and pollution make it pointless to try to restart growth. Let me just address one argument that you often hear in the debate: Technology will come to the rescue.

With technology, the argument goes, we can grow without using more resources – the so-called "decoupling" of growth and energy use. Heinberg considers this argument and finds that the world E/GDP (Energy-to-GDP) ratio has in fact decreased between 1980 and 2010; while world nominal GDP increased some 6 times (from 10 to 60 trillion USD), world consumption of primary energy barely doubled (from 280 quadrillion Btu to 500). However, when energy quality is accounted for, as well as the financialisation of the nominal GDP, the decoupling is less significant. And most importantly, energy use is still growing. Switching to renewables is good, but they have a relatively low EROI – less than 10:1 for solar photovoltaic energy (about the same as tar sands oil) and less than 30:1 for wind turbines. Wind turbines built to last 40 years sometimes only last 10. Again, we are running on the spot, getting nowhere fast.

In *Prosperity Without Growth* (2011), Tim Jackson puts the "myth of decoupling", as one of his chapters is called, to rest. He acknowledges some *relative* decoupling in the economy: Over the last 30 years or so we have been doing more with relatively less energy and other materials, especially so in China. However, *absolute* decoupling, which is what would really make a difference, is not happening anywhere. We still consume more and pollute more than we ever did. Jackson concludes: "[Absolute decoupling] simply doesn't exist at all for key indicators of environmental quality such as carbon emissions, resource extraction, municipal waste generation and species loss. As an escape from the dilemma of growth it is fundamentally flawed."

Part of the problem is that while technology is undeniably great, are we developing worthwhile technologies? I sympathise with Stephen Emmott, who is himself a data processing scientist, when he ridicules the fact that we spent 8 billion euros discovering the Higgs boson particle (why?), while the natural world is falling apart around us. Every time I see some happy astronaut float around in the International Space Station while enjoying the view and singing a sad song to his dear mother back on Earth, I cannot help but wonder, aren't there better things we could do with this capital? What's more important, finding out if there once was water on Mars or protecting the incredible variety of life we already have here on this planet before it disappears? I know people on Earth who cannot find just $1 million to prevent the Sunda Pangolin or the Helmeted Hornbill from going extinct – that is probably what a toilet seat on the space station costs, freight included.

What about technological advances in smartphones, which are touted to have set us free in so many ways? The connectivity we enjoy and the creativity unleashed on internet blogs and video-sharing sites is unprecedented, and most of it is good. All this has countered to some extent the stagnation in real wage growth and other declining measures of welfare, such as personal space and the quality of the environment. It doesn't matter so much that the real beaches are full of plastic garbage and chemicals when you can see beautiful clean beaches anytime you want on YouTube. Having that gadget with you at all times makes the reality of a tedious trip to work in an overcrowded commuter train a little more bearable. The digital age has contributed to our "weightless economy", as Diane Coyle and others call it, which has improved some aspects of our lives, even though it doesn't always show up in the GDP.

The weightless economy is all the stuff we enjoy for free now – like movies, music and newspapers – which we previously paid for. Remember what IDD calls cost in the 1980s? Today you can call anywhere in the world and chat and look at each other, virtually for free. While GDP over-represents some uneconomic elements of growth, as we saw before, it under-represents some aspects of welfare-generating spending. Quality improvements in products are not captured well by the GDP. A fridge today, at the same price as one bought 20 years ago, is most likely bigger and more energy-efficient. An ordinary family car today is certainly much more complex and quiet than a similar one at the same price just 10 years ago. And then there is the portion of economic transactions not captured by the GDP at all, such as volunteer work, people doing their own cleaning, gardening or DIY jobs. On top of that comes the whole informal sector of the economy, which in some countries with weak institutions can be substantial, i.e. unreported economic activity. In Europe, Bulgaria has the largest informal sector at 32.2% of GDP according to one source.[30] It is even bigger for most developing countries; the highest is estimated in Bolivia, where some 66.1% of GDP is in the so-called shadow economy.[31]

The conclusion is that while technology, innovation and hidden benefits within the new economy might cushion the impact somewhat, they will not save us from the end of growth. All these data centres and server warehouses around the world, which power the many digital services available, are now responsible for about 2% of global greenhouse gas emissions – a share similar to aviation.[32] The "weightless" economy is not totally weightless after all. Some 20–50 million tonnes of electronics waste is produced every year, while more than 20 million mobile phones are thrown away each year in China alone. Much of this waste ends up in land-fills, usually in developing countries in Africa and Asia, where it leaks chemicals and heavy metals into the environment.[33]

## Get used to it

At the end of the day, most environmental scientists and economists out there feel they have to be optimistic. Tim Jackson, for one, after making a case for how bad our situation is, says that if we just do this and this, things will get much better. His book has chapters such as "Flourishing – within limits", "Governance for prosperity" and "The transition to a sustainable economy". Check them out; they are full of things that we really should do, like reducing inequality as well as working hours, dismantling consumerism, putting the environment first, etc. Except we don't; this is all fantasy. And we are not going to in the foreseeable future, so get used to it.

In *Enough is Enough* (2013), two of Herman Daly's younger students, Dietz and O'Neill, try to provide an even more complete recipe for how we can move from uneconomic growth via degrowth to a steady-state economy. They implicitly acknowledge, however, that we most likely will have to go through a major crisis or an external threat of some sort before the public will accept the undertakings required, such as reducing population and consumption and stigmatising – instead of glorifying – greed.

Jørgen Randers, one of the authors of the 1972 book mentioned before, is still very much active in environmental academia, but fairly disillusioned by now. He described to Guardian.com on 19 January 2015 how voters tend to revolt when it comes to more regulation and higher taxes. He chaired a commission in Norway which in 2006 came up with a 15-point plan to solve the climate problem in the country. The plan would have allowed Norway to cut its greenhouse gas emissions by two-thirds by 2050 and be a case study other rich countries could learn from. Provided that every Norwegian was willing to pay just €250 each – equivalent to 1% more in income tax. "In spite of this small sacrifice, a vast majority of Norwegians were against the plan," Randers said. "To be frank, most voters preferred to use the money for other causes – like yet another weekend trip to London or Sweden for shopping." So Randers sees no sympathy for the environment among Scandinavian voters, and not among businesses either. "The capitalist system does not help," he added. "Capitalism is carefully designed to allocate capital to the most profitable projects. And this is exactly what we don't need today. We need investments into more expensive wind and solar power, not into cheap coal and gas. The capitalist market won't do this on its own."

World leaders face this problem too. Support from voters, consumers, businesses and the public in general for a better environment is simply not there. I honestly think that most leaders are well informed. They know where we are heading, and they genuinely want to do something about it. In France, already in 2008 President Sarkozy put Joseph Stiglitz and one of his academic colleagues in charge of a commission to rethink how GDP should be assessed, something we considered earlier. When launched, the report recommended a shift in emphasis to put people's well-being above just economic production and to put the sustainability of resources at the heart of any growth plan. Said Sarkozy: "We must change the way we live, consume, and produce."[34]

Remember President Obama's "green jobs" ideas when he got into office in 2009? That never happened. First Solar Inc was trading at around $190 per share then; today it is around $50. Meanwhile, Lockheed Martin, which makes cruise missiles and F-35 fighter jets among other goodies, has seen its share price go from $75 to $220. Green jobs never happened, but fracking for oil and gas jobs sure did. And that wasn't really Obama's fault; that's just the way consumers and the public want it.

Representing Asia during a meeting of world leaders discussing climate change at Davos, Switzerland in 2008, Prime Minister Lee Hsien Loong of Singapore gave a rare speech mainly about the environment. He highlighted that in Southeast Asia there are pressures to exploit fully the region's natural resources from minerals to timber and forest land. "It is impossible for anyone or any government to stop this", Lee said, adding that this push for rapid economic growth would mean more pollution. "Realistically, emissions are bound to increase ... this is human and economic reality." Lee suggested that countries like China, India and many in Southeast Asia should phase out subsidies for fossil fuels, which have led to overconsumption and waste: "If they phase out these subsidies, their economies will perform much better, and greener." Singapore, on its part, should make sustainable development a national effort, the Prime Minister said on that occasion.[35] An inter-ministerial committee was set up that year to "develop a comprehensive strategy to continue to grow economically in an environmentally sound way", as the report said.

But here is the reality: Politicians are just representing their electorates. When Malaysia and Indonesia a few years after this meeting started phasing out fossil fuel subsidies, people rioted in the streets. Subsidies for fossil fuels in Southeast Asia haven't changed much since then; although down from a peak in 2012 they are higher than in 2009; in 2014 they amounted to $36 billion; six out of 10 nations in the region provide financial incentives to burn more oil, gas, diesel and coal.[36]

PM Lee is right when he says that it is impossible to stop strip mining and forest clearance; it is here by popular demand. It will stop only when there is no land left to strip and no forest left to burn. The elite can have all the summit meetings and conferences they want; it is not going to make a difference. And in the meantime we all have to get on with our lives in the real world.

# So What Can I Do?

*"The stock market is filled with individuals*
*who know the price of everything,*
*but the value of nothing."*

— PHILLIP FISHER

## Position yourself to win

In the last chapter we saw how the world is going to hell in a hand-basket. In my view there are two things each of us can do about this. (1) We can be selfish and take care of ourselves. (2) We can work individually and collectively to monitor and understand what is happening and do our bit to give this world a viable future. I think we should do both.

Let us consider the first path. As we have seen, the global end of growth will be uneven. Just because your country is in a recession, that doesn't mean you couldn't do well personally. You could get a good education, rise above the average and excel while the rest are struggling. You could buy shares in a company that shoots up in value, even as the main index drops. It is a bit harder to do well while a retreating tide drops all boats, but it is by no means impossible. Be creative, innovative, flexible and above all service-minded. Save the money you make that way, just in case there is a storm coming, because there probably is. Tim Jackson in *Prosperity Without Growth* says: "The poorest will inevitably be hardest hit through the recession." I say: So don't be among the

207

poorest. "The best thing you can do for the poor is not be one of them," Andrew Matthews said in *Being Happy*, and I agree.

Likewise, there will be countries that can position themselves and progress even during the end of growth. Countries with good governance, strong institutions, secure borders and visionary leadership will still prevail. The rest not so much. "The overall picture is bleak," UN humanitarian chief Stephen O'Brien told a news conference in Geneva in December 2015. "Suffering in the world has reached levels not seen in a generation. Conflicts and disasters have driven millions ... to the edge of survival."[1] Some 125 million people are expected to require humanitarian assistance in 2016. Thomas Friedman, whom I mentioned earlier, puts it this way: "Every day now, you read about people fleeing the World of Disorder for the World of Order. There are more displaced people worldwide – some 50 million – than at any time since World War II. But here's the rub: We don't know what to do."[2]

It's rather funny that the places now being overwhelmed with migrants, like northern Europe and Scandinavia, were themselves pretty depressed countries until fairly recently. Just over 100 years ago, between 1870 and the early 1900s, some 1.3 million people left Sweden for the United States to escape poverty and hopelessness.[3] Of course, the difference being that at that time the world was not yet quite full, the emigration was fairly orderly, and there was plenty of land and resources in the western states, where the Scandinavians could settle and build a better life. Today the migrants are travelling in a chaotic fashion into areas that are already full of people.

Personally I don't see what is so great about living in Denmark or Norway, yet those two countries are near the top of various happiness surveys year after year. It is rainy and cold and miserable most of the time; half the year it is dark most of the day, the other half so bright you can hardly sleep; I guess they don't consider the weather in those surveys. Norway has a lot of land on paper, but most of it is just barren rock, people live cramped along a narrow strip of coastline, roads are narrow and jam-packed, housing and everything else is expensive, taxes are prohibitive and there is little to do after work but watch television and go for the occasional hike in the hills. Should this be the best we can come up with?

But apparently it is, and it has to do with governance. Regarding Norway, I remember the 1970s when the North Sea turned out to have oil under the seabed. The territorial lines at the time were a bit blurred. Norway, the UK, Denmark, Germany and the Netherlands all wanted the biggest share possible of the continental shelf for themselves. It was a potential powder keg, but the countries involved quickly found a solution through international arbitration. This is the way to long-term prosperity and a high ranking in the happiness indexes. May the countries sharing the South China Sea today learn from that.

So the message is, find a home for yourself with good governance. In such a place, you will have statistically better chances of riding out the storms ahead. John F. Kennedy said: "The time to repair the roof is when the sun is shining." Protect your capital and invest in value – this will be your ticket to personal freedom and a meaningful life in a finite world.

## The big picture

And then there is the second element to this, the big picture. Look at the realities for what they are; don't hide your head in the sand. Try to understand why your pay is not going up much. If there is no demand for what you are doing, how can you expect a pay rise? Try to understand what is happening in the wider economy; you will feel better that way.

Stop pestering the politicians for more subsidies and lower bus fares and welfare and pensions and free money – it doesn't work. Tell your elected representatives instead to tax consumption, fossil fuels and waste. Daly puts it this way: "Why tax what we want more of – employment and income? Why not tax what we want less of – depletion and pollution?" Even a moderate like Diane Coyle says: "Discourage spending, via taxes on consumption and especially high-carbon consumption."

I am proud to live in a country where we control our national borders, where we tax employment low (three-quarters of workers in Singapore do not pay income tax at all), and yet we have a balanced budget every year and money in the kitty. And it is all done by democratic consensus and regular free and fair parliamentary elections. If this little country that is just 50 years old as a nation can do it, why can't Europe with their high levels of education and enlightenment? That answer seems to be blowing in the wind.

At the level of international relations, it is best for problems to be solved amicably. Whatever contentions there are, they are not worth fighting for. Support mediation, reconciliation and the rule of law. Don't be like Africa, where wars stripped about US$284 billion from its economies between 1990 and 2005. That is 15% of growth lost and equal to the amount of money received in international aid during the same period. Only the international arms trade benefited from this. Some 95% of Kalashnikov rifles – the weapon of choice in the 23 regional conflicts identified in the survey by Oxfam International – came from outside the continent.[4]

I am not a security strategy expert, but I don't think you have to be one to establish that it is bad policy to bomb your neighbours into failed states, the way NATO has been doing regularly since the attack on Serbia in 1999. Regime-change wars are illegal, they don't work and we simply cannot afford them. Look at these countries that are doing pretty well: Singapore, Switzerland, Sweden, Finland, New Zealand. They are all non-aligned – maybe that is no coincidence.

It's not just about the social misery that war brings; it's about the Earth. At the opening session of the United Nations General

Assembly in 2015, Secretary-General Ban Ki-moon said: "The world continues to squander trillions in military funding. Why is it easier to find the money to destroy people and the planet than to protect them?"[5] I think I know what the answer to that question is: Because that is how you make more money. Some do anyway – the ones who supply the weaponry and the ones who rebuild afterwards. But like we saw in the broken window fallacy, we have to get away from that growth model.

We have to try something that people haven't had to cope with since the Industrial Revolution: We have to manage a shrinking economy. And this time we have to do it in a democratic fashion, by public consent and demand.

Previous attempts at forcefully steering the economy ended in social and economic tragedy and ruin, as we covered briefly in chapter 3. In Europe during the Cold War, Romania broke ranks with everyone else, and under Ceausescu in 1982 the leadership set out to pay back the country's large foreign debt. Sounds laudable, right? Wrong. This policy resulted in severe shortages of goods at home; without democratic controls the regime became more and more outlandish and repressive. The government collapsed in December 1989, and the head of state was captured by the army and accused of genocide and sabotaging the Romanian economy. Immediately after a trial that lasted about an hour, Ceausescu was executed by firing squad, together with his wife, for good measure. That was a lesson to everyone. No European leader has suggested paying back all their foreign debt since then.

Jørgen Randers may lament the shortcomings of the capitalist market economy and representative democracy, but as I am sure he would agree, it is still the best we've got. I don't see many people massing across the border to live in North Korea or Cuba, where they have experimented with other economic and political systems. Somehow we have to make this work, and it will only work if we rise to the challenge, each one of us.

Already in 2008, before the financial crisis that year, Professor Peter Victor in *Managing Without Growth* called into question "the primacy that we in rich countries give to economic growth as the overriding economic policy objective for government". We must incorporate this new paradigm into mainstream thinking, everyday economic and social management. We basically don't have a choice, and the sooner we do it, the smoother the transition will be to a no-growth condition.

After all, none of us grow forever. You might have a job for a while that pays a bundle, and then maybe the job is not worth it, and you find another at a lower pay but with better overall welfare. Towards the end of our careers we all downsize; we make less, spend less, and maybe move into a smaller home. That doesn't mean we are worse off. In fact we might have a better quality of life that way.

Now we have to do this on a larger scale, as a society. Make less, spend less, damage less, save more.

## What did nature ever do for me?

In Singapore alone we have many groups working on sustainable development. There's the World Business Council for Sustainable Development, whose tagline is "business solutions for a sustainable world". There's also TEEB, The Economics of Ecosystems and Biodiversity for Business Coalition, who have taken it upon themselves to focus on "making nature's values visible", as they say on their website; their principal objective is to mainstream the values of biodiversity and ecosystem services into decision-making at all levels. Local media company Global Initiatives organises events and conferences on responsible business practices and sustainable development issues.

One of the problems with our conventional methods of growing the economy has been the loss of much of our natural world and what it contains. This subject is well covered by many others, and is somewhat peripheral to this book, so I will not go into details here. The issue can get somewhat philosophical: Do we as humans have the moral right to exterminate other species and whole ecosystems? But even from a purely utilitarian and economic perspective, there is a concern.

It is well established that nature benefits us in many intangible ways. In *The Nature Principle* (2002), Richard Louv deals with many of these issues, and through research and personal evidence he shows how nature can boost mental acuity and creativity, promote health and wellness, strengthen human bonds, and help us in many other ways to live better, smarter and more productive lives. The habitat destruction and biodiversity extermination crisis is not just about morals; there is a practical argument for why we should keep nature healthy and conserve our biological diversity.

One concern is health. "By unsustainably exploiting nature's resources, human civilisation has flourished but now risks substantial health effects from the degradation of nature's life support systems in the future." This comes from a 2015 report written by 15 leading medical academics and published in the peer-reviewed medical journal *The Lancet*.[6] The thing is, when you do become financially free, you'll want to be a healthy person on a healthy Earth, to be able enjoy that freedom. Harming the environment is essentially harming your own prospects of freedom.

In Singapore, and I am sure in other countries, economists and academics are hard at work finding ways to express the value of nature in monetary terms. "The lack of monetary value on green spaces in no way diminishes their worth to people," write Euston Quah and Nicolas Neo for the *Straits Times*. And they conclude: "The dichotomy of economic growth and the environment has been a growing concern to Singapore. Cost-benefit analysis would be incomplete and erroneous if no attempt is made to measure the quantity and value of green goods."[7] I am sure this would be true not only for Singapore, but for all countries under development where natural capital is replaced with man-made stuff.

A few finance professionals are also troubled about what we are doing to our environment in the name of growth. Jeremy Grantham, an experienced hedge fund manager, has studied bubbles in the economy since long before the Japanese asset bubble burst in 1990, and has come to believe that our unrestrained use of fossil fuels for growth has led us into a gigantic partly-environmental and partly-financial bubble.

One thought-provoking issue that Grantham has raised is the so-called "Pascal's Wager". Blaise Pascal was a 17th-century mathematician and philosopher who concluded that a rational person would always choose to believe in God. That is because there are only two possible outcomes of this bet: God exists or he does not. You will find that out for sure only when you die. If God does exist, the upside of believing in him and serving him while you are alive is unlimited; you go to Heaven. The downside risk is catastrophic; you go to Hell. If God turns out not to exist when you die, it doesn't really matter one way or another. Grantham applies this probability problem to the fossil fuel issue and concludes that a rational person would always bet on conservation and green energy substitution. The cost of that is fairly small; the downside risk of getting it wrong and wrecking the planet is horrendous.

In a Bloomberg interview, Grantham brought up two points that work in our favour. First, with increased development, couples choose to have fewer children. This is a well-established demographic fact, and China found that out in the 2010s when they gradually relaxed the one-child policy; many couples simply stuck to it voluntarily. If this trend continues, Grantham foresees a much-needed decline in human population; he is on record as saying that the world can only sustainably support a population of 1.5 billion – not 7 and certainly not 9 or 10 as projected now.

The other favourable point concerns our energy capabilities.

For the first time ever, it would actually be possible to convert most of our energy use to renewable sources like solar, wind, geo-thermal and hydro-electric power. Germany generates some 30% of its electricity from renewables already. China is coming up fast in this field. Markets alone will not do it, as coal is still the cheapest and most abundant energy source we have, as well as one of the dirtiest. Public governance (legislation/force) is required. But we could actually do it, convert to renewable energy.

I believe in freedom; I don't really like Big Government. But I also realise that total personal freedom could wreck our environment. When I see unregulated gold miners ravage the rainforests of Indonesia and Peru, I realise that unlimited freedom doesn't work. The strict environmental standards enforced by the government in the US may appear heavy-handed at times – and I know it is resented by many private artisanal gold miners in places like Alaska – but it sure keeps the Brooks Range looking nice and the rivers there spotlessly clean. Where public order breaks down, like in Uganda during the chaotic years in the 1970s, wildlife populations are the first to suffer.[8] So we do need public institutions, we need legislation and we need enforcement, even if they are sometimes a hassle and go too far in their powers.

I'm sure many individuals and organisations struggle with this issue – the freedom of the individual versus the common good. I know I do. It is a balance we continuously have to fine-tune.

## There are alternatives

Now that we have identified some of the existential dangers that we face in the form of uneconomic growth, habitat destruction, biodiversity loss and climate change, we might want to do something about it, each one of us. The thing is, in conservation there is no "one size fits all".

My wife and I bought a hybrid electric car around 2006 when the improved Toyota Prius came out. A hybrid car does not draw power from the grid; it simply uses the power of the vehicle much more efficiently by capturing, storing and reusing the energy usually lost in city driving during braking and deceleration; at red lights it shuts down completely. At that point in time I was willing to accept some sacrifice for the benefit of our environment; surely urban transport is one of these easy nuts to crack. I can see why some poor people want to grow and develop, sometimes at the cost of the environment. But I cannot for the life of me understand why someone living in a tropical city would buy a huge SUV with oversized wheels to get to the office, or a long limousine with a 4.5-litre engine that is just a hassle to park. And guess what, the hybrid car was not even a sacrifice to own. It turned out to be quicker, quieter, as roomy and cheaper to own than the 2-litre gas-guzzling Ford Mondeo we had before! Yet, after 10 years, hybrid cars in Singapore are less than 2% of the car population. I can see why Jørgen Randers is pulling his hair in frustration over consumer habits!

But then, I eat meat, almost every day. Many of our green friends point out that this is one of the worst things you can do to the environment. Meat production gobbles up resources on a much larger scale than vegetarian foods, and that is not even considering the ethical and health issues associated with meat. I used to race around in fast cars, I kept birds in cages as a hobby when I was in primary school, I even hunted animals for a short period of time when I was a kid. I worked in the oil business. I flew around the world on pointless sightseeing trips. I am not proud of any of that. But to me it just goes to show that people have the capacity to change. If you still race around senselessly in a performance car or shoot big game animals when you are over 40 years old in this day and age, maybe you should study the facts, see the light and get your priorities straight.

There are alternative lifestyles, and we don't all have to go back to living in caves or like hippies in the woods. All over the world, millions of people are experimenting with unconventional paths to development and success. I am thinking of the Barefoot College in India, President Rafael Correa's alternative development plans for Ecuador, and many more. There are hundreds of such initiatives going on, some coming from the grassroots, others supported by NGOs and/or governments, and some even by commercial companies, once a demand develops.

The digital revolution facilitates all this. Global connectivity has helped make a more shared and frugal economy possible. Car-sharing services (think Uber), house-sharing (think Airbnb), peer-to-peer lending bypassing the commercial banks – all these will in my view cushion the effects of an economy and a middle-class struggling due to lack of space and resources. DIY hardware kits, free cooking instruction videos, online foreign language courses, etc, will increasingly make it easier for you to do more with less. That is exactly the subtitle of a new book by Navi Radjou and Jaideep Prabhu, *Frugal Innovation: How To Do More With Less*.[9] Check it out when you get the chance.

A "downshifting movement" is gaining ground. According to Tim Jackson in *Prosperity Without Growth*, a staggering 83% of Australians felt society was too materialistic; 28% of Americans have taken some steps to simplify their lives; 62% expressed a willingness to do so; and similar results have been found in Europe. Jackson concludes that "consuming less, voluntarily, can improve subjective well-being – completely contrary to the conventional model". So next time you hear cute terms like "shop till you drop" or "retail therapy", stop and think: Is shopping and eating really therapeutic for you, or are you just being manipulated by the advertising and the consumer industry to borrow money and buy stuff you don't need, which clutter your life and harm the environment?

In Singapore, Kishore Mahbubani has made himself a spokesman for a car-less society. He wrote in the *Straits Times*: "When we worship material goods like cars, we will be perpetually unhappy. Someone else will always have a better car than ours. Happiness does not come from owning the most expensive car, but from living a life of greater meaning and purpose."[10] I couldn't have put it better myself. Mahbubani went on to quote Bertrand Russell: "It is the preoccupation with possessions, more than anything else, that prevents us from living freely and nobly."

In the mathematical equation that determines your level of financial freedom, there are two variables. One is your income as well as your return on capital, the other one is your expenses. Remember Piketty's formula in the previous chapter, $r > g$? Here is my formula: $F = r - e$. Your freedom is your return on capital minus expenses. Keep your consumerism impulses in check and your "e" value low, and you are that much closer to financial freedom.

## Vote with your wallet

I don't want to pick on democracy, because experience shows us that democratic controls in society are vital to avoid despotism, corruption and misery. But let's face it, as voters we only get to exercise our powers once every four years or so. Many (like me) cannot vote in the country that they reside in, and cannot vote in their country of birth because they are not living there. Even then, it is rare for only one vote to separate two candidates, so in reality your vote as a citizen doesn't make that much direct difference anyway.

But as a consumer, you do vote virtually every day. Every time you buy something, you cast a vote, and this vote has a direct and significant bearing on events and developments. It could be that you read the labels on your purchases in the supermarket and consciously avoid produce with corn syrup, GMO-modified ingredients, etc. If you shop from the organic section or buy biodegradable plates for your picnic instead of plastic, you will help increase the aggregate demand for these products.

Taking this concept a step further, you could also partici-pate in public campaigns on social media to put pressure on cer-tain businesses with bad practices. When the "annual" haze in Singapore from plantation fires in Sumatra and Borneo finally got too much for the general public in 2015, the threat of a consumer boycott prompted some supermarket chains to remove paper products from the shelves originating from companies suspected of contributing to the burning.

When consumers change, business will change as well. Don't listen to me; take it from the biggest capitalist of all time. At Berkshire Hathaway's AGMs – what Warren Buffett calls "Woodstock for capitalists", where 40,000 people gather to cel-ebrate this successful investment company and its billionaire founder – environmental sustainability is not really the foremost item on the agenda; profits are. However, at the 2015 AGM there was one confrontational question about Berkshire's stakes in com-panies like Coca-Cola that sell highly sugared products. For the record, sugary drinks may cause severe health damage and up to 184,000 deaths a year worldwide according to one survey pub-lished in the journal *Circulation*.[11] Buffett's reply: "Companies can change as consumer tastes evolve."[12]

So there you have it, you change your consumption pattern, and big business and the world will change with it. This is real power in your hands.

I know there are forces working against you. Tobacco compa-nies urge you to smoke, and then you get hooked and can't stop. Pharmaceutical companies and doctors recommend that you pop pills which just make you weaker, so that you need to pop more pills. "Through the aggressive marketing of ultra-processed food and drink, multinational companies are now major drivers of the world's growing epidemic of chronic diseases such as heart dis-ease, cancer and diabetes." So said a global analysis published in *The Lancet* in 2013.[13] This is done by "building financial and institutional relations" with health professionals, charities and health agencies, distorting research findings and lobbying politicians to oppose health reforms, the report said. So, as a consumer, the cards may be somewhat stacked against you. But that doesn't free you from liability. The gambling, tobacco, booze and junk-food business might be manipulative, and their products highly addictive, but that doesn't mean you don't have responsibility. You always have the choice to say no, to kick the habit and get out. Just do it.

In conservation, things are not always what they appear to be. For instance, did you know that electric cars pollute more than conventional vehicles? A study by WWF in Germany in 2009 concluded that an electric car running on electricity from a coal-fired power plant released 33% more $CO_2$ than a conventional VW Golf.[14] This has been confirmed by several other reports, including one from the Norwegian University of Science and Technology published in the *Journal of Industrial Ecology*. The research team looked at the life-cycle impact of conventional and electric vehicles and concluded: "Electric cars might pollute much more than petrol or diesel-powered cars. Electric car factories also emitted more toxic waste than conventional car factories."[15] The secret is to have the electric vehicle powered by renewable energy such as solar or wind farms. "In regions where fossil fuels are the main source of power, electric cars offer no benefits and may even cause more harm," the 2012 report said.

Likewise, recycling is good, right? Not always. You know the mantra: reduce, reuse and recycle. It sounds fine, but regarding the last entry it is important how you go about it. "[Recycling] is seen as virtuous but there is evidence that the process is often costly and ineffectual", said an article in the *New York Times*.[16] Recycling is labour-intensive and puts more trucks on the road hauling the stuff around; the rinsing, sorting and re-processing of garbage is in itself energy-intensive, and the overall gain might be very small.

It seems to me that this needs to be studied better. But I would intuitively think that of the three "r"s, the first one is the most important. Simply reduce! Spend less and stop the waste at its source. If you must use, then reuse. Buy or take over quality stuff second-hand, or pre-owned if you will, use it for as long as you can. Discarding completely and recycling should be the last resort.

## A do-gooder's guide to investing

If as a consumer you are conscientious about not buying from companies that flagrantly cause environmental destruction, what about as an investor? The companies' actions may not be as transparent (who owns what?), but the same principle holds. It doesn't make sense to contribute towards the depletion of the Earth, and by extension, the undermining of your own future freedom – financial and otherwise. Again, though, like your lifestyle choices, this is a highly subjective matter, and I don't think there is one size that fits all. But I urge you to keep these issues in mind.

Let us quickly get the terminology sorted out; there are a lot of different expressions floating around.

*Sustainable development:* Probably the most misunderstood term of all. If you listen to Herman Daly, this is development without economic growth; all other development would be unsustainable to him. But the concept is usually defined as development that doesn't use up finite natural capital faster than it can be replenished (renewable resources) or substituted (non-renewable resources). In practice, the phrase is applied vaguely during business conferences to include economic development and growth with some consideration shown to the natural environment.

*Sustainable investing/finance:* The official definition runs like this: "The practice of creating economic and social value through financial models, products and markets that are sustainable over time."[17] So the definition uses the word that should be defined ... not very useful.

*Socially responsible investing / Sustainable and responsible investing (SRI):* No wonder if you are confused: SRI first meant the former, but increasingly now it means the latter! Anyway, either way this is an investment strategy that aims to consider financial returns as well as social consequences in a wider sense. An individual or institutional fund that practises SRI will use positive or negative screening, i.e. positively select favourable projects that make money as well as improve the environment or community, and negatively avoid others. The negative screening usually includes companies involved in alcohol, tobacco, gambling, pornography, animal testing and probably also military hardware, especially nuclear weapons and landmines. These are the so-called "sin stocks". SRI also looks for companies with solid labour rights, equal opportunity employment and a good human rights record.

*Responsible investing:* The UN uses this term in their PRI, i.e. principles for responsible investment. This is the government bureaucrats' version of SRI. Institutional investment managers can sign on and get the PRI accreditation for their funds, and half of them have in fact done so worldwide.[18]

*Ethical investing:* This is really another word for SRI. The positive screening includes renewable energy companies or organic food producers; usually all arms producers and military contractors are screened out, as well as logging and mining companies, lately also increasingly coal and oil and gas producers. Ethical funds also apply "engagement" as a tool to get influence, i.e. they use their shareholder's status to push for changes within the company to improve its record on the environment and social governance.

*Green investing:* A very narrow type of SRI where only "green" companies are positively screened. This usually involves companies engaged in the following sectors only: wind, solar, water, fuel cells, waste management, pollution control and organic farming. Green investment strategies and funds have a mixed record. With few established green companies making steady boatloads of money, these funds usually end up investing in rocky start-ups and unproven business models with a high failure rate. I bought a copy of Jack Uldrich's *Green Investing* when it came out in 2008, and I still pull it out and go through it once in a while. There is a good lesson in that: Most of the green companies that Uldrich recommended then are trading below their valuations in 2008; some have gone bust. That doesn't mean you should never try green investing, it just means you should be careful.

*Impact investing:* This is a bit different as a concept and is usually applied by private equity managers and venture capitalists. Impact investors actively select projects and start-ups that they think will have a positive impact on the environment or the community and make them happen by providing funds in exchange for a stake in the company.

*Social investing:* This is the ultimate do-gooder investment policy. Unlike in impact investing, where you are willing to take high risk but still aim for a return on investment, in social investing you don't really expect financial gain. You invest in the community and the people to improve their conditions; any financial gain is secondary and you are even willing to accept a loss.

*Environmental, social and corporate governance (ESG):* This is a key concept used in SRI; the three areas of concern are evaluated as the key guiding principle to rank companies when ethical criteria are applied in investment decisions.

*Corporate social responsibility (CSR):* Probably the broadest of the measures mentioned here and used since the 1960s. Very few companies would not sign on to this – which corporation wants to be socially irresponsible? It covers everything from transparent accounting practices and regulatory policies to turning down the light in the office and making sure there are clean towels in the washroom. It says nothing about what the company does; even Philip Morris International (tobacco) and Northrop Grumman (nuclear-capable stealth bombers) have high CSR ratings.[19]

## Ethical investing in practice

Out of the many terms, let us go with this one, ethical investing. If you Google this, you will find a lot of useful resources. For instance, there is a complete manual to ethical investment funds on Blueandgreentomorrow.com. After all, anything that is not ethical must be unethical, and who wants to be an unethical investor? Actually, it seems to me that most of us don't mind!

Let me elaborate. Ethical investing increasingly hits the news. According to a 2014 report from US SIF (The Forum for Sustainable and Responsible Investment), one out of six dollars under professional management in the US ($6.57 trillion to be exact) is now invested according to SRI strategies.[20] A useful benchmark for performance would be the ETF from iShares tracking the MSCI KLD 400 index. This selection of stocks has been screened positively according to ESG (environmental, social and governance) characteristics. According to my own quick calculations, this index has actually matched the S&P 500 quite well. An investment in 2006 would have grown about 83% till 2015; had you bought the S&P index ETF, your money would have grown 78%. If anything, you would have made a bit more money by screening out the sin stocks!

This contradicts a story by Goh Eng Yeow, who wrote for the *Straits Times*: "[Sin stocks] outperform those in other industries by far, thanks to unstoppable demand for liquor, tobacco and gambling." Goh thinks that sin stocks outperform others partly due to "the refusal of some investors to buy their shares, thus artificially depressing their prices and ensuring a high return for those with fewer scruples."[21] This argument might not really work; most companies try to generate demand for their shares; and if you look at the small print, Goh uses a 115-year time horizon to make his point about above-average return. It could be a case of past performance not being indicative of future returns, as the disclaimer goes. Investor sentiment can change pretty quickly, as we saw recently when fossil fuel stocks suddenly fell out of favour with investors, and many coal- and oil-related companies saw their market capitalisation crash.

That said, Singapore – and Asia as a whole, I suspect – cannot be said to be a hotbed for ethical investment radicalism. I have been to many investment fairs and talks and seminars over the years, and I have not been struck by any overwhelming concern for the environment among participants. In fact, I have never heard the environment mentioned – not even once! The presenters even brag about making a ton of money on tobacco stocks, for example. You know, great dividend, steady capital gain, what could be better? I think of those who have to clean up the mess that smoking makes. According to N. Sivasothi, a senior lecturer teaching biodiversity at the National University of Singapore who organises coastal clean-up activities, 36% of the trash that his group of volunteers picks up on the beaches is smoking-related. Should we finance this filth as investors? Surely there must be other ways we can put our capital to work and make money.

When I started out in the oil business on the rigs in the Norwegian sector of the North Sea, we had these young engineers from a government agency called Statoil come out to see us. In brand new bright-orange overalls they would quietly eye us and try to figure out what we were doing. My southern American colleagues said about the Statoil guys: "They don't know s*** from wild honey." Well, look at Statoil now, a full-fledged oil company in their own right, listed on the NYSE with a market cap of over $50 billion. I bought shares in Statoil ASA in my youngest son's name shortly after he was born – they are of somewhat sentimental value to me. And yes, the stock has done pretty well. Otherwise, I avoid fossil fuel stocks, and that's not just because they contribute to environmental devastation and global warming. More and more institutional investors shy away from them, such as pension funds and college endowment funds with SRI policies. Even the $860 million Rockefeller Brothers Fund announced in 2014 that they would divest out of fossil fuels.[22] Which is somewhat ironic, because the family fund was founded by Standard Oil, later ExxonMobil!

The huge Norwegian sovereign wealth fund is in a similar dilemma. With US$860 billion under management, it might be the largest SWF in the world – not bad for a small country of some 5 million people which 50 years ago did not have much going for it. Anyway, the Norwegians couldn't really divest out of fossil fuels, since all their assets by definition originate from oil revenues and royalties from the Norwegian offshore oil and gas industry. However, the fund does have an SRI policy, and they announced in 2015 that they would work to ban coal investments. The Norwegian parliament decided to mandate the fund to gradually divest from some 50 to 75 companies with more than 30% of their revenue from coal, an estimated $4.5 billion in total.[23]

Ethical guidelines are a moving target. The Norwegian fund negatively screens companies involved in tobacco, illegal logging, cluster bombs and nuclear weapons. Singapore Technologies Engineering is among their excluded companies as it is reported to make anti-personnel landmines which kill indiscriminately and contaminate war zones for decades after a conflict ends. But guess who owns ST Engineering? The Singapore government. The company is listed on the SGX, and has a market cap of around S$10 billion. Temasek Holdings own 51% of the shares, DBS Bank (another government-linked company) owns 11%. So what is wrong for one government is OK for another. It goes to show that you have to find your own ethical boundaries and shift them dynamically as you learn more about the consequences of your actions as citizen, consumer, investor and inhabitant of the Earth.

## Find your own way

Many big financial fund managers such as Schroders, Deutsche Bank, HSBC and ABN AMRO have so-called climate change funds for sale. When I look at them, however, they don't make much sense. The Schroders Global Climate Change Equity fund's number one holding is Amazon.com – what does Amazon have to do with climate change? The equivalent product from Deutsche Bank has Siemens AG as its number one holding. Yes, Siemens AG makes some wind turbines, but look at this statement from its website: "Expanding its oil and gas field equipment portfolio, Siemens strengthens its position as global strategic partner for Oil and Gas customers." So much for countering global climate change.

What about banks that finance all this? In Singapore neither one of the two public wealth funds (GIC and Temasek Holdings) have specific SRI policies, unlike the much larger Norwegian fund mentioned earlier. The managements make regular public statements that they aim to protect the environment. Temasek chairman Lim Boon Heng put it like this recently: "Growth should not come at the expense of sustainability – protection of our environment can and should go hand in hand with development, jobs and prosperity."[24] Yet, there are no binding SRI guidelines. For Singapore, protecting and growing taxpayers' money comes first.

The three fully licensed Singapore banks also do not have ethical guidelines. In fact, the whole financial sector in Southeast Asia lags behind in this matter. This was highlighted in a study by the WWF published in 2015, which found "an alarming gap between regional ASEAN financial institutions and the environmental, social and governance (ESG) standards adopted by their international counterparts".[25] Shortly after this report was released, and with the haze from plantation fires in Indonesia a big issue later that year, the Association of Banks in Singapore finally came out with some guidelines to encourage their members, the Singapore banks, to consider the environmental and ethical practices of their clients. Non-binding, but a beginning.[26] Things can change, and sometimes, when the time is right, they can change very quickly.

So if you buy a bank stock, you can be pretty sure that you contribute to deforestation, strip-mining for coal and global warming. If you buy the index, as I advised you to do earlier, what do you get? In Singapore you get of course the three local banks, but also Wilmar International Ltd (palm oil and deforestation), Noble Group (fossil fuels and mining), Genting Singapore (gambling) and yes, of course ST Engineering, which the Norwegians didn't want to touch.

And what about the S&P 500? You have Philip Morris, Reynolds American Inc (tobacco), Freeport McMoRan (dirty mining), Northrop Grumman Corp, Boeing Company, Honeywell Inc, Textron Inc, General Dynamics, Lockheed Martin, Jacobs Engineering, Raytheon (nuclear weapons and/or cluster bombs), Wal-Mart Stores Inc (labour rights), etc. These are all S&P 500 component stocks which are also on the Norwegian government's exclusion list.

You may soon find that if you negatively screen out any company contributing to climate change or fossil fuels or mining or logging or palm oil, you won't have that many investment opportunities left.

So what is there to do? In a perfect world I would like to make all my money just investing in good companies. Wouldn't we all? I look at the SGX, and I can only find a handful of locally listed companies that I would include if I were to put together an actively managed fund investing only in green companies. I calculated that about 1.7% of the market capitalisation of SGX listed companies would qualify – companies like Hyflux, SIIC Environment, United Envirotech (clean water), Ecowise and Enviro-Hub Holdings (recycling). Once you get into companies like Sembcorp Industries and Keppel Infrastructure Trust, you are dealing with conglomerates doing environmental services as well as fossil fuel projects. If you go overseas, the choice of green companies is obviously much greater.

But this is not a perfect world. There is no guarantee that these companies doing good will make money. Like I said, we all have to develop our own personal guidelines and find an equitable balance. I cannot tell you what to do, but I can tell you what we do in our family. In our case, yes, we also have a bit of stock in banks, telecom companies, and some health companies like Novo Nordisk A/S and Religare Health Trust. At least they don't do that much harm. I also do try to find do-gooder companies to invest in – companies involved in environmental services and clean energy – but only if I think they can pass a fundamental analysis test and make money, not just do good. I wish I could afford to be into pure social investing, but I can't.

However, I am proud to say that I don't own a single stock linked directly to tobacco, deforestation, mining, gambling or arms. It is not necessary. Those companies have to find their capital somewhere else; they won't get any from me.

I think of it this way: If I invest in a company known to be involved directly in deforestation, each dollar I make from it now is in a sense debited from the future, as the loss of each hectare of forest will assuredly bring us one step closer to ecological limits. And as we've seen, those limits are a scary place to be – we have established a link between ecological limits, environmental collapse and social unrest. You don't want to end up in a highly unstable situation in which it will be harder to preserve your financial freedom and your quality of life. So think about the long tail of consequences of your investment decisions. You're not just doing it for the Earth or society or humankind, you're doing it for yourself.

# Enjoy Your Freedom

*"In the truest sense, freedom cannot be bestowed; it must be achieved."*

— FRANKLIN ROOSEVELT

## The great disconnect

I devoted the longest chapter in the book (chapter 10) to the finite nature of our natural world. Because our planet is finite it imposes constraints on how much we can alter it. I quoted from economists and strategists who believe that our economic growth, as we have known it since the Industrial Revolution, cannot continue due to these constraints, these limits. Today I agree with that. I have come to that conclusion from my experience as a worker, an investor and as a citizen economist. In chapter 11 I gave you some suggestions regarding what you can do as an investor, in view of these limits.

But, you may still wonder, why hasn't the rest of the world realised this yet? As I have mentioned, most analysts and investors don't consider environmental constraints as an economic factor at all. DBS's chief investment officer Lim Say Boon wrote in the *Straits Times* in January 2016: "There are many complex factors behind the sluggishness of the world economy, post-global financial crisis. Among them, high levels of indebtedness, over-investment in commodities, developed economies' unwillingness to endure the pain of structural reforms, China's reluctance to destroy excess industrial capacity, low global productivity rates and ageing demographics. None of these will be solved by printing more cheap money and racking up more debts."[1]

All this is so true. But as usual there is no mention of the environment. Lim's approach is typical in the world of economics and finance. Yet the environment really is the missing piece in the puzzle; without it you cannot see the whole picture of our economy. The true situation is that we have exhausted the carrying capacity of the Earth.

There is indeed a disconnect here. It is the disconnect between those who realise that our Earth is crashing and those who run our economy. In late 2014 I attended a presentation in Singapore by Dr Marco Lambertini; at that time he had just been appointed Director General of WWF International. The hall was full of influential people from the government, academia and green NGOs. Dr Lambertini made the point that there are two areas in which Singapore, as a sovereign nation with a first-class reputation around the world, can make significant contributions to a more sustainable world economy: (1) as a financial centre channelling capital into green projects, and (2) as a shopping destination encouraging responsible consumption. Everyone in the room nodded and applauded this.

The funny thing is, I had just come from an even bigger event where financial investment advisers spoke to a hall full of retail investors. The message there was not to save the Earth; the issue there was how to make money. Including how to spot investment opportunities in the armament industry, as the world was becoming a more violent place, and so arms manufacturers provided great returns, etc. And responsible shopping? It is just not happening. In Singapore, shoppers don't even bring their own bags to the store, they don't source for fair-trade items, they look for the lowest prices and the most prestigious products. The disconnect between the two meetings, between lofty words and the reality, was glaring. We need to get across this disjuncture.

As an investor, what is important for you to understand is that we have reached the end of economic growth, i.e. of growth that improves our welfare. Much of what goes on in the economy today is uneconomic growth. Some developer might tear down a perfectly good residential building that is just a little more than 10 years old in something called an "en-bloc sale". A new, taller building is put in its place. It all looks like growth, but the people living in the new smaller and more expensive units are actually not better off, they are worse off. GDP is up, but GPI is down.

As we have established, drawing from experts' opinions, we are in a deflationary period caused by over-capacity and lack of demand. We are simply too many people on Earth making lots and lots of stuff that no one needs. We are drowning in man-made things and waste and fumes and garbage. The deflation and the stagnation is just a symptom of that. Yet central banks don't want to accept that. They say we need to get "back to growth", and they try to generate inflation by expanding the money supply furiously. Consumers should be rejoicing over the lower prices, but instead surveys establish again and again that they only feel worse off! You cannot understand these disconnects unless you accept that we have come to the limits of our growth due to overpopulation and a deteriorating natural environment.

## How do you cope?

That is why it is imperative that you build up financial muscle to withstand the end of welfare-generating economic growth. I showed you how to do that by controlling your spending. I also showed you how to manage the savings you accumulate with a balanced portfolio. Forget the daily and weekly and monthly chatter generated by the financial experts. Take the long view. Look at chapter 9 again and position yourself for the long haul.

Have you watched the programme "Doomsday Preppers" on National Geographic Channel? If you haven't, catch it on YouTube, it is quite entertaining. The show is about ordinary Americans who prepare themselves for the end of the world, or at least nuclear war, magnetic pole shift or some other sudden and catastrophic event that will cause calamity and social unrest. I am not so sure about the pole shift hypothesis, but I do urge you to become a "financial doomsday prepper". So don't go out and fill your bunker with guns, ammo and canned food, but stock up on plenty of safe financial assets for when the storm comes.

There are outfits out there which promise you that if you just invest like Warren Buffett you will be a millionaire in no time. They advertise in the newspapers and on financial websites; they charge thousands of dollars for a two-day seminar. But it is not that simple. Warren Buffett lost 11% of his wealth during 2015, and so did many of his faithful followers. Times are tough, and you have to be patient. Don't quit your day job till you are good and ready.

The bad news is that the end of growth does not provide you with exceptional investment opportunities as such. The future green economy cannot be completely market-driven – we saw Jørgen Randers drive that point home. It will have to rely on government manipulation and subsidies. In practice, this makes investments in things like clean energy difficult to evaluate and predict.

The good news is that there will be opportunities. Vestas Wind Systems A/S is listed on the Copenhagen Stock Exchange, and if you feel that wind turbines are the future for us, you might consider the stock. Look at the chart of its share price over the last five years (Fig. 18). Quite amazing, right? And notice that the scale is logarithmic; a linear Y-axis would show even steeper slopes! You buy at 40 and sell at 400 a few years later. But what a rollercoaster too. You need good nerves for something like this, and make sure

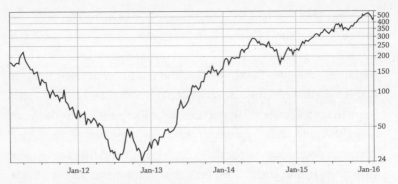

**Fig. 18: Vestas Wind Systems recent share price (DKK)**

that 90% of your funds are always securely placed in other more dependable financial products.

What else? No, don't buy oil futures. Commodities are just stuff that don't work and don't generate value. Remember that real wealth can only come from work, from the input of capital as well as labour and productivity. Among commodities only consider gold. Marc Faber is on record saying that he keeps 25% of his assets in gold, not to generate returns but to protect against future economic calamities. In general, buy into good companies that will benefit from the nature of our economy in the future. I agree with Richard Heinberg, quoted in chapter 10, when he says that the end of growth will not mean the end of human development.

We covered the first two Industrial Revolutions in previous chapters. The first was based on steam generated by the power of wood and coal, the second was based on petroleum and petroleum converted into electricity. As I mentioned before, politicians and business head honchos all have to be optimistic and put a positive spin on things; if they don't they will get fired. So you might have heard them enthusiastically talk about the fourth Industrial Revolution. In case you missed the third, that was presumably the digital developments from the 1970s and to this day. The fourth, so the optimists assert, will revolutionise industrial production and leisure time with robotics, artificial intelligence and unlimited connectivity.

It might sound like a load of hogwash, but try to keep an open mind. There will be a few big winners, but also many losers among companies involved in this; if you are not sure which are which, you should look at buying a technology-based ETF rather than try to pick individual companies in this space. Undoubtedly there will be opportunities in the future economy. There is a tremendous need for infrastructure developments in Asia, as well as on other continents. Put your capital to work here and you might be doing well for a while.

Just don't forget about the limits – they will be coming home to roost. Get a copy of *Limits to Growth* and study it carefully. This century will be crunch time. The end is near – not the end of the world, but the end of growth. See how industrial production, food production and then shortly after that life expectancy, population numbers and the human welfare index drop off. It will be the "new normal". Just make sure you are ready for it.

Have you noticed how the public debate has shifted in recent years regarding environmental problems? We used to discuss solutions; now a gradual realisation is setting in, that there aren't any of those. The UN Climate Change Conference, COP 21, in Paris in 2015 confirmed this. The new key words are "resilience" and "adaptation". Global warming is coming, and it cannot be stopped now, so nations prepare by developing flexible responses and by adapting. In Singapore the Marina Barrage is already in place to protect the downtown area from future flooding and we are in the process of raising Changi Coast Road and Nicoll Drive by a metre or so. So develop your own resilience. Build a financial barrage to protect your wealth.

And remember the old saying: Money isn't everything. There will be times when your investments go south and you cannot see the point of what you are doing. Then it is important to have other interests, other values that can cheer you up. From what I see, having a lot of money doesn't always make you happy. I have heard of rich people who took an overdose of pills or put a gun to their head because they weren't happy, in spite of their wealth and success. However, not enough money can definitely make you very unhappy. The logical solution to that is to have enough money, and then find another way to be happy. My way is to be productive, and then occasionally stretch out with a long walk in the woods. Find yours.

## By the way, what happened to me?

So if you recall from the first chapter of the book, I was 33 years old when I retired. That was in 1986. I didn't really know what I wanted to do; I just knew that I was finished with the oil business. I was married but with no kids. I didn't have to work – my bond holdings provided me with a steady income. That summer, I watched all the FIFA World Cup matches – Diego Maradona and Argentina won that year – but after that television got a bit boring. I picked up an old hobby from my school days and started photographing birds. There were few other people doing that at the time in the region, just two in Singapore, one in Malaysia and one in Indonesia. Today there are thousands of wildlife photographers in Southeast Asia, many of them much better than I ever was.

I always believed that our natural environment is important, and I felt that if I could show the biodiversity out there to people, they would start to be grateful for it and develop an urge to protect and conserve it. There is a lot more awareness about nature in Southeast Asia now than there was then. But that interest hasn't translated into conservation. In fact, the opposite happened. We have a lot less rainforest and mangroves and wild places now than we did 30 years ago. So in that regard I failed. We didn't manage to steer the concern and the appreciation for the natural world into concrete action to defend it and grow it. It shrank instead.

One of my first field projects as a wildlife photographer was travelling to Bali to survey the Bali Myna (*Leucopsar rothschildi*), found only on that island, and there only on the Prapat Agung peninsula inside the Bali Barat National Park. I went there several times in 1986 and 1987, and with special permission I walked all across the peninsula to study and count the birds. I had a couple of Indonesian rangers with me as escort. That part of Bali must be one of the most beautiful places on Earth. There was no plastic on the beaches in those days, just snow-white sand. The monsoon savannah forests in the hills behind were pristine, lush and wet in December, dry and open in June. The rangers with me worked for the Ministry of Environment and Forestry; they were well taken care of and there were lots of training and promotion opportunities available to them at the time. They were paid to be here, in this Garden of Eden. To me, those young guys had the best job in the world. One evening one of them asked me: "When you go back to Singapore, can I come with you and work as your driver?" I knew then that there was no hope. We could do everyting in our power to inform and campaign about conserving nature. What people really want is to be in a city and drive through the traffic jams all day long for a living – that is Heaven to them.

In Indonesia there are about 5,000 active birdwatchers. This is according to an old ecologist friend of mine, Colin Trainor, who was based in the country for many years. Let's presume that is correct. In the country as a whole, there are some 250 million people. Now imagine a football stadium packed to capacity with 100,000 people, something like Wembley Stadium in London on a good day. The bird team is playing against developers. Two guys will be supporting nature; the other 99,998 spectators will be enthusiastically cheering on the bulldozers. That's what is happening in the world today.

My life after retirement held some surprises. In 1993, after my first three kids were born, I ended up back in Denmark. But that didn't work out for me, and my wife and I divorced in 1999. It was tough on the kids, but it was the best thing that ever happened to me. I was 46 years old and broke; I left everything there and travelled back to Singapore with 20 kg of luggage – that was all I had. I got a chance to work for the woman who is now my wife, Ng Bee Choo, and although I don't like to be in debt, I am indebted to her for everything that happened after that. In 2002 our first and my fourth child, Mark, was born.

My interest in nature, birds, photography and the environment took me into the book business. I wrote a few and sold many more as marketing manager for my wife's company, Nature's Niche Pte Ltd. I took my last photograph in 2009 and sold off all my analog SLR equipment shortly after that – two duffel bags full of cameras and lenses and accessories. I think we have enough bird pictures by now, don't you? Search Google Images and you will see what I mean.

Instead I picked up my old interest in finance and economics. Partly because I like it – and that's a pretty good reason to me – but also partly because I wanted to understand how economics and environmental issues are linked. I did my last bird book in 2013 (*Hornbills of the World*) and closed my publishing company, Draco Publishing and Distribution Pte Ltd, shortly after that. In the meantime I studied to qualify as a financial fund manager and adviser. I passed the tests required in 2013 and 2014; as mentioned in chapter 4, they are prepared by the IBF (Institute of Banking and Finance) and approved by MAS. I took CMFAS modules 3, 5, 6 and 6A. It was a great experience. What a well organised and professional operation the IBF runs. You get your results on your way out of the examination room!

## Plan for your liberty

So now I am retired again. But I also think that retirement is overrated. Who wants to sit on his butt all day long and watch television or YouTube? That's no life. The American baby boomers (those born around 1946–64) put it this way: "Retired? Hey, I ain't even tired yet!" I'm glad I found that out very early in life. So forget retired. Financially independent, however, that's a goal worth aiming for. David Kuo, whom I mentioned earlier, has a term I like: salary independent.

You want to be in a position where you are not desperately living from paycheck to paycheck. I know that can be hard if you don't make much. The **r > g** phenomenon will work against you – we talked about that in chapter 10 – but you can help yourself if you follow the steps covered in chapter 1. "When prosperity comes, do not use all of it." Those are not my words; Confucius said that sometime around 500 BC! And 600 years later, Cicero had the same bright idea: "Cannot people realise how large an income is thrift?" At least accumulate some "I quit" money, invest it and gradually build a nest-egg up from that; make sure you know how to hold on to it and make it grow. Stay with a modest lifestyle, even when you don't have to any longer. Consider what Pablo Picasso said: "I'd like to live as a poor man with lots of money." That is exactly what he did.

This advice works best in a low-tax environment, where you are allowed to manage your own money. If we take the case of Singapore, the total tax burden is 16% of GDP, as calculated by the OECD; in Denmark it is 49%. A high-tax environment is typically expensive to run, and it siphons money away from the productive section of the economy. In Singapore, the low tax burden has enabled real median household income in Singapore to increase by 39% from 2005 to 2015; in the US the number dropped by 5% during the same period. It was +37% versus –8% respectively after allowing for taxes and transfers.

In a low-tax economy, inequality will of course be higher. Looking at Singapore versus Denmark again, the Gini coefficient is 0.44 and 0.43 for the two nations respectively – not much difference, right? But it is 0.37 versus 0.25 after taxes and transfers (a lower ratio means more equal income distribution). But then social mobility is low for Denmark, with only 11.7% of children born to parents in the bottom 20% of income reaching the top 20% of income during this survey; in Singapore it was 14.3%.[2]

You can discuss the benefits and drawbacks of taxation all night long; I will not go into it here. I will just point out that in the Western world, taxes have increased tremendously together with the stagnation and the financialisation of the economy that started with the debt culture in the late 1970s. When I was a kid, we had no retail sales taxes in Denmark. The first came in at 9% in 1967. Today the rate is 25%, and altogether the state will take from you about half of what you make. It all makes it a bit harder to be free.

## Pensions and annuities

The relevance regarding your retirement is that in a welfare state you are taxed hard on your income while you work; the state keeps the money and then gives you some pocket money when you are old. In Europe it is called an old age pension; in America, a bit confusingly, social security.

These countries might also have company-based pension schemes – it is pretty big in some countries like America and Germany. This doesn't work at all, in my opinion. I was deducted some pension money years ago when I worked for American companies. I have no idea where that money is now that I near "retirement age". The companies I worked for then were bought up by others long ago and no longer exist! This type of pension makes no sense.

In Singapore, CPF is a funded pension system covering all citizens and permanent residents. Like in the West, you are taxed on your income when you work, but instead of paying concurrently to other people's pensions, you get your own account. Your money stays your money, and what you pay in is what you get out, plus a bit of interest, as we discussed earlier. Should you move out of the country, you get all your money back immediately, right then and there!

This is the most obvious way of managing national retirement benefits. It is a simple and yet ingenious arrangement, and it really works. It is fair and transparent and cheap to run. Why in the world other much older and more established developed democracies cannot work this out is a puzzle to me. In most developed countries, savers are penalised with high taxes on income as well as on dividends from investments. It makes managing your own money very hard. For the individual it makes self-financed retirement difficult; for the national economy it generates an unseen time bomb of future liabilities from unfunded entitlement plans.

So, if you live in a low-tax society, you are lucky. Your freedom is just around the corner. If you live in a country with high taxes, you may have to wait a bit longer. If you don't trust yourself to manage your retirement funds, you can consider buying an annuity. In fact, although I previously advised you not to work with insurance companies, this is one product that I think you should consider. That is because with an annuity you bet on yourself, not against. The longer you live, the more your counterparty – the insurance agency – has to fork out.

So cover yourself by putting not all, but some of your capital into a secure annuity. In Singapore you are lucky (again!), the state will arrange an annuity for you, so you don't have to feed the insurance giants. When you reach the age of 55, CPF deducts money from your Special and Ordinary accounts under the CPF Life scheme. The amount will depend on the sum you have in your accounts, but I would advise you to top up your Special Account well in advance to make sure you get the full benefit of this excellent scheme. Then when you reach 65 years of age, CPF Life will start to make regular monthly payments, the size of which will depend on the money you deposited of course, as well as prevailing conditions at that time. The payments are for life.

If you don't live in Singapore, you have to go onto the private insurance market to buy a similar annuity. The concept is the same. You pay in a lump sum to an insurance company; they will then guarantee you monthly payments for life once you reach the agreed age. It will most likely be a bit more expensive than if you invest yourself, but I would still advise it. You should definitely be able to get a better return on the rest of your nest-egg that you invest yourself, but just so as to cover even the most unlikely scenarios, like your super-safe well-diversified portfolio crashing, an annuity plan lets you sleep better at night.

In welfare states, children are not expected to take care of their parents when they grow old. In fact, many middle-aged people expect an inheritance from the old folks instead. Maybe the aged parents live in a nice house that can be sold off, or they have savings and an antique collection. A survey by HSBC published in 2015 found that among working-age people in America, nearly half expect to receive a legacy that will support them later in life. Of those who had received or expect to receive an inheritance, some 3 in 10 believe it will fully or partly fund their retirement. However, the same survey also found that the older American households, in general, seem less inclined to leave an inheritance to the next generation. Nearly a quarter of old people said they would rather spend all of their savings while they were around to enjoy it and let their children create their own wealth. Less than 1 in 10 plan to save as much money as possible to pass on to the next generation.[3] So please be aware of this discrepancy.

## When will I be free?

This is an important question. In general you will be free when you feel you have enough funds to last you till the end. And how much then is that? That will depend on your lifestyle and how much you expect you will need. Here is another formula for our little formula collection: $S = Y/R$ (or $Y = S \times R$ of course). This one is also homemade but I find it helpful. S is the savings you need when you retire. Y is your yearly required income from savings. R is the future return you expect to generate from your savings, your capital, your nest-egg if you will.

Say you want \$3,000 per month to live, then $Y = \$36,000$. You reckon you can match GIC in return and generate 6% p.a. from you super-safe portfolio. What is your S? $S = \$36,000/0.06 = \$600,000$. That is how much you need to retire safely.

Keep two things in mind. With this formula you spend all your returns; there is no reinvesting of returns. Remember, though, that the Singapore government investment agencies reinvest half of the returns they generate. This might work against you in the long haul if inflation creeps back up. But the other thing to keep in mind is that when I say "retire", I mean become salary independent. Most people at a young age would still want to stay active and work for fun, even after they drop out of the rat race; so this will work in your favour.

Don't feel bad about leaving your chosen career early. In fact, you will do the younger people in your workplace a favour; this gives them a chance to move up the ladder a bit quicker. As we saw in some of the previous chapters, with a global surplus of people there simply isn't enough work to go around. We also saw that some observers have started to question one of the myths in conventional economics, that more education is the answer to the oversupply of human capital. But if education is not the answer, what is? Personally I think that only fewer people is; and then maybe shorter working hours as well as more gap years between jobs.

A few years ago, the New Economics Foundation, a UK think tank, suggested that a reduction in working hours would help to ease unemployment and overwork. It observed that although unemployment was high, we worked longer hours than 30 years ago. Reducing the working week to 21 hours would help boost the economy and improve quality of life. The foundation admitted people would earn less, but said they would have more time to carry out worthy tasks. Anna Coote, co-author of the report, said to the BBC: "So many of us live to work, work to earn, and earn to consume, and our consumption habits are squandering the Earth's natural resources. Spending less time in paid work would help us to break this pattern. We'd have more time to be better parents, better citizens, better carers and better neighbours – less stressed, more in control, happier in our jobs and more productive."[4]

Once you are salary independent, step aside and let others do the daily grind. Once you don't work nine to five, you will find that you need less. It is expensive to commute, to always wear new clothes; you are under pressure to entertain and constantly upgrade to the latest most expensive digital gadgets. Your health probably suffers from stress and lack of sleep and exercise. With more time on your hands, you can fix all that and save more. You can travel anytime you like, not just over Chinese New Year and Christmas when hotels and flights are all packed and much more expensive.

Don't worry too much about being able to get back into the workforce, should you want to later. The workplace is changing as well. In the future there will be more part-time work and project work available. Many people will find themselves changing jobs more often, even switching careers. Professor Arnoud De Meyer, president of Singapore Management University, says: "We need to prepare students for a longer professional life that will not be a sequence of jobs but may well be a portfolio of careers. The sort of linear progression typical in current organisations may be replaced by a life over which we have different careers, perhaps interspersed with gap years or sabbaticals."[5] Professor De Meyer does not explain how these gap years are going to be financed. I say: Make sure you have the reserves to manage, or better still, simply be salary independent.

## Keep going

Now you can work because you want to, not because you have to. And I suggest you do keep working. Stay productive. My wife for a while had a retired banker working for her in one of her shops; it was a nice place and part of the gorgeous Singapore Botanic Gardens. He made much more from his investments and the fancy properties he owned and rented out, but he worked diligently as a cashier in the shop because he got to meet interesting people and enjoyed the venue. He was one of the best employees we ever had. This is confirmed by one of these happiness surveys in Canada, which found that paid employment was the most satisfying activity for people over the age of 65.[6]

Personally I think that volunteering is overrated. Don't volunteer; ask for payment for what you do, even if it is just a nominal sum. Just because you love what you do, that doesn't mean you shouldn't get paid doing it. For instance, if you guide people around, charge for it, even if you take pleasure in it. Remember that there are other people out there trying to make a living as tour guides; don't take their livelihoods away from them.

As for consumption, we don't have to come to a total grinding halt just because we are frugal. I like this quote from George Best, the British footballer. Few people remember him now from his playing career, but he was one of the greatest ever. He said about his life: "I spent a lot of money on booze, birds and fast cars – the rest I just squandered." He could probably sympathise with Errol Flynn, who said: "My problem lies in reconciling my gross habits with my net income." We only go around once, and we should be free to enjoy it, if that is what we want, as long as we don't bother others.

Continue to invest in your own future through your consumer "vote". There are lots of fair-trade and ethical products out there. John Perkins in *Hoodwinked* (2011) says: "Paying more for products made by companies that are socially and environmentally responsible is always an investment in the future." Perkins is also not so impressed with the philanthropy of tycoons like Warren Buffett and Bill Gates. In the case of Bill Gates, Perkins says: "As a young founder and CEO (of Microsoft), Gates had a reputation for brutally beating down competitors." His company has faced hundreds of class action and antitrust lawsuits; it was fined $613 million by the European Union, the largest fine in EU regulatory history. Through unethical and sometimes illegal business practices, underpaying his workers and overcharging his customers, Gates built up enormous wealth and he is now giving it away. Perkins' response to this is: "Why not run a company that concentrates on improving social and environmental conditions through its daily operations instead? That's a lot more efficient, and ultimately more satisfying."

I mentioned Iain Ewing in chapter 1, as a case study of someone who gained financial independence and personal freedom. Before he died, Iain was content and satisfied with his life, but he confided in me that there was one thing he would have done differently in hindsight: "I wish I had been nicer to people." I thought Iain was pretty nice; but I am sure there were events in his life where his wasn't, and towards the end of it, that was his only regret. By being kind you not only make life better for others, you actually help yourself. Many studies confirm this. Dr David Hamilton wrote a book about this, *Why Kindness is Good For You*, in which he concludes: "Scientific evidence has proven that kindness changes the brain, impacts the heart and immune system, and may even be an antidote to depression." Think about that the next time someone tries to cut into your lane in traffic. Just let him – you will feel better and get a stronger immune system!

## Why this book

I was editor-in-chief of *Nature Watch* for a while, the membership magazine of the Nature Society (Singapore). I resigned in 2011; my last issue was the Jan–Mar 2012 issue. In it I wrote: "Do you know what we need today? Rational, ethical and competent *financial management*! I want to re-invent myself as an honest financial adviser – yes; I know it sounds like a contradiction in terms for most people. But you have to set your goals high and believe that you can make a difference."[7] That editorial was picked up by Marshall Cavendish and ended up in a textbook for secondary school kids. So I did make a little difference with that. And now, four years later, I am trying with this book.

So you might ask me: What makes you qualified to write a book like this? Why should I listen to you? I wish I had bought a book by Jack Welch, Jim Rogers or George Soros. Those guys are real tycoons, they made millions, surely they can teach me how to get filthy rich like them. Maybe they can, but then again maybe not. I don't think their life experience can really be applied to most ordinary working people. Mine can.

I have showed you that it is possible for virtually anyone to obtain a life of freedom. You don't need to be chairman and CEO of General Electric or own a billion-dollar hedge fund. You don't even need rich parents or a college education (although admittedly that would probably help!).

What you need is a desire to learn, and you need strong work ethics. That is a requirement, but it is not enough. Importantly you also need to develop the discipline to control your spending, and you need to know how to protect the money you save that way and how to make it grow. I have showed you step by step how to do that. I have also been honest about the mistakes I made along the way: I probably retired a bit too early, I didn't diversify my assets correctly for many years, I bought shares in companies that went bankrupt, I lost most of what I had at one stage during a messy divorce. Try to avoid all the mistakes I made and get it right the first time.

Once you are financially free and salary independent, your life will be wonderful, I can assure you of that. Financial freedom is the key to everything else. While money in itself cannot buy you happiness, it is a prerequisite for a meaningful and interesting life. With enough capital and passive income to get by, you can travel and live anywhere you want to, you can follow your heart and work with whatever you are passionate about. You can get the famous work-life balance right; you can take a job, but you don't ever again have to beg for one.

Only, there is one more important issue to consider: You cannot enjoy your freedom if the world is coming apart.

That is why I dedicated two chapters of the book to the world's ecological limits and the implications they have for your financial freedom and general well-being. I try to look at the long term; and in fact the term might not be that long after all, before the ecological limits start to close in on our economy and our finances. Virtually every other book I know of this kind totally ignores the environment. Maybe except for *Prosper!* by Martenson & Taggart (2015) – but their US-focused advice of moving to the boondocks and setting up a self-sustained solar-powered homestead on 160 acres of land might not work for many. Most other financial books simply pretend the natural world doesn't exist.

I don't know why the other financial professionals don't see this issue, why they refuse to deal with it. If you follow their get-rich-quick mantra and their unscrupulous business ethics you are in fact unwittingly planting the seeds of your own future financial grief. How can you be free and happy if you are running out of space and food and water and power and eventually money? If you are facing perpetual overcrowding in your community, shortages, economic collapse and then finally riots in the streets and mass migration? Does it sound like scare-mongering? It is the daily reality for hundreds of millions of people around the world already.

So become salary independent as soon as you can, build up financial resilience for the tough times ahead, enjoy your freedom. And remember, what you do makes a difference.

# Notes

### Chapter 1: Retire at 30?

1. www.who.int/gho/road_safety/mortality/traffic_deaths_ number/en/

2. Tan, Lorna. 2015. "Guidelines on public selling of financial products." *The Straits Times,* 24 July.

### Chapter 2: Spend Less

1. Parts of this were first published in Strange, Morten. 1998. "Spar en tusse – på 20 måder." *Readers Digest,* Copenhagen, May.

2. www.denstoredanske.dk/Kunst_og_kultur/Bog-_og_ biblioteksv%C3%A6sen/Encyklop%C3%A6dier/Den_Store_ Danske_Encyklop%C3%A6di

3. news.asiaone.com/news/singapore/more-families-hiring- two-or-more-maids

### Chapter 3: Interest in Economics

1. en.wikipedia.org/wiki/Invisible_hand

2. www.intelligencesquared.com/events/democracy-is-not-always- the-best-form-of-government/

3. www.youtube.com/watch?v=gN7wNdGL2FM

4. www.tradingeconomics.com/

5. www.mti.gov.sg/ResearchRoom/Pages/default.aspx

6. www.mti.gov.sg/ResearchRoom/Documents/app.mti.gov.sg/data/ pages/885/doc/econ.pdf

## Chapter 4: Derivatives

1. www.fintools.com/docs/Warren%20Buffet%20on%20 Derivatives.pdf

2. www.marketwatch.com/story/warren-buffetts-investing-tip

3. www.mti.gov.sg/MTIInsights/Pages/Financial-Services-Sector.aspx

4. mathworld.wolfram.com/GamblersRuin.html

5. www.thecalculatorsite.com/articles/finance/the-gamblers-fallacy.php

6. Leong, Grace. 2015. "MBS' earnings take a hit in Q2." *The Straits Times*, 24 July.

7. Boon, Rachael. 2015. "Fitness buff has his career all worked out." *The Straits Times*, 26 July.

## Chapter 5: Investing in Stuff

1. en.wikipedia.org/wiki/Rogers_International_Commodity_Index

2. en.wikipedia.org/wiki/Price_elasticity_of_demand

3. econweb.ucsd.edu/~jhamilto/understand_oil.pdf

4. www.democraticunderground.com/discuss/duboard.php?az= view_all&address=114x85928

5. www.eia.gov/forecasts/steo/report/global_oil.cfm

6. www.lta.gov.sg/content/dam/ltaweb/corp/PublicationsResearch/ files/FactsandFigures

7. www.goodreads.com/quotes/tag?id=gold&page=2&utf8=%E2 %9C%93

8. www.businessinsider.sg/why-investing-in-art-is-a-terrible-idea-2015-4/#.Vd7cWiWqqkp

9. www.nytimes.com/2007/06/20/business/worldbusiness/20iht-money.4.6234700.html?_r=2&

10. www.cnbc.com/id/49533493

## Chapter 6: Bonds and Property

1. www.brainyquote.com/quotes/quotes/w/warrenbuff409211.html

2. www.tcf.org/blog/detail/graph-how-the-financial-sector-consumed-americas-economic-growth

3. www.srx.com.sg/cooling-measures

4. en.wikipedia.org/wiki/Japanese_asset_price_bubble

5. www.moneysense.gov.sg/Understanding-Financial-Products/Investments/Types-of-Investments/Real-Estate-Investment-Trusts.aspx


## Chapter 7: Shares

1. Chong, Koh Ping. 2015. "UK ends quarterly reports – how about Singapore?" *The Straits Times*, 17 December.

2. Goh, Eng Yeow. 2015. "Why the Facebook model holds currency." *The Straits Times*, 30 November.

3. www.goodreads.com/quotes/29255-be-fearful-when-others-are-greedy-and-greedy-when-others

4. en.wikipedia.org/wiki/Microsoft_Corp_v_Commission

5. www.investopedia.com/terms/i/irrationalexuberance.asp


## Chapter 8: Getting Started

1. Wong, Wei Han. 2015. "SGX grilled by concerned shareholders at AGM." *The Straits Times*, 24 September.

2. www.investinganswers.com/financial-dictionary/technical-analysis/standard-deviation-4948

3. en.wikiquote.org/wiki/Niels_Bohr

4. www.statista.com/statistics/188165/annual-gdp-growth-of-the-united-states-since-1990/

## Chapter 9: Mix It Up

1. blogs.terrapinn.com/total-asset/2013/08/22/warren-buffett-average-person-invest-stock-market-buying-equities/

2. Goh, Eng Yeow. 2015. "ETFs a cheaper, low-risk option for stock investors." *The Straits Times*, 18 July.

3. Kung, Geoffrey. 2015. "Marketing of endowment plans needs regular review." *The Straits Times*, 8 October.

4. www.goodreads.com/quotes/76863-compound-interest-is-the-eighth-wonder-of-the-world-he

5. Wong Wei Han. 2015. "GIC posts steady returns but warns of tougher times ahead." *The Straits Times*, 30 July.

6. www.gic.com.sg/report/report-2014-2015/investment_report.html

7. dqydj.net/sp-500-return-calculator/

8. *New York Times*. 2015. "Besieged US hedge funds closing down." *The Straits Times*, 19 May.

9. Steven Rattner. 2013. "Markets irrational, thus beatable." *The Straits Times*, 24 November.

10. Heng, Janice. 2015. "Many CPF investors get their fingers burnt." *The Straits Times*, 15 June.

## Chapter 10: It's a Finite World

1. O'Keefe, Brian. 2015. "Chevron's Cheap-Oil Playbook." *Fortune*, April 1.

2. Bourne, Joel K. 2007. "Green Dreams." *National Geographic*, October.

3. *Los Angeles Times*. "Biofuels make climate change worse, say studies." *The Straits Times*, 9 February.

4. Daly, Herman E. 2005. "Economics in a Full World." *Scientific American*, September.

5. wwf.panda.org/about_our_earth/all_publications/living_planet_report/

6. news.nationalgeographic.com/news/2003/05/0515_030515_fishdecline.html

7. Jin, Keyu. 2015. "Getting the Chinese to open up their wallets." *The Straits Times*, 21 November.

8. www.investopedia.com/ask/answers/08/broken-window-fallacy.asp

9. Bloomberg. 2008. "Fed may cut interest rates to near zero." *The Straits Times*, 28 October.

10. Reuters. 2015. "Top brands vow to halve food waste." *The Straits Times*, 26 June February

11. Agence France Press. 2014. "Obesity growing into big global problem." *The Straits Times*, 30 May.

12. Agence France-Press. 2014. "Sweet talk." *The Straits Times*, 3 Dec.

13. www.unep.org/geo/geo4/report/geo-4_report_full_en.pdf

14. www.nytimes.com/2014/01/22/opinion/friedman-wikileaks-drought-and-syria.html?_r=0

15. *New York Times*. 2014. "Climate change a security threat: Pentagon." *The Straits Times*, 15 October.

16. Agence France Presse. 2015. "Barrier Reef corals eating plastic: Study." *The Straits Times*, 25 February.

17. Bloomberg. 2015. "Plastic waste dumped into ocean on Titanic scale." *The Straits Times*, 14 February.

18. en.wikipedia.org/wiki/List_of_countries_by_percentage_of_population_living_in_poverty

19. Choudhury, Ziauddin. 2015. "Bangladesh's shame in the refugee crisis." *The Straits Times*, 26 May.

20. www.facing-finance.org/en/database/cases/working-conditions-in-foxconn-factories-in-china/

21. Chuan, Toh Yong. 2013. "S'pore staff 'not engaged' at work." *The Straits Times*, 6 December.

22. Reuters. 2015. "Indonesian youth hit hardest as jobs vanish." *The Straits Times*, 22 June.

23. www.ifa.sg/cost-to-raise-a-child-in-singapore/

24. www.socialeurope.eu/2015/01/economic-stupidity/

25. Blasi, Freeman & Kruse. 2015. "Need for a more inclusive capitalism." *The Straits Times*, 20 July.

26. Mishel, Lawrence. 2015. "Wages must be key US economic focus." *The Straits Times*, 3 March.

27. Marin, Dalia. 2014. "Education in the second machine age." *The Straits Times*, 27 November.

28. Fleming, Sam & Chris Giles. 2015. "Why slowing productivity growth is acute problem worldwide." *The Straits Times*, 2 June.

29. Boon, Lim Say. 2015. "Ghosts of deflation past are back to haunt us." *The Straits Times*, 26 August.

30. www.grreporter.info/en/share_informal_economy_2012_243_gdp/7331

31. www.investopedia.com/financial-edge/1012/countries-with-the-largest-shadow-markets.aspx

32. Vaughan, Adam. 2015. "Watching videos, using apps all add to global warming." *The Straits Times*, 29 September.

33. Associated Press. 2008. "Dire warnings as electronics waste piles up." *The Straits Times*, 27 June.

34. Lim, Teresa. 2012. "Britain's capital of misery." *The Straits Times*, 10 March.

35. Fernandez, Warren. 2008. "Asia's dilemma: Go green or pursue growth." *The Straits Times*, 26 January.

36. www.iea.org/publications/freepublications/publication/WEO2015_SouthEastAsia.pdf

**Chapter 11: So What Can I Do?**

1. Agence France-Presse. 2015. "UN makes record $28b aid appeal." *The Straits Times*, 8 December.

2. Friedman, Thomas. 2015. "Hillary, Jeb and the new world of disorder." *The Straits Times*, 27 May.

3. en.wikipedia.org/wiki/Swedish_emigration_to_the_United_States

4. Reuters. 2007. "Africa aid 'swallowed up by armed conflict'." *The Straits Times*, 12 October.

5. Au Yong, Jeremy. 2015. "Obama urges China, Russia to pursue diplomatic solutions." *The Straits Times*, 29 September.

6. AFP. 2015. "Scientists warn of major threat to human health." *The Straits Times*, 17 July.

7. Quah, Euston & Nicolas Neo. 2015. "Look beyond market value in preserving green spaces." *The Straits Times*, 16 May.

8. www.ugandawildlife.org/news-a-updates-2

9. Project Syndicate. 2015. "Rise of the frugal economy." *The Straits Times*, 14 February.

10. Mahbubani, Kishore. 2015. "The road to a car-less Singapore." *The Straits Times*, 12 December.

11. AFP. 2015. "Sugary drinks 'kill 184,000 people a year'." *The Straits Times*, 1 July.

12. Reuters. 2015. "Buffett marks 50 years at Berkshire with 5-hour dialogue." *The Straits Times*, 4 May.

13. Reuters. 2013. "F&B, alcohol firms 'undermine health policies'." *The Straits Times*, 13 February.

14. From, Lars & Michael Bækgaard. 2009. "Elbiler forurener mere end andre biler." *Jyllandsposten*, 29 August.

15. www.bbc.co.uk/news/business-19830232, 4 October 2012.

16. *New York Times*. 2015. "How recycling is wasteful." *The Straits Times*, 11 October.

17. responsiblebusiness.haas.berkeley.edu/programs/sustainablefinance.html.

18. Goh, Eng Yeow. 2015. "'Sin' stocks make good buys." *The Straits Times*, 23 February.

19. www.csrhub.com

20. www.ussif.org/sribasics

21. Goh, Eng Yeow. 2015. "'Sin' stocks make good buys." *The Straits Times*, 23 February.

22. *New York Times*. 2014. "Heirs to oil fortune join drive to divest from fossil fuels." *The Straits Times*, 23 September.

23. Bloomberg. 2015. "Norway's sovereign wealth fund turns its back on coal." *The Straits Times*, 2 June.

24. Lee, Su Shyan. 2015. "Temasek building icons to pay it forward." *The Straits Times*, 20 January.

25. www.wwf.sg/?246790/WWF-ASEAN-regional-banks-and-investors-behind-on-Environmental-Social-and-Governance-standards

26. Yahya, Yasmine. 2015. "Good credit rating, but did you pollute the earth?" *The Straits Times*, 4 November.

## Chapter 12: Enjoy Your Freedom

1. Lim, Say Boon. 2016. "Markets are staring at a failure of policy." *The Straits Times*, 27 January.

2. Shanmugaratnam, Tharman. 2015. "Uniquely Singapore story: Broad-based social uplifting." *The Straits Times*, 17 August.

3. www.cnbc.com/2015/05/04/retirement-plan-workaround-inherit-enough-to-live-on.html

4. news.bbc.co.uk/go/pr/fr/-/2/hi/business/8513783.stm

5. De Meyer, Arnoud. 2015. "The jobs – they are a-changing." *The Straits Times*, 9 November.

6. Mulgan, Geoff. 2015. "Happiness by design." *The Straits Times*, 28 November.

7. Strange, Morten. 2012. "Reflections on Making a Difference." *Nature Watch*, Volume 20 No 1, Jan–Mar.

8. en.wikipedia.org/wiki/World_Wide_Fund_for_Nature

# Glossary

Accredited investor: In Singapore this is a legal term defined by the MAS as an investor with more than S$2 million to invest or an annual income of over S$300,000.

Aggregate: The collective whole formed by several different parts. Aggregate demand is all the demand across the whole of the economy.

AGM: Annual general meeting.

Arbitrage: Making a risk-free profit by buying low in one market and simultaneously selling the same product high in another.

ASEAN: The Association of Southeast Asian Nations, an economic and political organisation of 10 nations in that region.

Bloomberg Television: An American 24-hour financial cable TV channel reaching more than 300 million homes worldwide.

Bretton Woods: A village in New Hampshire, USA, that was the venue for meetings in 1944 that led to a new system of monetary policies, exchange rate mechanisms and international financial institutions.

Cash: This is of course banknotes and coins; but in investments it is used synonymously with cash equivalents such as liquid bank deposits and short-term government bonds.

CDP: Central Depository Pte Ltd; a subsidiary of SGX where shares are deposited electronically.

CEO: Chief Executive Officer; the most senior executive in a private corporation; he or she reports to the board of directors.

CNBC: An American 24-hour cable TV channel covering financial news and competing neck-and-neck with Bloomberg Television.

Contrarian investors: Investors that make a point of going against the prevailing trends and what they see as herd mentality; Marc Faber, Peter Schiff and Jim Rogers come to mind.

CPF: Central Provident Fund; a compulsory social security savings scheme for Singaporean citizens and permanent residents.

CPFIS: CPF Investment Scheme; allows CPF members to invest their funds in selected products approved by the CPF Board.

CPI: Consumer Price Index; a measure of inflation rates; core inflation is the CPI basket of consumer goods stripped of food and energy items.

EROI: Sometimes EROEI; energy returned on energy invested, the ratio of how many units of energy are recovered for each one used up to achieve the result.

ETF: exchange traded fund; a type of mutual fund that tracks an index or asset class, but usually with lower cost and better liquidity.

Fiat currency: "Paper" money decreed by government regulation, without base in a commodity such as gold.

Fiscal policy: Government policy to regulate public taxation and spending levels in order to promote economic growth and welfare.

GDP: Gross Domestic Product; a measurement of the total output in the national economy.

GIC: The Government of Singapore Investment Corporation Pte Ltd; the sovereign wealth fund of Singapore investing most of the country's public savings and pensions funds.

Gini coefficient: A measure of a country's income inequality; the higher the ratio, the more unequal the income distribution within that population; 0.5 and above is considered high, below 0.3 is low.

GNP: Gross National Product; similar to GDP but measures the output of citizens (only) from a given country, whether based at home or abroad.

GST: Goods and Services Tax; this is the term used for the sales tax or value-added consumption tax in Singapore (currently 7%).

HDB: Housing & Development Board; Singapore's public housing authority.

Hedge fund: A mutual fund that uses derivatives to enhance risk as well as return; large initial investment can be difficult to redeem.

IRAS: Inland Revenue Authority of Singapore; the tax department.

iShares: A range of ETFs managed by BlackRock, the world's largest asset manager.

Laissez-faire: A free market economic system with no state intervention in the form of regulations or subsidies.

Macroeconomics: Economics dealing with the larger national and international concepts such as national income, trade, employment, savings and interest rates.

MAS: Monetary Authority of Singapore. The central bank of Singapore; conducts monetary policy, issues currency, supervises banks and manages the official foreign reserves in order to promote sustained non-inflationary economic growth.

Microeconomics: Economics dealing with businesses and consumers, supply and demand, and price formation.

Mixed economy: An economic system that mixes free market capitalism with some state intervention to regulate markets and reduce inequality.

Monetary policy: The policy of central banks to control the money supply and interest rates in order to promote growth and full employment in the economy.

MRT: Mass Rapid Transit; commuter train system of Singapore.

MSCI: Morgan Stanley Capital International (MSCI Inc); a New York-based provider of stock market indexes and other financial analysis tools.

Mutual fund: A fund of pooled investments actively managed by professional managers according to the terms set out in a prospectus.

NASDAQ: Second only to the NYSE as the largest stock exchange in the world; based in New York; many technology companies list here.

NATO: The North Atlantic Treaty Organization; a military alliance comprising most Western European countries as well as USA, Canada and Turkey.

NAV: Net Asset Value; the value of all assets minus liabilities in a mutual fund. Divide this by number of shares to get NAV per share.

NGO: Non-Governmental Organisation; a non-profit organisation set up and funded by ordinary citizens.

NYSE: New York Stock Exchange; the big board of American listed companies and by far the largest exchange in the world by capitalisation.

OECD: Organisation for Economic Co-operation and Development.

OTC: Over-the-counter; a financial deal done between two parties directly, without the use of an exchange.

p.a.: Per annum; usually used for interest or yield paid or calculated over one year.

PCE: Personal Consumption Expenditures price index; a measure of inflation mainly used in the United States.

QE: Quantitative easing; the policy of central banks to buy government bonds and thereby expand the money supply, i.e. to "print money".

S&P 500: An index tracking 500 major companies listed on the NYSE as well as NASDAQ; considered the best indicator of the performance of American listed companies.

SGX: Singapore Exchange Ltd; a listed company in Singapore functioning as an exchange for stocks, bonds, derivatives and other securities products.

SPDR funds: Standard & Poor's Depositary Receipts, pronounced "spider"; a range of ETFs managed by State Street Global Advisors.

STI: Straits Times Index; the benchmark index for Singapore's stock market; tracks 30 large-capitalisation component stocks as calculated by Singapore Press Holdings, SGX and FTSE Group.

Tea Party: An informal group of conservative American Republican Party supporters promoting a libertarian agenda of lower taxes and less state intervention.

Temasek: Often used in short form for Temasek Holdings Pte Ltd; an investment company wholly owned by the Singapore government and regarded as a national wealth fund.

WWF: World Wide Fund for Nature; an international NGO working for biodiversity conservation and the reduction of humanity's footprint on the environment.

# Persons referred to

Abbey, Edward P. 1927–1989. American writer end environmentalist.

Attenborough, David F. Born 1926. English broadcaster and writer; famous for his work with the BBC Natural History Unit.

Ban, Ki-moon. Born 1944. South Korean diplomat and politician; currently secretary-general of the United Nations.

Best, George. 1946–2005. British footballer playing for Manchester United and the Northern Ireland national team; great player to watch in his prime but struggled with alcoholism in later years.

Browne, John P. E. Born 1948. Also Baron Browne of Madingley. British businessman and author; CEO of BP 1995–2007.

Buffett, Warren E. Born 1930. American investor and philanthropist; the guru and inspiration to countless other value investors.

Bush, George H.W. Born 1924. 41st President of the United States (Republican) 1989–1993.

Bush, George W. Born 1946. 43rd President of the United States (Republican) 2001–2009.

Camus, Albert. 1913–1960. French philosopher and writer associated with absurdist and existentialist thinking.

Ceausescu, Nicolae. 1918–1989. Romanian politician; General-Secretary of the Communist Party and head of state 1967–1989.

Churchill, Winston. 1874–1965. British politician; he served as Prime Minister 1940–1945 and again 1951–1955.

Cicero, Marcus T. 106–43 BC. Influential Roman speaker, writer, philosopher and politician serving during the end of the Roman Republic.

Clooney, George T. Born 1961. American actor and movie producer.

Cobb, John B. Born 1925. American environmentalist, philosopher and writer; collaborated with Herman Daly to explore ecological economics.

Columbus, Christopher. c1451-1506. Italian explorer working for Spain who discovered the Americas.

Confucius. 551–479 BC. Chinese philosopher and teacher; he emphasised family loyalty, honesty and justice in personal and public affairs.

Correa, Rafael. Born 1963. Ecuadorian economist and politician; since 2007 president of the country.

Daly, Herman E. Born 1938. American economist, professor at the University of Maryland specialising in ecological economics.

Einstein, Albert. 1879–1955. German-born physicist and philosopher; best known for developing the general theory of relativity.

Emmott, Stephen J. Born 1960. British computer scientist and environmentalist; professor at Microsoft Research, University College London and Oxford University.

Faber, Marc. Born 1946. Hong Kong-based Swiss investor, financial analyst and media commentator; director of Marc Faber Ltd, which publishes the *Gloom, Doom and Boom Report* newsletter.

Fargo, Donna. Born 1945. Born Yvonne Vaughan. American country music singer and song-writer.

Farley, Warren. Australian oil field executive who arranged for me to move to Singapore in 1980. Thank you, Warren!

Fisher, Philip A. 1907–2004. American stock investor and best-selling author.

Flynn, Errol L. T. 1909–1959. Australian-born actor; became an American and starred in Hollywood movies in the 1930s and 40s.

Franklin, Benjamin. 1706–1790. American writer, scientist, politician and statesman; one of the founding fathers of the United States.

Friedman, Milton. 1912–2006. American economist; taught at University of Chicago; free-market advocate and adviser to conservative politicians like Ronald Reagan and Margaret Thatcher.

Friedman, Thomas L. Born 1953. American journalist and author; currently with the *New York Times*; three-times winner of the Pulitzer Prize.

Galbraith, John K. 1908–2006. Canadian-American economist; one of the most influential academics and economic policy advisers during the 20th century with a strong liberal bias.

Gandhi, Mahatma. 1869–1948. Indian political leader; he advocated non-violence to free India from British colonial rule.

Gates, William H. Born 1955. Bill Gates is the American co-founder of Microsoft and one of the world's richest people.

Conant, James B. 1893–1978. American scientist, academic and diplomat; President of Harvard University 1933–1953.

Gore, Albert A. Born 1948. American politician and environmentalist; served as Vice President from 1993 to 2001.

Grantham, Jeremy. Born 1938. British American-based investor and fund manager; an expert in analysing "bubbles" in the economy and the environment.

Greenspan, Alan. Born 1926. American economist; chairman of the Federal Reserve from 1987 to 2006.

Heinberg, Richard. Born 1950. American journalist, author and senior fellow at the Post Carbon Institute.

Henriksen, Henrik L. 1896–1987. Danish schoolmaster and passionate Danish nationalist who promoted conservative democratic values in the German/Danish border region; and also my grandfather.

Hubbard, Frank M. 1868–1930. American writer, humorist and illustrator.

Jackson, Alan E. Born 1958. American country music singer-songwriter.

Jackson, Tim. Born 1957. British economist and professor of sustainable development with the University of Surrey.

Johnson, Stacy. American financial author and TV journalist, known for the *Money Talks* show.

Kennedy, John F. 1917–1963. 35th President of the United States (Democrat) 1961–1963; assassinated 22nd November.

Kennedy, Robert F. 1925–1968. American politician (Democrat); member of the Senate; leading candidate for president in the 1968 election when he was assassinated.

Keynes, John Maynard. 1883–1946. British economist; his work forms the basis for Keynesian economics, which favours state intervention to moderate macroeconomic cycles.

King, Martin L. 1929–1968. American Christian minister and civil rights leader for the black community.

Kiyosaki, Robert T. Born 1947. American investor, motivational speaker and author, famous for his *Rich Dad Poor Dad* books.

Krugman, Paul R. Born 1953. American economist, writer and commentator with liberal Keynesian views; professor at Princeton University.

Kuo, David. Born 1956. British financial analyst and commentator with the Motley Fool financial services group.

Lambertini, Marco. Born 1958. Italian scientist, author and nature conservationist; since 2014 Director General of WWF.

Larson, Doug. Born 1926. American journalist and editor.

Lee, Hsien Loong. Born 1952. Singaporean politician; since 2004 and currently serving as 3rd Prime Minister.

Mahbubani, Kishore. Born 1948. Singaporean former diplomat; currently Dean of the LKY School of Public Policy, National University of Singapore.

Malthus, Thomas J. 1766–1834. English cleric and economist; predicted that overpopulation would lead to economic and social collapse, somewhat prematurely as it turned out.

Maradona, Diego. Born 1960. Argentinian footballer and one of the all-time greatest; played for his country in four FIFA World Cups.

Marx, Karl. 1818–1883. Born in Germany but worked out of Paris and London. Economist, philosopher and writer; the founder of Marxism and co-founder of Communism.

Matthews, Andrew. Born 1957. Australian self-help writer, illustrator and public speaker.

Meadows, Dennis L. Born 1942. American environmental scientist and writer; currently professor at the University of New Hampshire.

Meadows, Donella H. 1941–2001. American environmental scientist; co-author with her husband Dennis and Jørgen Randers of *The Limits to Growth*.

Monet, Oscar-Claude. 1840–1926. French impressionist painter.

Morrison, Toni. Born 1931. American academic and award-winning author.

Ng, Bee Choo. Born 1965. Singaporean naturalist and nature-related businesswoman; former mechanical engineer; also my wife since 2002.

Orwell, George. 1903–1950. Born Eric Arthur Blair; English novelist; author of *Animal Farm* (1945).

Pascal, Blaise. 1623–1662. French mathematician, physicist, philosopher and writer.

Paycheck, Johnny. 1938–2003. Born Donald E. Lytle. American country music singer.

Perkins, John. Born 1945. American economist; former corporate consultant, now writer and speaker campaigning against the ills of exploitive capitalism.

Picasso, Pablo. 1881–1973. Spanish painter and sculptor; lived and worked most of his life in France.

Ponzi, Charles. 1882–1949. Italian-born businessman based in the U.S.; gave name to the financial swindle scheme where you pay investors huge "dividends" with money from new investors, until the money flow stops and the investors lose their deposits.

Porter, Michael E. Born 1947. American professor with the Harvard Business School; known for his work on competitive forces and strategies within businesses and nations.

Randers, Jørgen. Born 1945. Norwegian environmentalist and writer; currently professor of climate change at BI Norwegian Business School.

Rankin, Eddie. American oil field inventor and executive, and my boss 1977–1979. The best boss a young man could have.

Reagan, Ronald W. 1911–2004. 40th President of the United States (Republican) 1981–1989.

Ricardo, David. 1772–1823. British economist of the classical school; his work on comparative advantage among nations forms the theoretical foundation for free trade.

Rivkin, Rene W. 1944–2005. Australian stockbroker and investment adviser.

Rogers, James B. ("Jim"). Born 1942. American, Singapore-based, investor and author with a libertarian and contrarian outlook.

Roosevelt, Franklin D. 1882–1945. 32nd President of the United States (Democrat) 1933–1945.

Russell, Bertrand A.W. 1872–1970. British aristocrat, logician, humanitarian philosopher and writer.

Samuelson, Paul A. 1915–2009. American Nobel Prize-winning economist and author of the best-selling book on economics of all time.

Santelli, Rick. Former financial futures trader; now financial journalist with CNBC television promoting a libertarian free-market agenda.

Sassen, Saskia. Born 1949. Dutch-American sociologist and professor at Colombia University.

Schiff, Peter D. Born 1963. American businessman, financial analyst and commentator with a contrarian outlook.

Scully, Frank. 1892–1964. American journalist, humorist and author.

Sendak, Maurice. 1928–2012. American writer and illustrator; best known for his children's books.

Seow, Ashleigh. Born 1956. Australian, Singapore-born, Malaysia-based naturalist; works for the MYCAT conservation alliance.

Shanmugaratnam, Tharman. Born 1957. Singaporean politician; currently Deputy Prime Minister and Chairman of MAS.

Singal, Saurabh. Born 1969. Indian, Singapore-based mathematician, computer programmer and financial fund manager.

Sivasothi, N. Born 1966. Biodiversity lecturer at Faculty of Science, National University Singapore, and coordinator, International Coastal Cleanup Singapore.

Smith, Adam. 1723–1790. Scottish economist and philosopher; author of *The Wealth of Nations* and regarded as the intellectual father of free market capitalism.

Soros, George. Born 1930. Billionaire Hungarian-American hedge fund owner, political activist, financial commentator and writer.

Spitz, Mark A. Born 1950. American champion swimmer; winner of nine Olympic gold medals between 1968 and 1972.

Stiglitz, Joseph E. Born 1943. American economist, writer and liberal anti-austerity commentator; professor at Columbia University.

Strange, Ebba M. 1929–2012. Born Henriksen. Danish pedagogue and politician, member of parliament 1973–1994; also my mother.

Tobin, James. 1918–2002. American economist with a Keynesian outlook; gave name to the proposed "Tobin tax" on financial transactions and the "Tobin Q ratio" used in stock market evaluations.

Trump, Donald. Born 1946. American business tycoon, TV personality and Presidential candidate.

Welch, John F. ("Jack"). Born 1935. Super-rich American businessman and author; former CEO of General Electric.

# References

**Major works used when preparing this book**

Alpert, Daniel. 2014. *The Age of Oversupply: Overcoming the Greatest Challenge to the Global Economy*. New York: Penguin Group.

Browne, John. 2013. *Seven Elements: That Have Changed the World*. London: Weidenfeld & Nicolson.

Coyle, Diane. 2011. *The Economics of Enough: How to Run the Economy as if the Future Matters*. New Jersey: Princeton University Press.

Daly, Herman E. 1996. *Beyond Growth: The Economics of Sustainable Development*. Massachusetts: Beacon Press.

Diamond, Jared. 2011. *Collapse: How Societies Choose to Fail or Succeed*. New York: Penguin Books.

Dietz, Rob and Dan O'Neill. 2013. *Enough is Enough: Building a Sustainable Economy in a World of Finite Resources*. San Francisco: Berrett-Koehler Publishers.

Emmott, Stephen. 2013. *Ten Billion*. New York: Vintage Books.

Fergusson, Adam. 2010. *When Money Dies: The Nightmare of the Weimar Hyper-Inflation*. London: Old Street Publishing.

Galbraith, John Kenneth. 2004. *The Economics of Innocent Fraud*. London: Penguin Books.

Green, Alexander. 2008. The Gone Fishin' Portfolio. New Jersey: John Wiley.

Heinberg, Richard. 2011. *The End of Growth: Adapting to Our New Economic Reality*. Canada: New Society Publishers.

IBF. 2013a. *Module 6 Study Guide: Securities Products and Analysis*. Singapore: The Institute of Banking & Finance.

IBF. 2013b. *Module 6A Study Guide: Securities & Futures Product Knowledge*. Singapore: The Institute of Banking & Finance.

Jackson, Tim. 2009. *Prosperity Without Growth: Economics for a Finite Planet*. New York: Earthscan.

Johnson, Stacy. 2005. *Life Or Debt*. New York: Ballantine Books.

Klein, Peter J. 1998. *Getting Started in Security Analysis*. New York: John Wiley & Sons.

Louv, Richard. 2012. *The Nature Principle: Reconnecting with Life in a Virtual Age*. New York: Workman Publishing.

Matenson, Chris and Adam Taggart. 2015. *Prosper! How to Prepare for the Future and Create a World Worth Inheriting*. Arizona: Peak Prosperity Books.

Meadows, Donella, Jorgen Randers & Dennis Meadows. 2004. *Limits to Growth: The 30-Year Update*. Vermont: Chelsea Green Publishing.

Myers, Norman. 1979. *The Sinking Ark*. Oxford: Pergamon Press.

Niederhoffer, Victor and Laurel Kenner. 2003. *Practical Speculation*. New Jersey: John Wiley & Sons.

Perkins, John. 2011. *Hoodwinked*. New York: Random House.

Pettifor, Ann. 2014. *Just Money*. London: Commonwealth Publishing.

Piketty, Thomas. 2014. *Capital in the Twenty-First Century*. Massachusetts: Howard University Press.

Ray, Debraj. 1998. *Development Economics*. New Jersey: Princeton University Press.

Robin, Vicki, Joe Dominguez and Monique Tilford. 2008. *Your Money Or Your Life*. New York: Penguin Books.

Rogers, Chris. 2014. *Capitalism and Its Alternatives*. London: Zed Books.

Samuelson, Paul. 1970. *Economics: International Student Edition*. 8th Edition. New York: McGraw-Hill Book Company.

Sassen, Saskia. 2014. *Expulsions: Brutality and Complexity in the Global Economy*. Massachusetts: Howard University Press.

Stiglitz, Joseph. 2002. *Globalization and Its Discontents*. London: Penguin Books.

Saw, Swee-Hock. *Investment Management*. 4th Edition. Singapore: Prentice Hall.

Taleb, Nassim Nicholas. 2007. *Fooled by Randomness*. London: Penguin Books.

Victor, Peter A. 2008. *Managing Without Growth*. Massachusetts: Edward Elgar Publishing.

## Useful websites

For general definition of financial terms and videos:
www.investopedia.com
For calculating compound interest and annuities:
www.thecalculatorsite.com/finance/
Many sites like Yahoo and Bloomberg carry financial news, events, stock
prices and charts. For Singapore shares I recommend this site:
www.shareinvestor.com/sg
Although somewhat UK-centred in focus, this site is useful if you are
concerned about sustainable investment policies:
blueandgreentomorrow.com/invest/

**MORTEN STRANGE** (born 1952, Denmark) is a Singapore-based IBF-certified independent financial analyst. Since becoming salary-independent and retiring at the age of 33, he has pursued his interests in economics and finance, writing, photography, and environmental conservation.

*"Be Financially Free* by 'citizen economist' Morten Strange is not just a good book, it is a fantastic piece of entertainment, common sense economics, and wisdom about life, and how to achieve financial independence, and to 'live', as Pablo Picasso said, 'as a poor man with lots of money'. Strange will not win a Nobel Prize with *Be Financially Free*, but he has my respect for having written a highly readable, funny and cynical financial essay, which actually makes sense."

— DR MARC FABER
Financial analyst, international fund manager,
and publisher of the *Gloom Doom & Boom Report*